Jim Henson's
BENEATH THE
DARK CRYSTAL™

ADAM
SMITH

ALEXANDRIA
HUNTINGTON

VOLUME THREE

Published by
ARCHAIA™

Jim Henson's
BENEATH THE
DARK CRYSTAL ™

Written by **Adam Smith**
Illustrated by **Alexandria Huntington**
Lettered by **Jim Campbell**

Cover and Chapter Break Art by **Benjamin Dewey**

Series Designer **Marie Krupina**
Collection Designer **Jillian Crab**
Assistant Editor **Allyson Gronowitz**
Editor **Matthew Levine**

Special Thanks to **Brian Henson, Lisa Henson, Jim Formanek, Nicole Goldman, Carla DellaVedova, Karen Falk, Blanca Lista, Jessica Mansour**, the entire Jim Henson Company team, **Wendy Froud, Brian Froud, Francesco Segala, Jason Lusk, Cameron Chittock**, and **Sierra Hahn**.

JIM HENSON'S BENEATH THE DARK CRYSTAL Volume Three, February 2020. Published by Archaia, a division of Boom Entertainment, Inc. ™ & © 2020 The Jim Henson Company. JIM HENSON's mark & logo, BENEATH THE DARK CRYSTAL, mark & logo, and all related characters and elements are trademarks of The Jim Henson Company. Originally published in single magazine form as BENEATH THE DARK CRYSTAL No. 9-12. ™ & © 2019 The Jim Henson Company. All rights reserved. Archaia™ and the Archaia logo are trademarks of Boom Entertainment, Inc., registered in various countries and categories. All characters, events, and institutions depicted herein are fictional. Any similarity between any of the names, characters, persons, events, and/or institutions in this publication to actual names, characters, and persons, whether living or dead, events, and/or institutions is unintended and purely coincidental.

BOOM! Studios, 5670 Wilshire Boulevard, Suite 400, Los Angeles, CA 90036-5679.

Printed in China. First Printing.

ISBN: 978-168415-191-2, eISBN: 978-164144-636-5

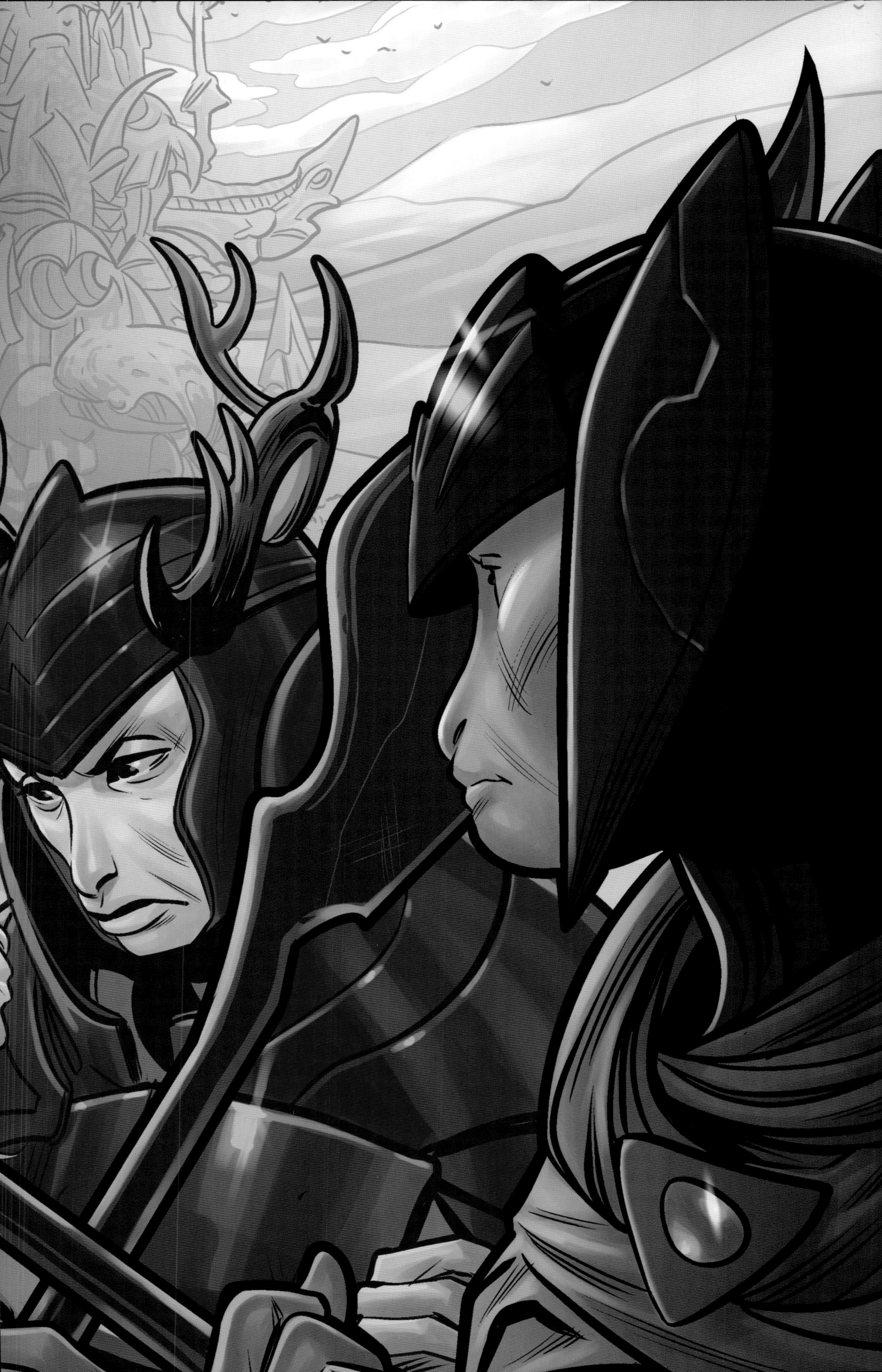

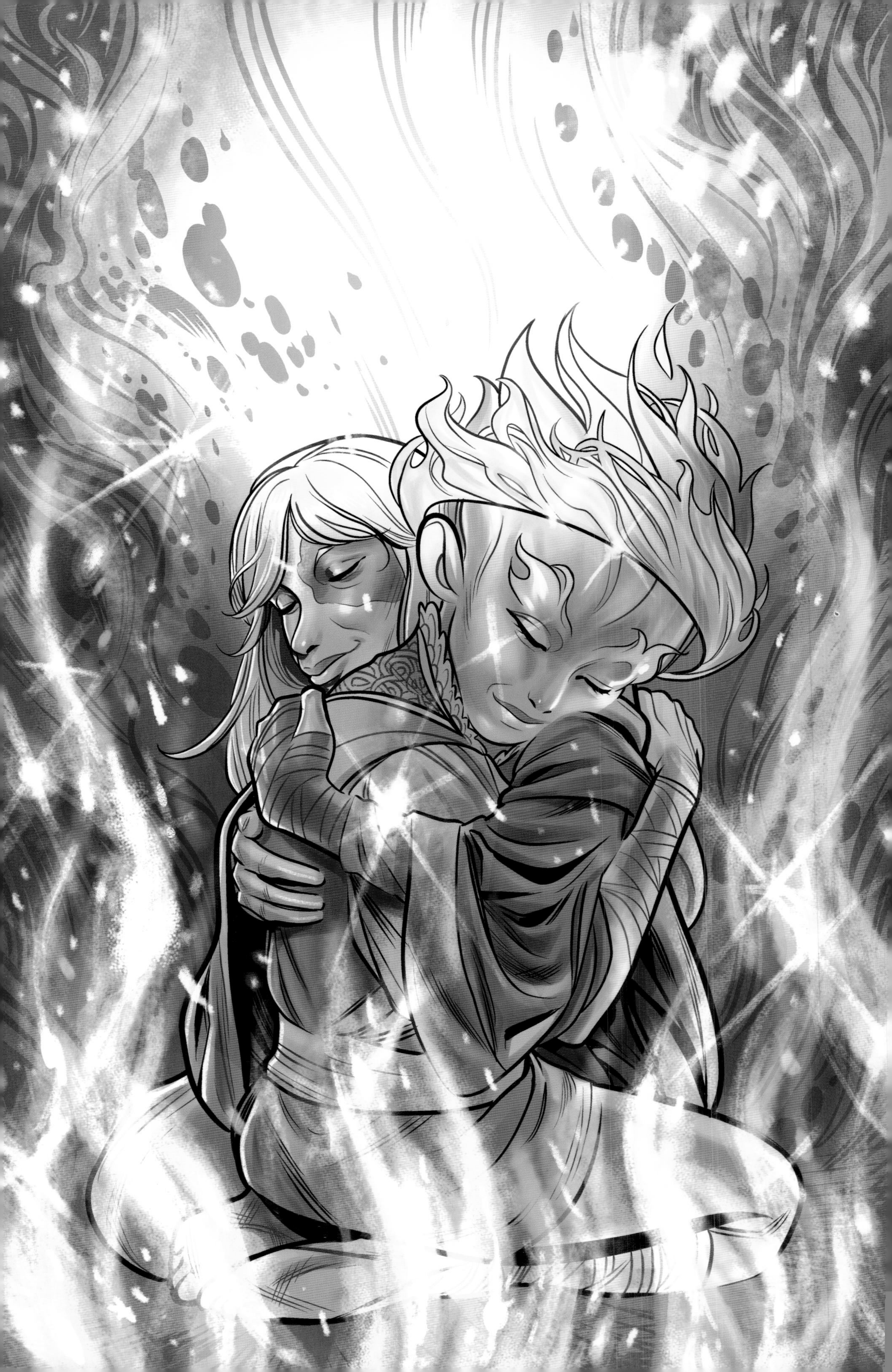

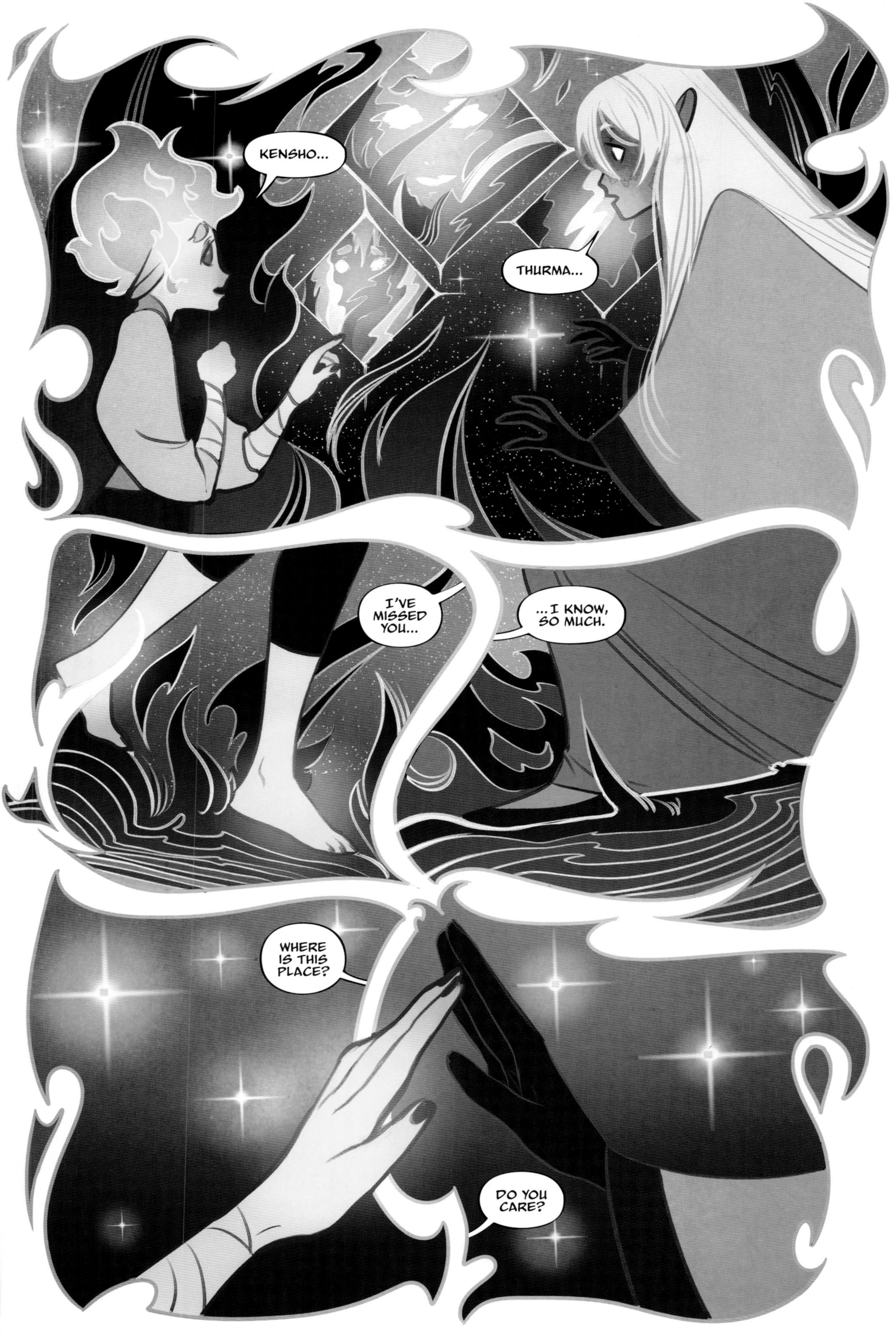
KENSHO...
THURMA...
I'VE MISSED YOU...
...I KNOW, SO MUCH.
WHERE IS THIS PLACE?
DO YOU CARE?

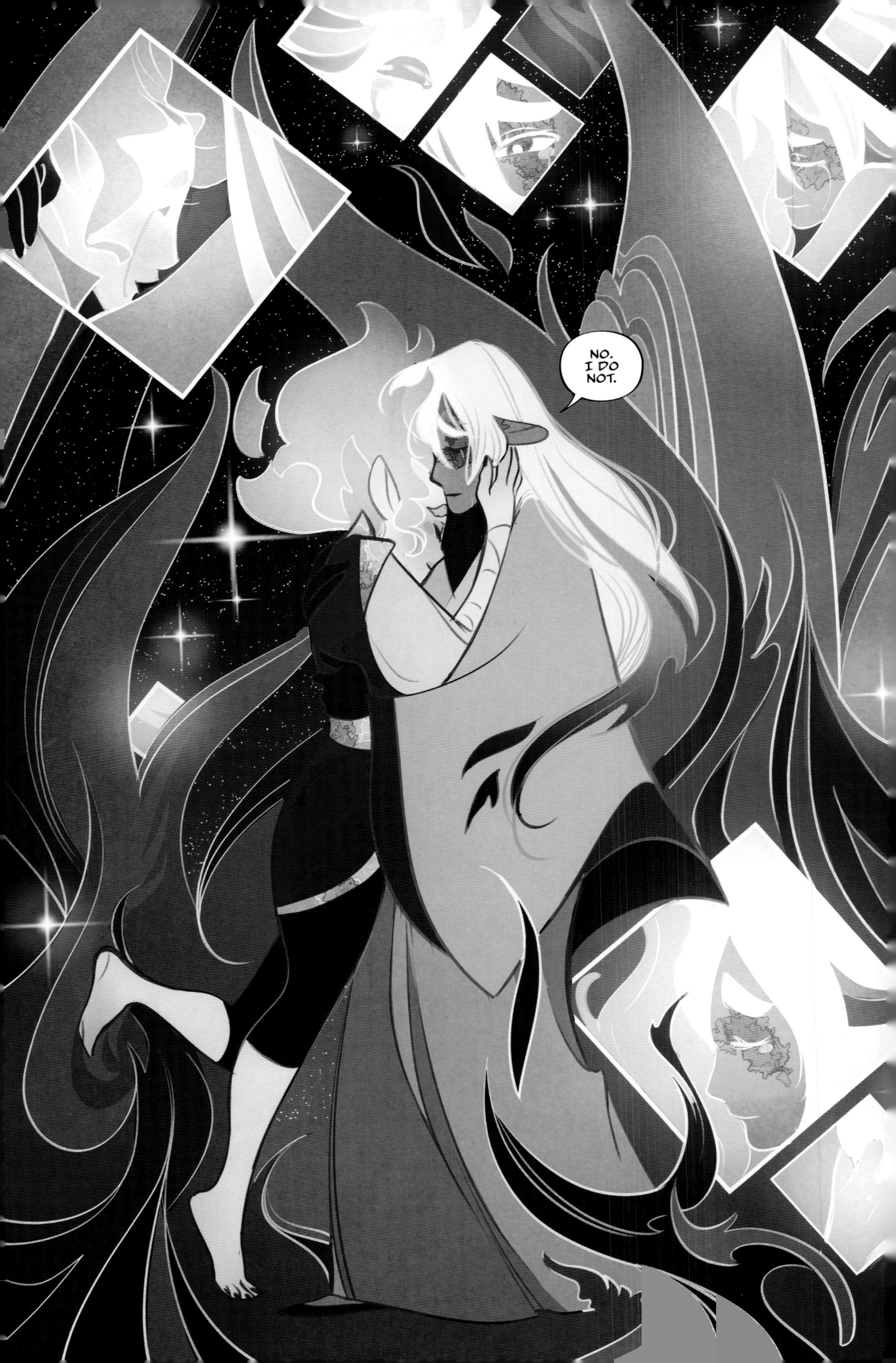
NO. I DO NOT.

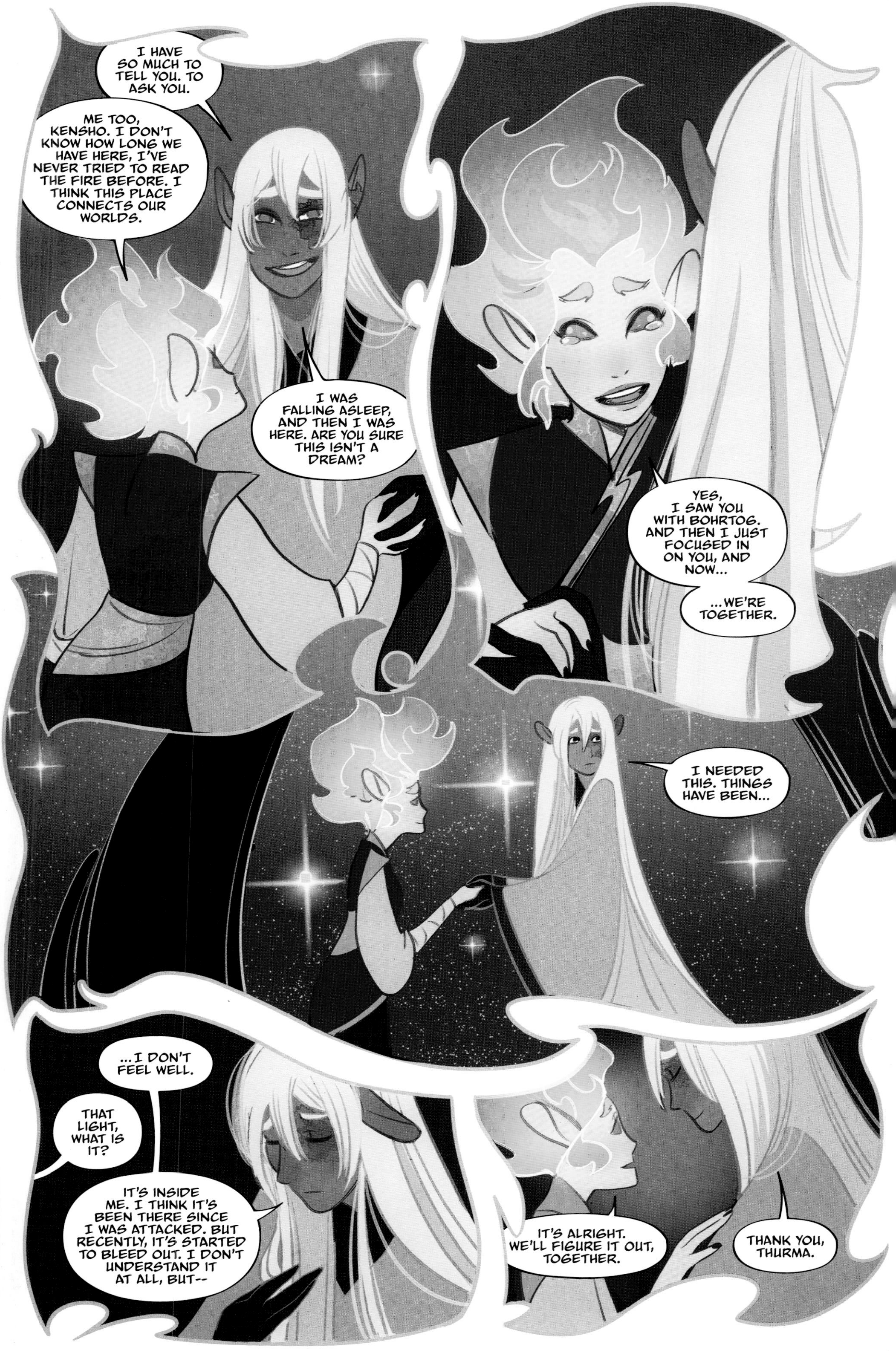
I HAVE SO MUCH TO TELL YOU. TO ASK YOU.
ME TOO, KENSHO. I DON'T KNOW HOW LONG WE HAVE HERE, I'VE NEVER TRIED TO READ THE FIRE BEFORE. I THINK THIS PLACE CONNECTS OUR WORLDS.
I WAS FALLING ASLEEP, AND THEN I WAS HERE. ARE YOU SURE THIS ISN'T A DREAM?
YES, I SAW YOU WITH BOHRTOG. AND THEN I JUST FOCUSED IN ON YOU, AND NOW...
...WE'RE TOGETHER.
I NEEDED THIS. THINGS HAVE BEEN...
...I DON'T FEEL WELL.
THAT LIGHT, WHAT IS IT?
IT'S INSIDE ME. I THINK IT'S BEEN THERE SINCE I WAS ATTACKED. BUT RECENTLY, IT'S STARTED TO BLEED OUT. I DON'T UNDERSTAND IT AT ALL, BUT--
IT'S ALRIGHT. WE'LL FIGURE IT OUT, TOGETHER.
THANK YOU, THURMA.

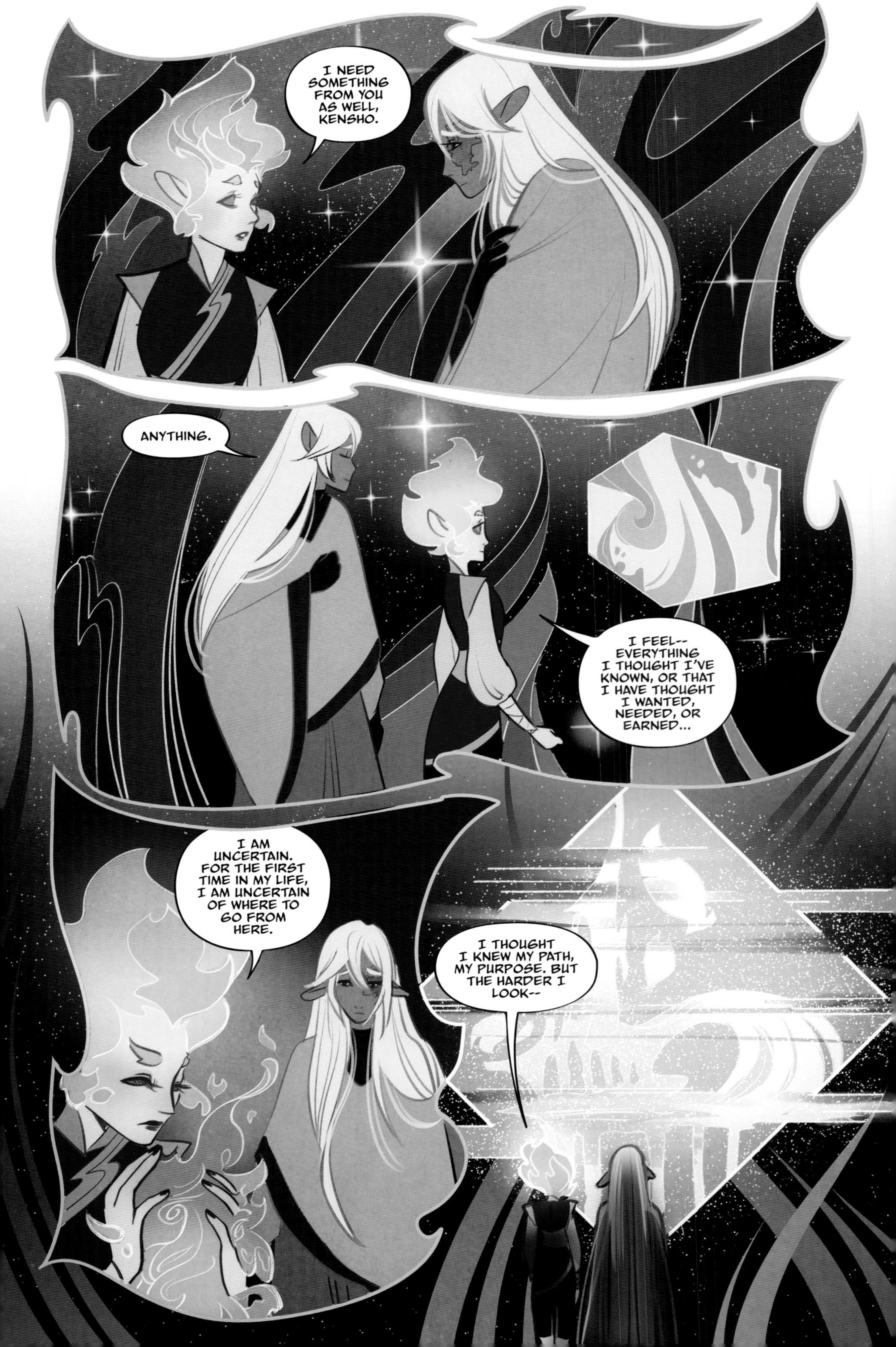
I NEED SOMETHING FROM YOU AS WELL, KENSHO.
ANYTHING.
I FEEL-- EVERYTHING I THOUGHT I'VE KNOWN, OR THAT I HAVE THOUGHT I WANTED, NEEDED, OR EARNED...
I AM UNCERTAIN. FOR THE FIRST TIME IN MY LIFE, I AM UNCERTAIN OF WHERE TO GO FROM HERE.
I THOUGHT I KNEW MY PATH, MY PURPOSE. BUT THE HARDER I LOOK--

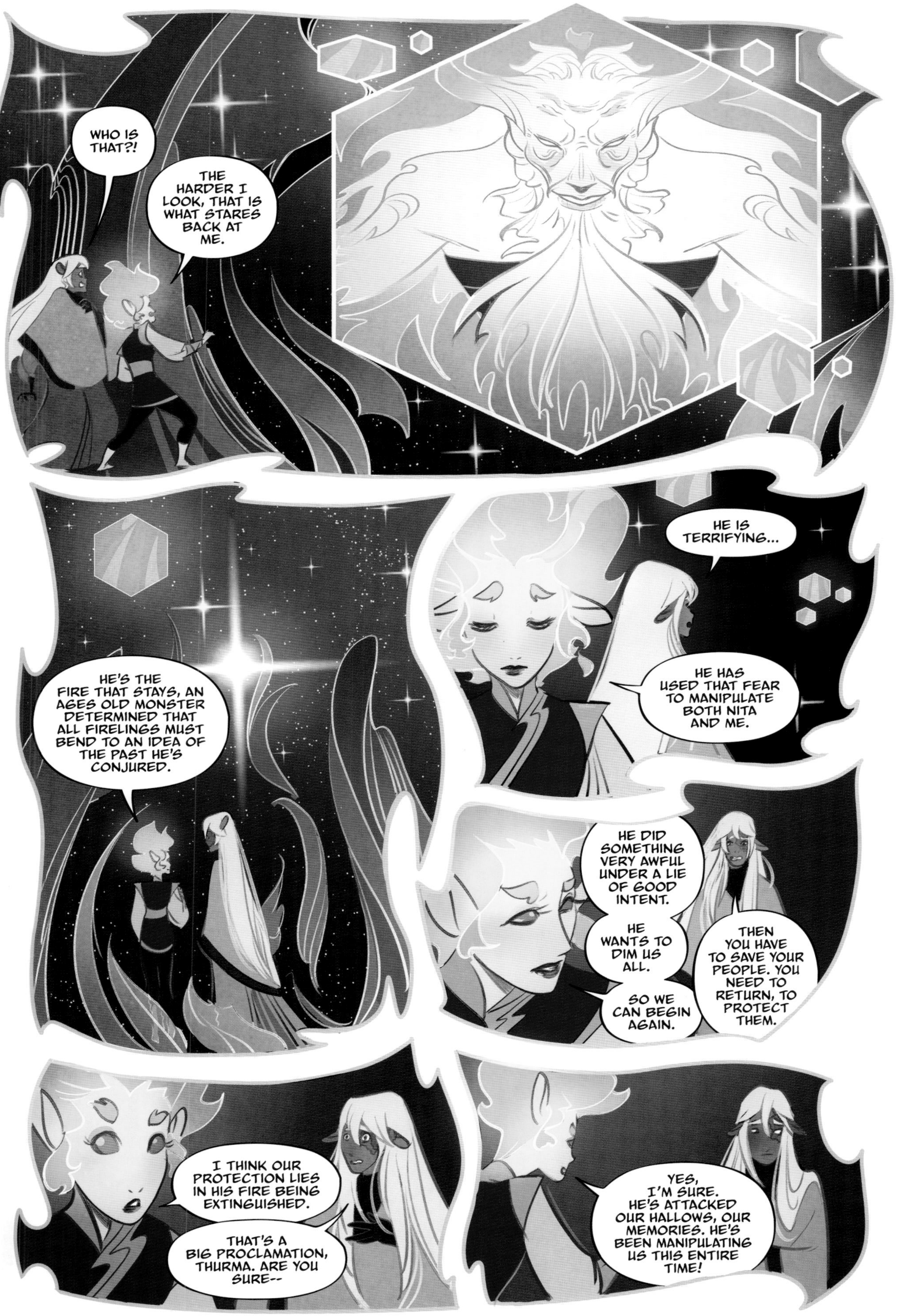
WHO IS THAT?!
THE HARDER I LOOK, THAT IS WHAT STARES BACK AT ME.
HE'S THE FIRE THAT STAYS, AN AGES OLD MONSTER DETERMINED THAT ALL FIRELINGS MUST BEND TO AN IDEA OF THE PAST HE'S CONJURED.
HE IS TERRIFYING...
HE HAS USED THAT FEAR TO MANIPULATE BOTH NITA AND ME.
HE DID SOMETHING VERY AWFUL UNDER A LIE OF GOOD INTENT.
HE WANTS TO DIM US ALL.
SO WE CAN BEGIN AGAIN.
THEN YOU HAVE TO SAVE YOUR PEOPLE. YOU NEED TO RETURN, TO PROTECT THEM.
I THINK OUR PROTECTION LIES IN HIS FIRE BEING EXTINGUISHED.
THAT'S A BIG PROCLAMATION, THURMA. ARE YOU SURE--
YES, I'M SURE. HE'S ATTACKED OUR HALLOWS, OUR MEMORIES. HE'S BEEN MANIPULATING US THIS ENTIRE TIME!

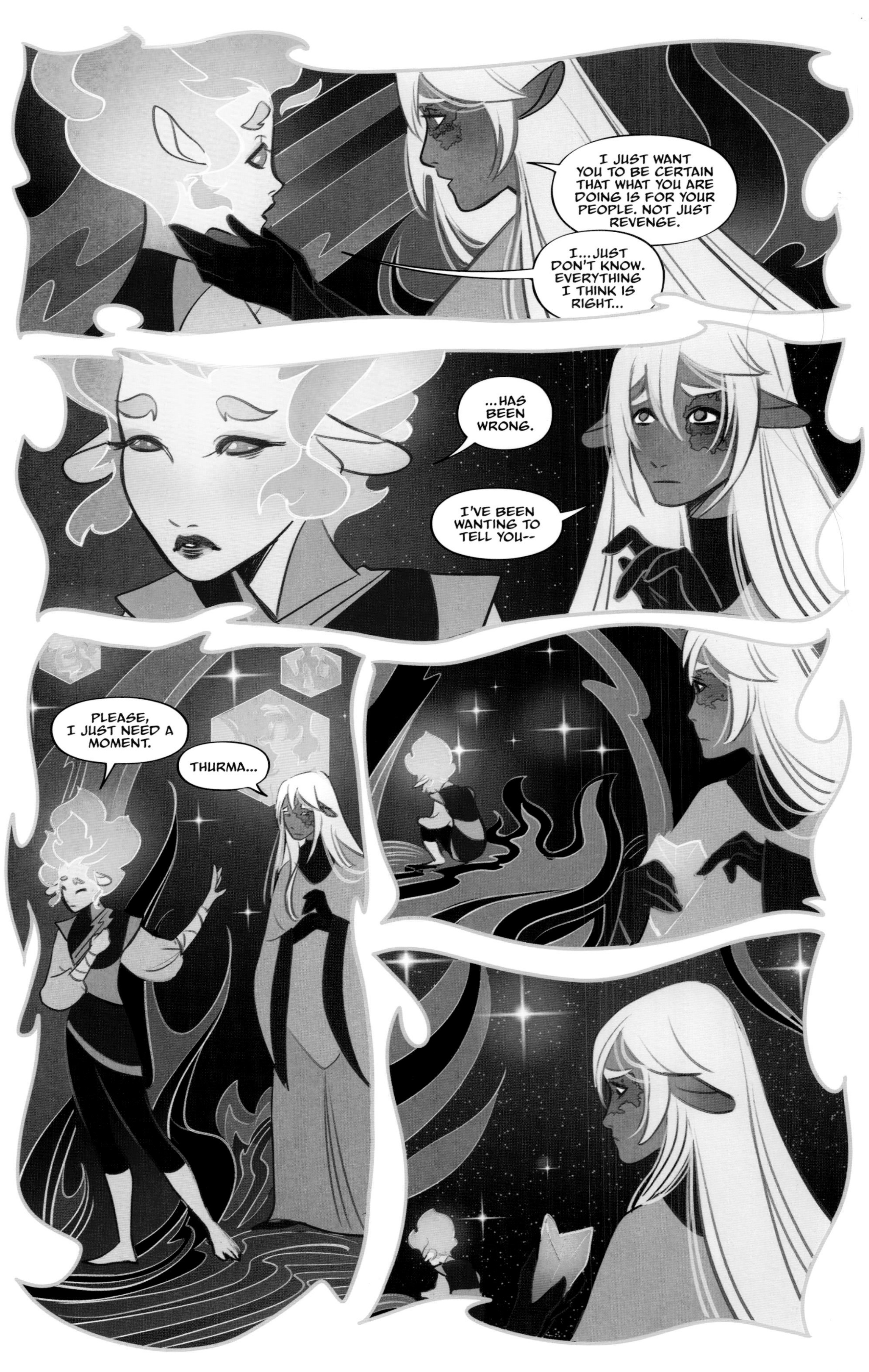
I JUST WANT YOU TO BE CERTAIN THAT WHAT YOU ARE DOING IS FOR YOUR PEOPLE. NOT JUST REVENGE.
I...JUST DON'T KNOW. EVERYTHING I THINK IS RIGHT...
...HAS BEEN WRONG.
I'VE BEEN WANTING TO TELL YOU--
PLEASE, I JUST NEED A MOMENT.
THURMA...

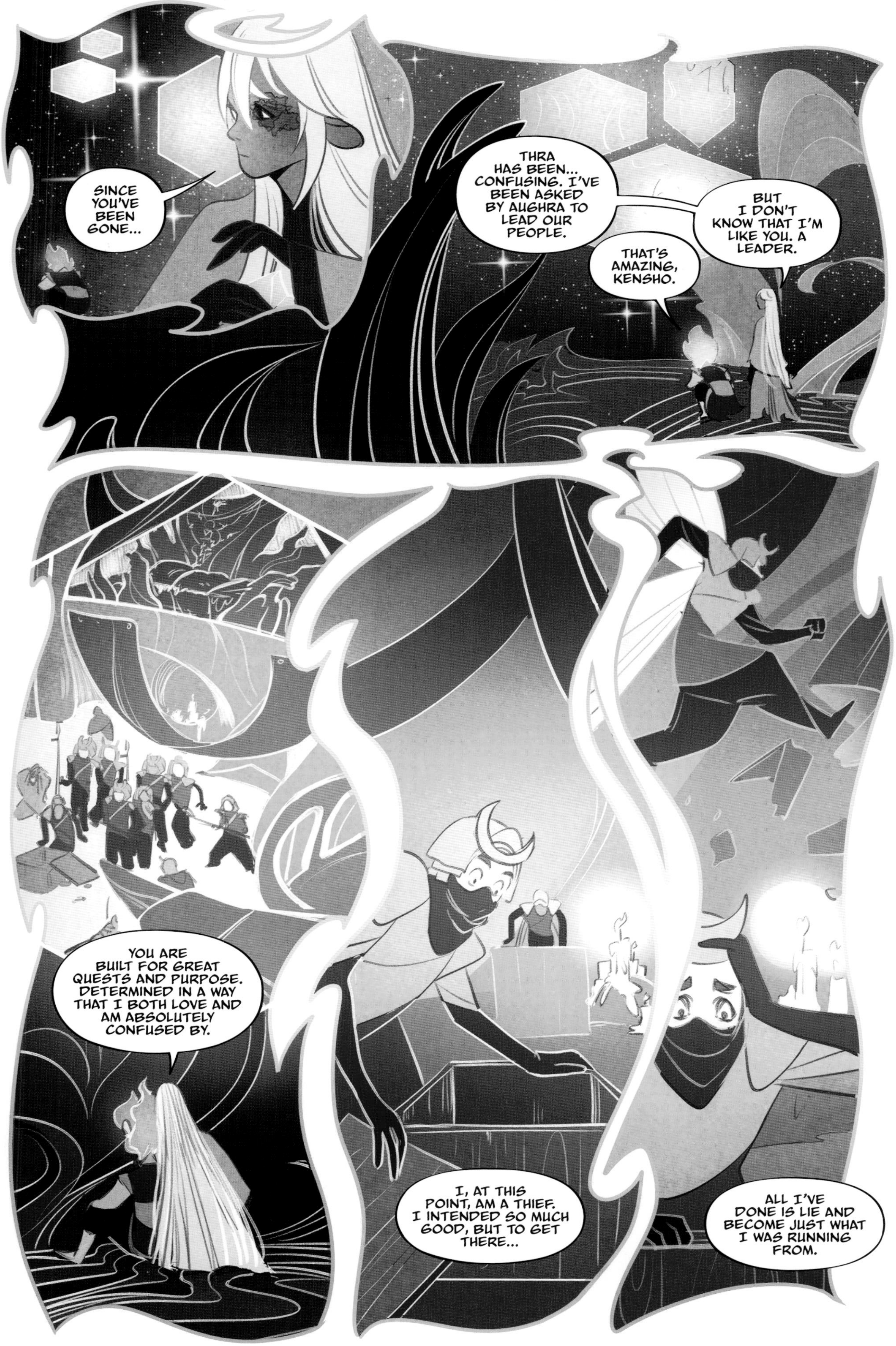
SINCE YOU'VE BEEN GONE...
THRA HAS BEEN... CONFUSING. I'VE BEEN ASKED BY AUGHRA TO LEAD OUR PEOPLE.
BUT I DON'T KNOW THAT I'M LIKE YOU. A LEADER.
THAT'S AMAZING, KENSHO.
YOU ARE BUILT FOR GREAT QUESTS AND PURPOSE. DETERMINED IN A WAY THAT I BOTH LOVE AND AM ABSOLUTELY CONFUSED BY.
I, AT THIS POINT, AM A THIEF. I INTENDED SO MUCH GOOD, BUT TO GET THERE...
ALL I'VE DONE IS LIE AND BECOME JUST WHAT I WAS RUNNING FROM.

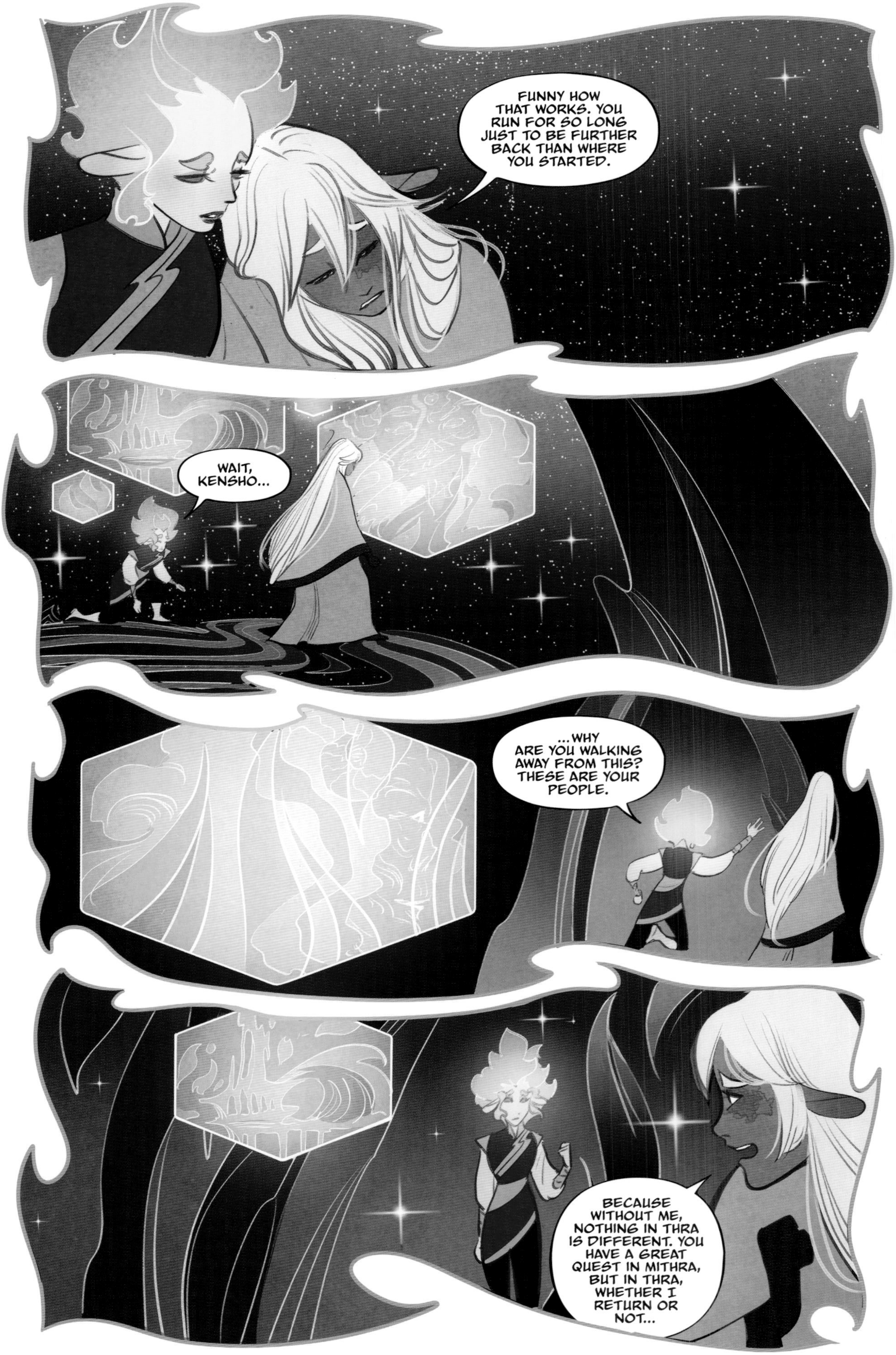
FUNNY HOW THAT WORKS. YOU RUN FOR SO LONG JUST TO BE FURTHER BACK THAN WHERE YOU STARTED.
WAIT, KENSHO...
...WHY ARE YOU WALKING AWAY FROM THIS? THESE ARE YOUR PEOPLE.
BECAUSE WITHOUT ME, NOTHING IN THRA IS DIFFERENT. YOU HAVE A GREAT QUEST IN MITHRA, BUT IN THRA, WHETHER I RETURN OR NOT...

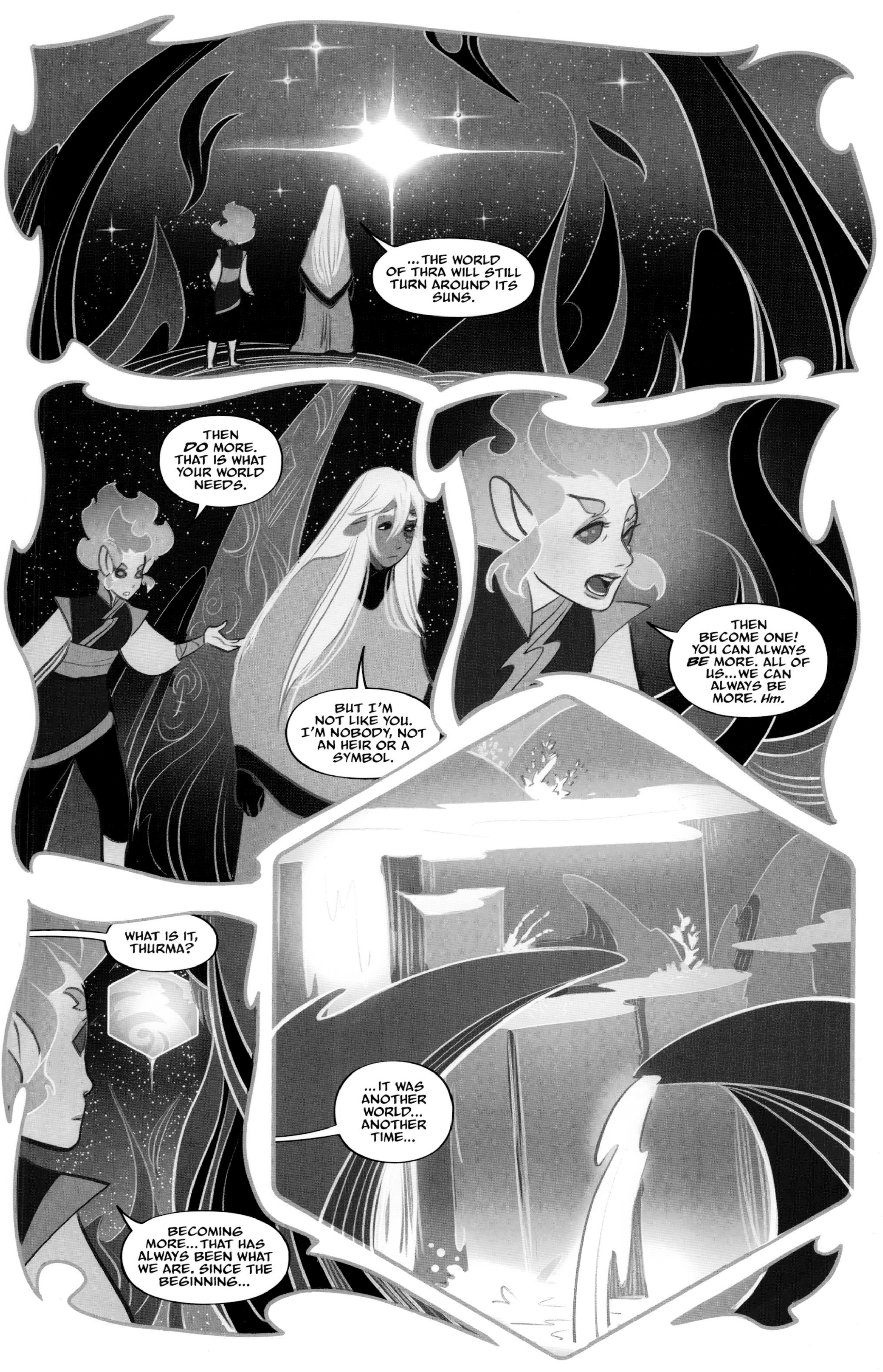
...THE WORLD OF THRA WILL STILL TURN AROUND ITS SUNS.
THEN *DO* MORE. THAT IS WHAT YOUR WORLD NEEDS.
BUT I'M NOT LIKE YOU. I'M NOBODY, NOT AN HEIR OR A SYMBOL.
THEN BECOME ONE! YOU CAN ALWAYS *BE* MORE. ALL OF US...WE CAN ALWAYS BE MORE. *Hm.*
WHAT IS IT, THURMA?
...IT WAS ANOTHER WORLD... ANOTHER TIME...
BECOMING MORE...THAT HAS ALWAYS BEEN WHAT WE ARE. SINCE THE BEGINNING...

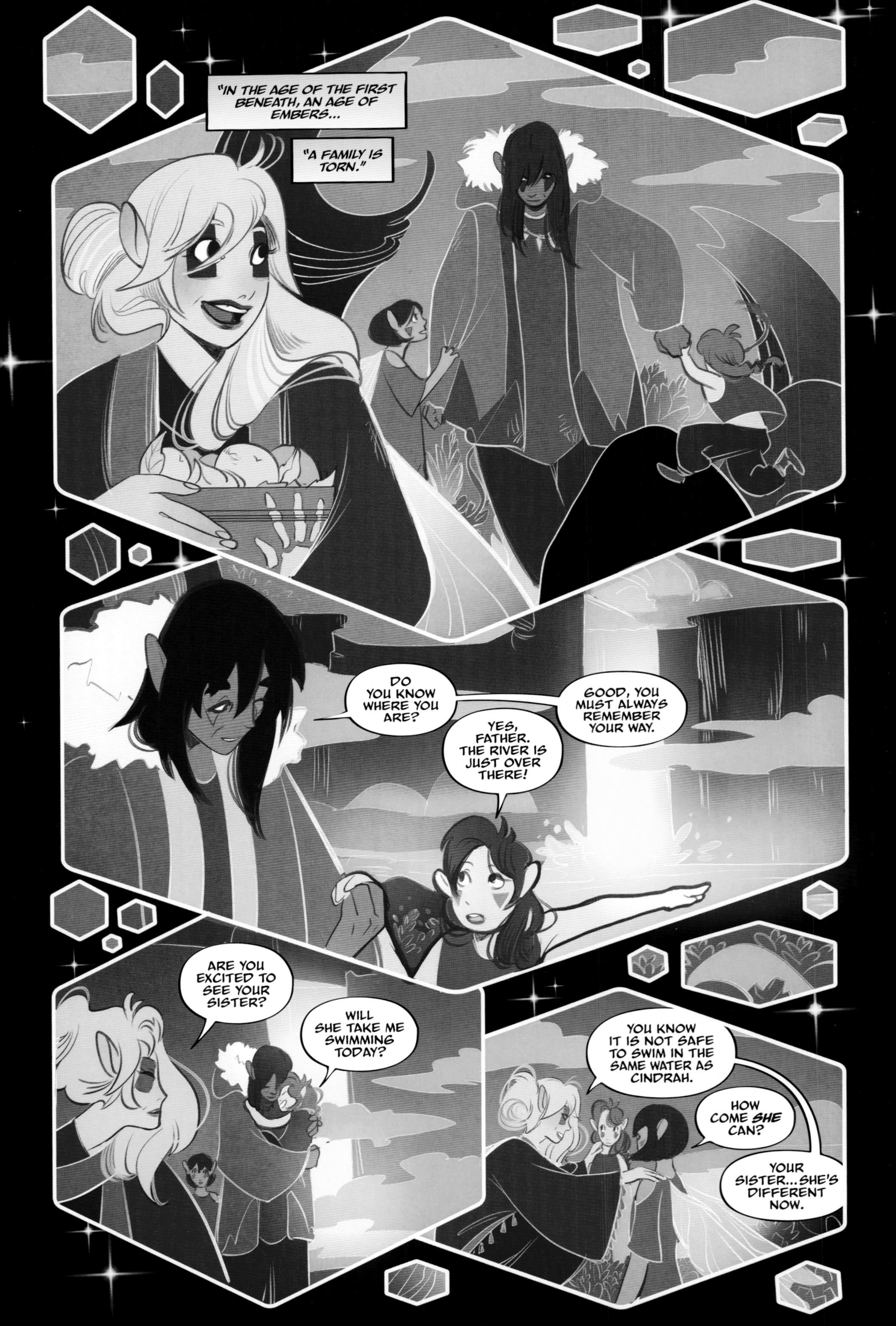
"IN THE AGE OF THE FIRST BENEATH, AN AGE OF EMBERS...
"A FAMILY IS TORN."
DO YOU KNOW WHERE YOU ARE?
YES, FATHER. THE RIVER IS JUST OVER THERE!
GOOD, YOU MUST ALWAYS REMEMBER YOUR WAY.
ARE YOU EXCITED TO SEE YOUR SISTER?
WILL SHE TAKE ME SWIMMING TODAY?
YOU KNOW IT IS NOT SAFE TO SWIM IN THE SAME WATER AS CINDRAH.
HOW COME *SHE* CAN?
YOUR SISTER...SHE'S DIFFERENT NOW.

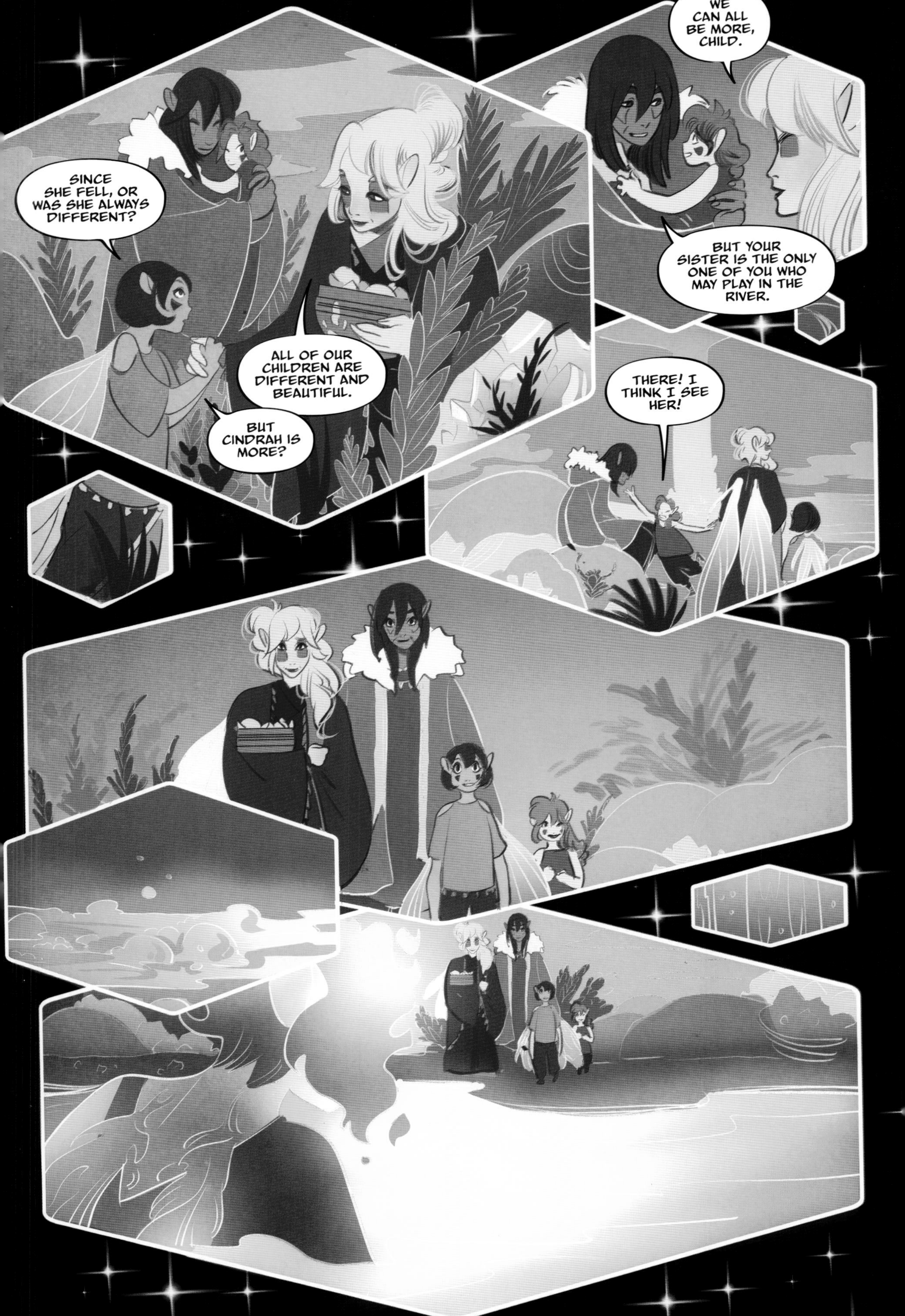
SINCE SHE FELL, OR WAS SHE ALWAYS DIFFERENT?
ALL OF OUR CHILDREN ARE DIFFERENT AND BEAUTIFUL.
BUT CINDRAH IS MORE?
WE CAN ALL BE MORE, CHILD.
BUT YOUR SISTER IS THE ONLY ONE OF YOU WHO MAY PLAY IN THE RIVER.
THERE! I THINK I SEE HER!

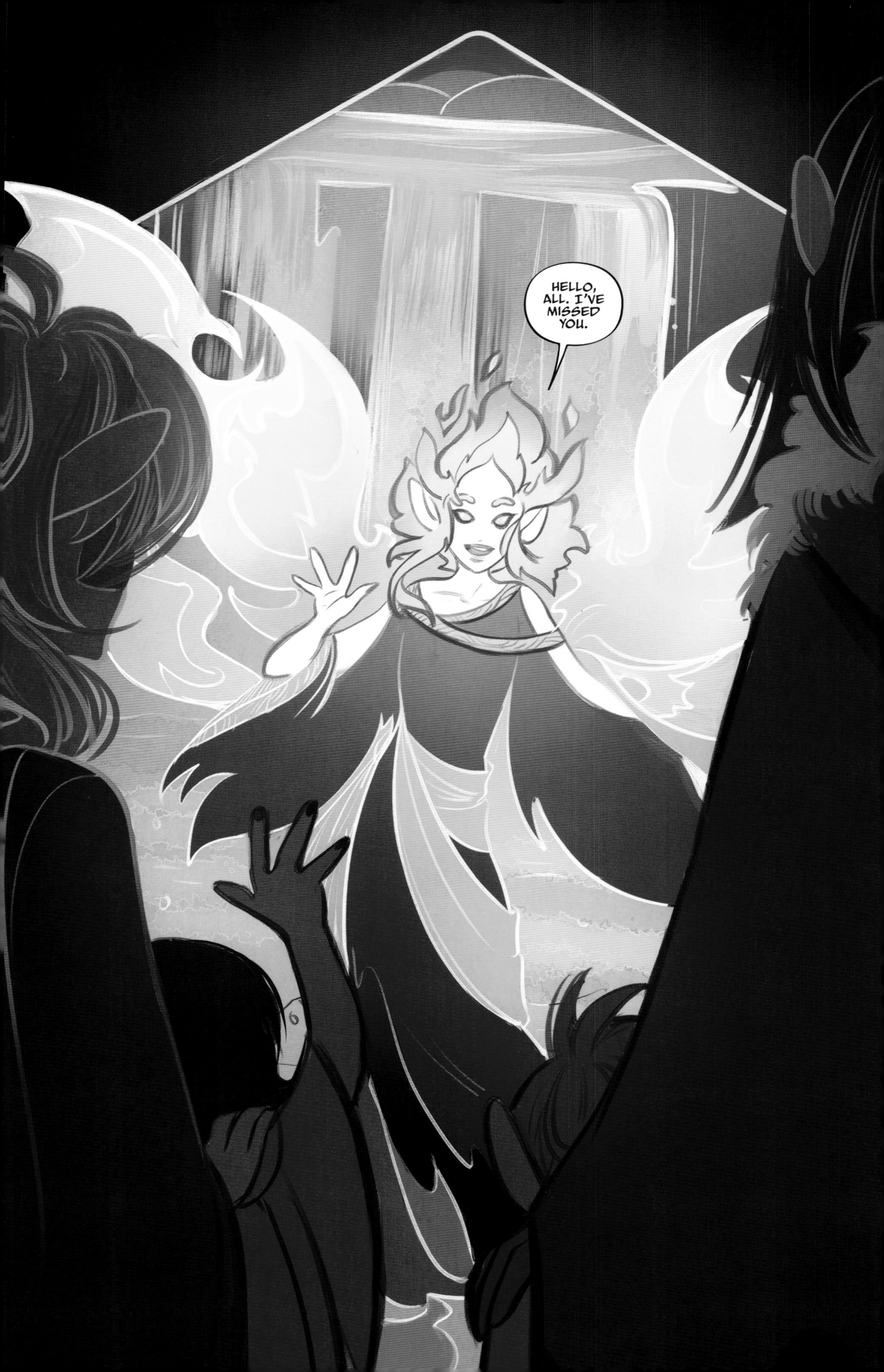
HELLO, ALL. I'VE MISSED YOU.

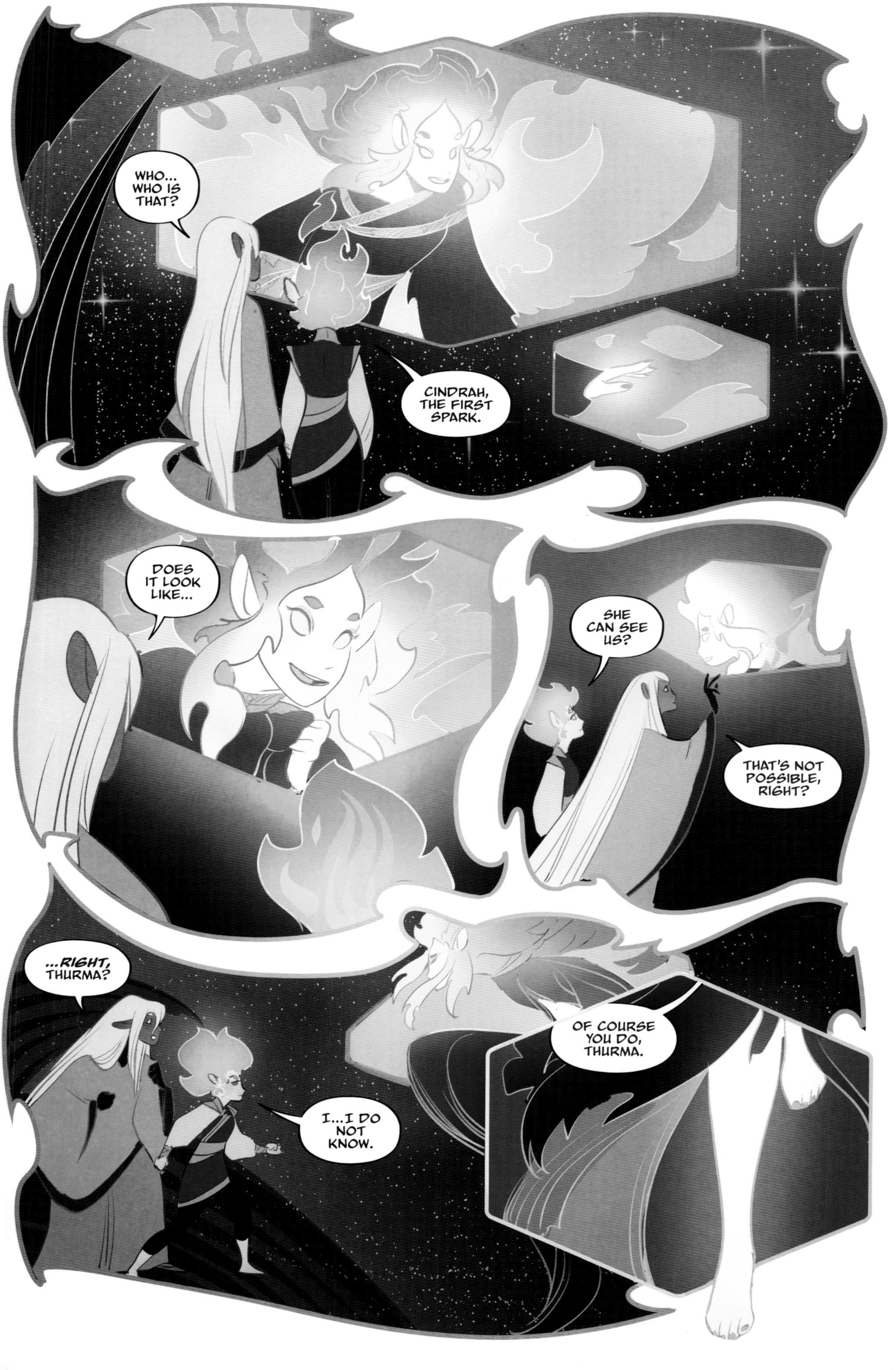
WHO... WHO IS THAT?
CINDRAH, THE FIRST SPARK.
DOES IT LOOK LIKE...
SHE CAN SEE US?
THAT'S NOT POSSIBLE, RIGHT?
...RIGHT, THURMA?
I...I DO NOT KNOW.
OF COURSE YOU DO, THURMA.

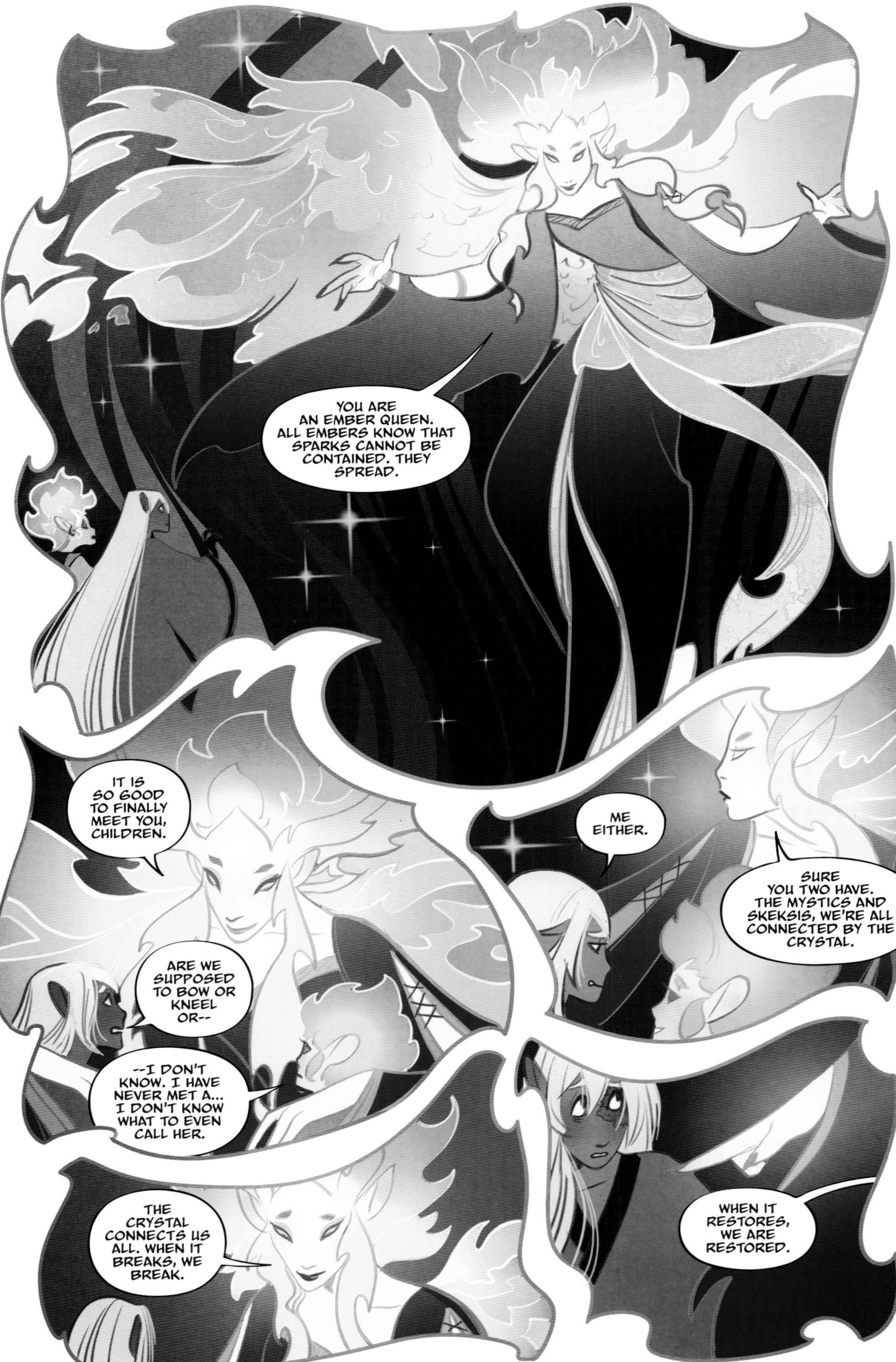
YOU ARE AN EMBER QUEEN. ALL EMBERS KNOW THAT SPARKS CANNOT BE CONTAINED. THEY SPREAD.
IT IS SO GOOD TO FINALLY MEET YOU, CHILDREN.
ARE WE SUPPOSED TO BOW OR KNEEL OR--
--I DON'T KNOW. I HAVE NEVER MET A... I DON'T KNOW WHAT TO EVEN CALL HER.
ME EITHER.
SURE YOU TWO HAVE. THE MYSTICS AND SKEKSIS, WE'RE ALL CONNECTED BY THE CRYSTAL.
THE CRYSTAL CONNECTS US ALL. WHEN IT BREAKS, WE BREAK.
WHEN IT RESTORES, WE ARE RESTORED.

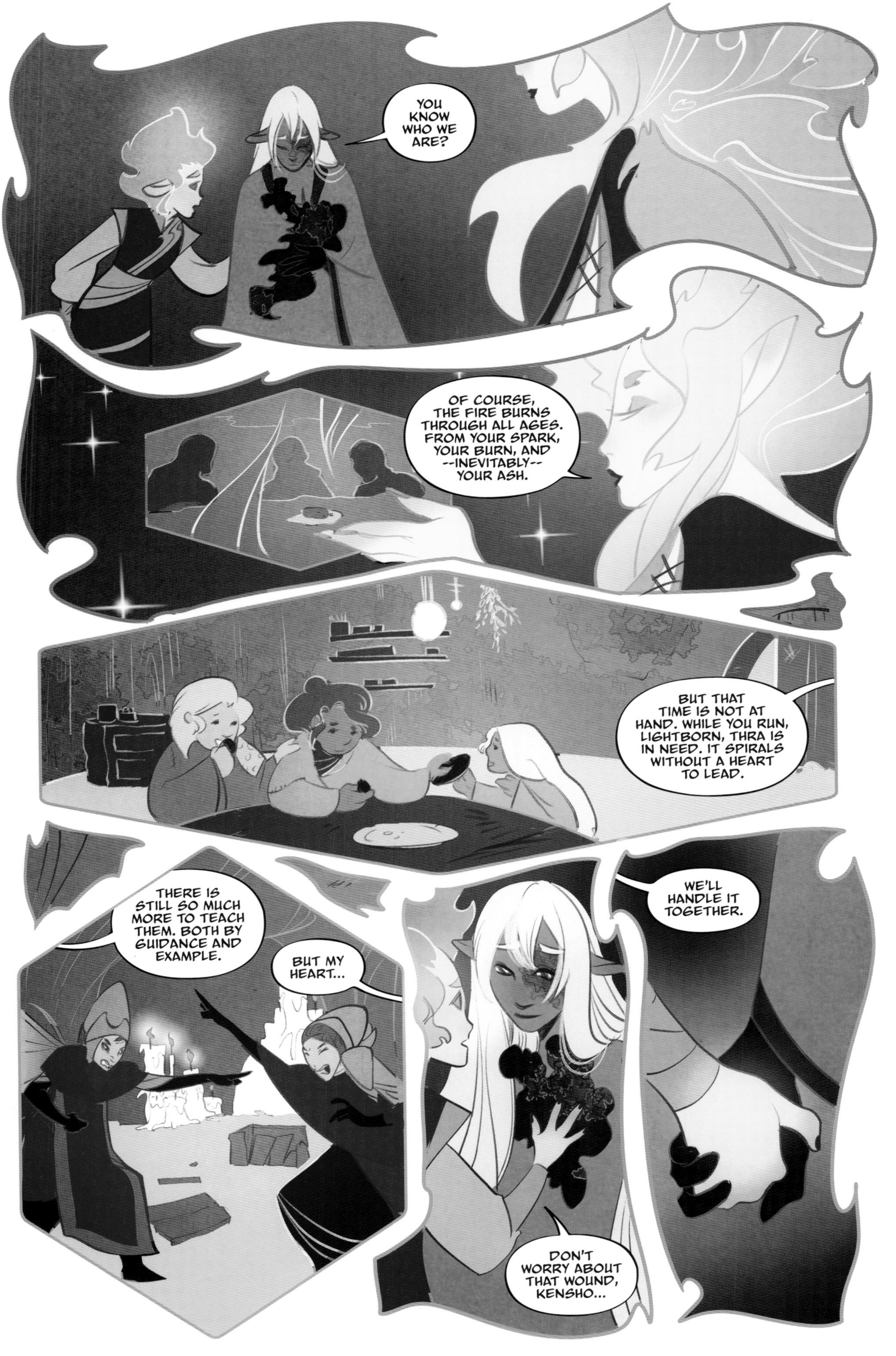
YOU KNOW WHO WE ARE?
OF COURSE, THE FIRE BURNS THROUGH ALL AGES. FROM YOUR SPARK, YOUR BURN, AND --INEVITABLY-- YOUR ASH.
BUT THAT TIME IS NOT AT HAND. WHILE YOU RUN, LIGHTBORN, THRA IS IN NEED. IT SPIRALS WITHOUT A HEART TO LEAD.
THERE IS STILL SO MUCH MORE TO TEACH THEM. BOTH BY GUIDANCE AND EXAMPLE.
BUT MY HEART...
WE'LL HANDLE IT TOGETHER.
DON'T WORRY ABOUT THAT WOUND, KENSHO...

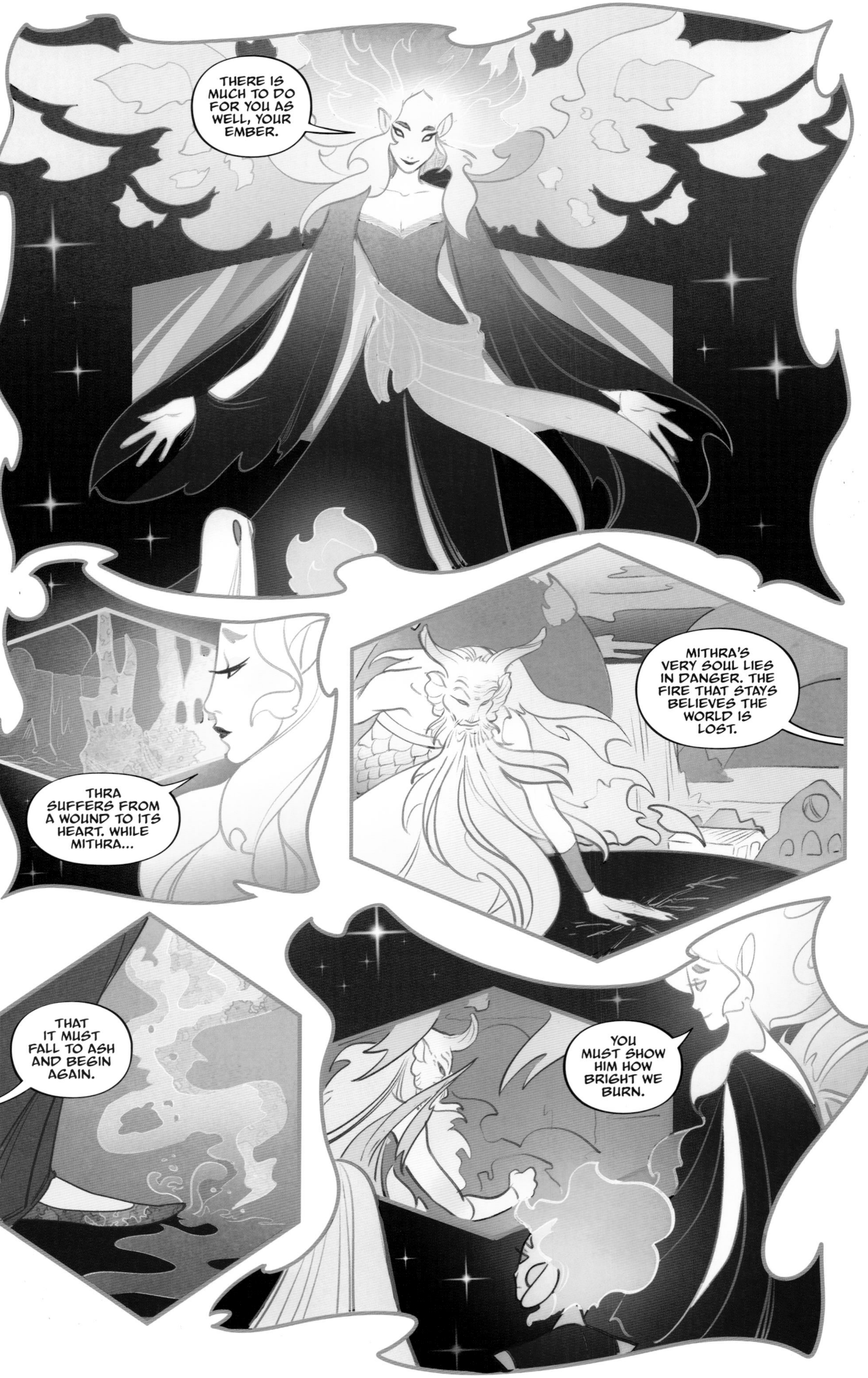
THERE IS MUCH TO DO FOR YOU AS WELL, YOUR EMBER.
THRA SUFFERS FROM A WOUND TO ITS HEART. WHILE MITHRA...
MITHRA'S VERY SOUL LIES IN DANGER. THE FIRE THAT STAYS BELIEVES THE WORLD IS LOST.
THAT IT MUST FALL TO ASH AND BEGIN AGAIN.
YOU MUST SHOW HIM HOW BRIGHT WE BURN.

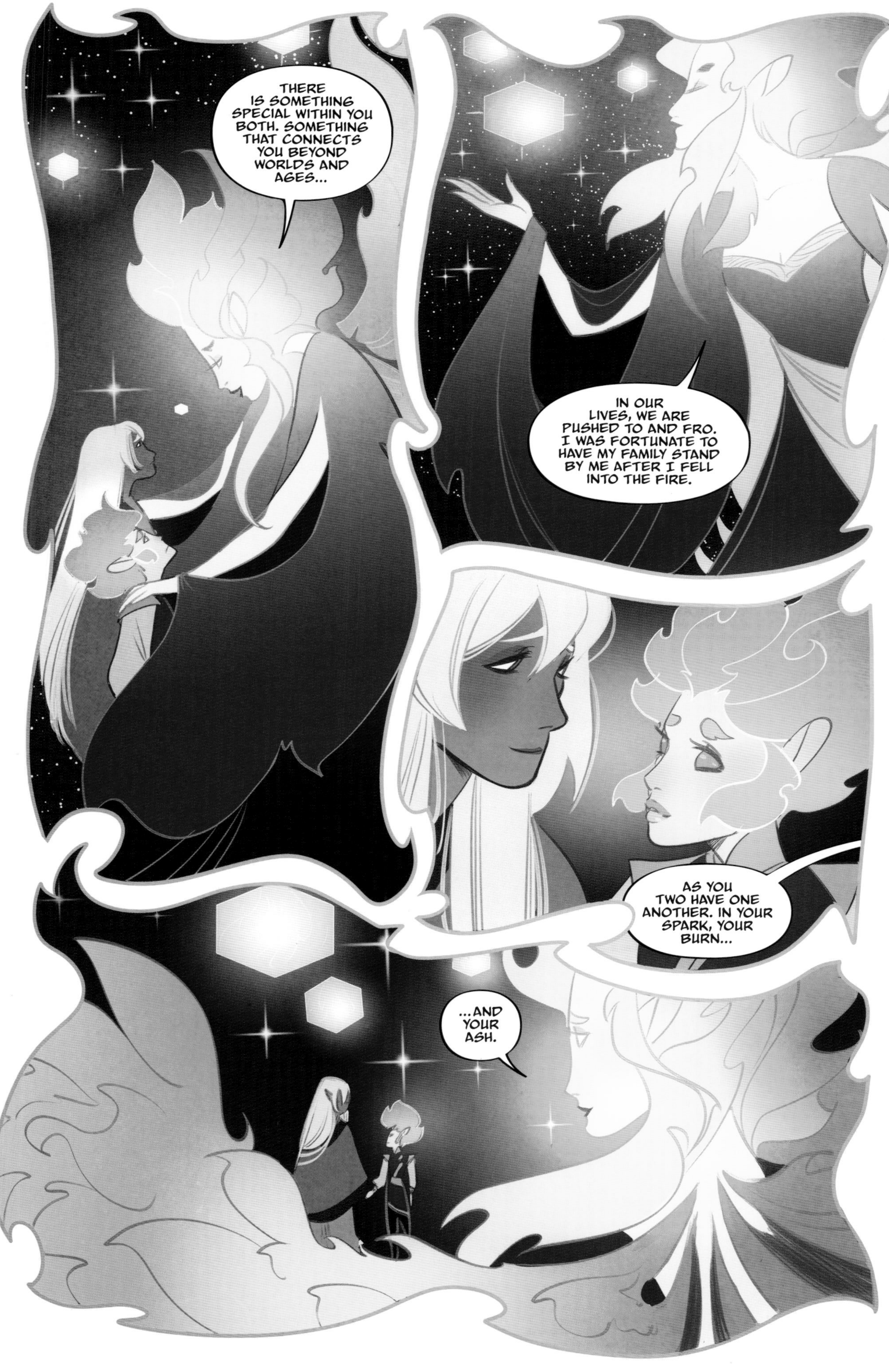
THERE IS SOMETHING SPECIAL WITHIN YOU BOTH. SOMETHING THAT CONNECTS YOU BEYOND WORLDS AND AGES...
IN OUR LIVES, WE ARE PUSHED TO AND FRO. I WAS FORTUNATE TO HAVE MY FAMILY STAND BY ME AFTER I FELL INTO THE FIRE.
AS YOU TWO HAVE ONE ANOTHER. IN YOUR SPARK, YOUR BURN...
...AND YOUR ASH.

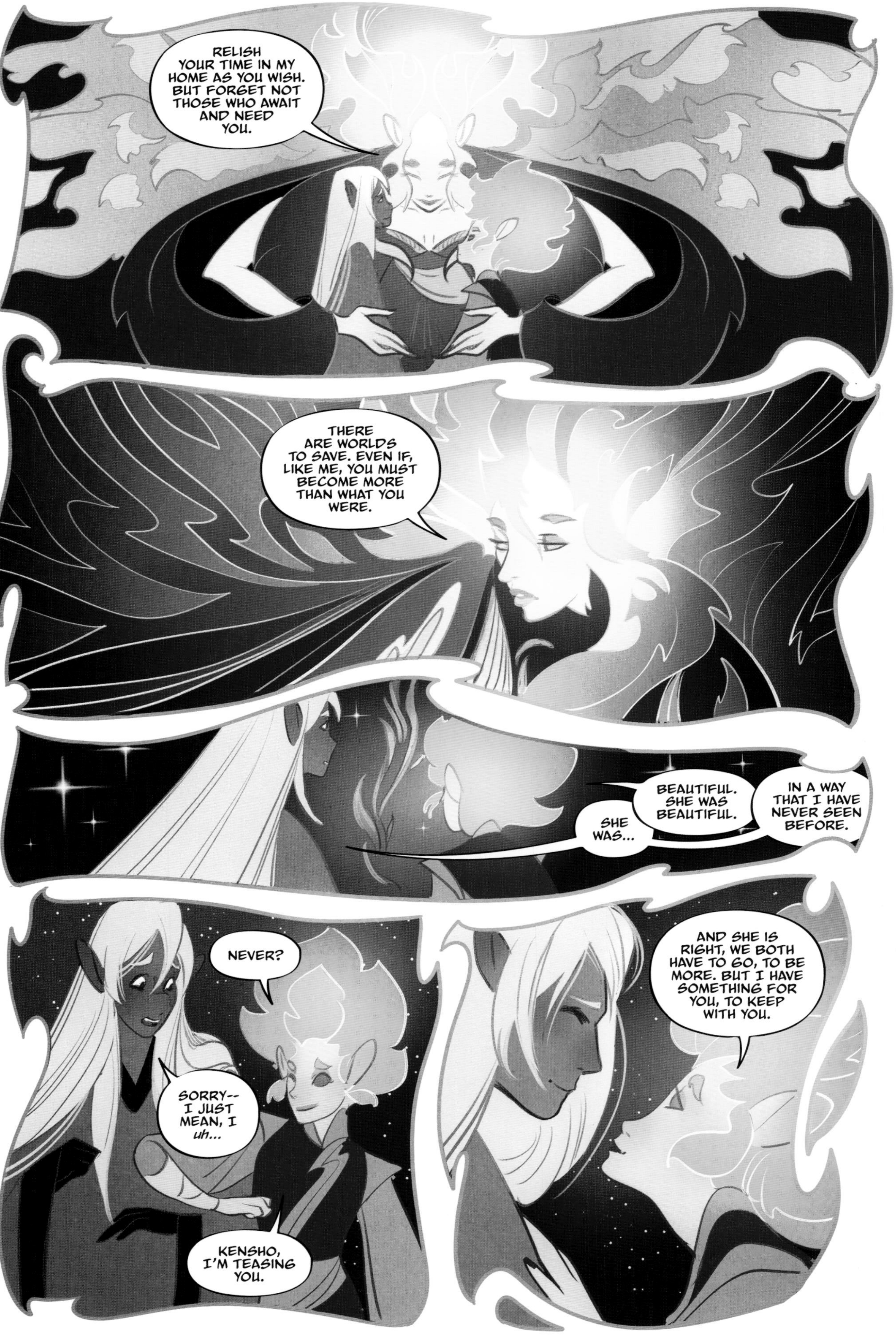

RELISH YOUR TIME IN MY HOME AS YOU WISH. BUT FORGET NOT THOSE WHO AWAIT AND NEED YOU.
THERE ARE WORLDS TO SAVE. EVEN IF, LIKE ME, YOU MUST BECOME MORE THAN WHAT YOU WERE.
SHE WAS...
BEAUTIFUL. SHE WAS BEAUTIFUL.
IN A WAY THAT I HAVE NEVER SEEN BEFORE.
NEVER?
SORRY-- I JUST MEAN, I *uh*...
KENSHO, I'M TEASING YOU.
AND SHE IS RIGHT, WE BOTH HAVE TO GO, TO BE MORE. BUT I HAVE SOMETHING FOR YOU, TO KEEP WITH YOU.

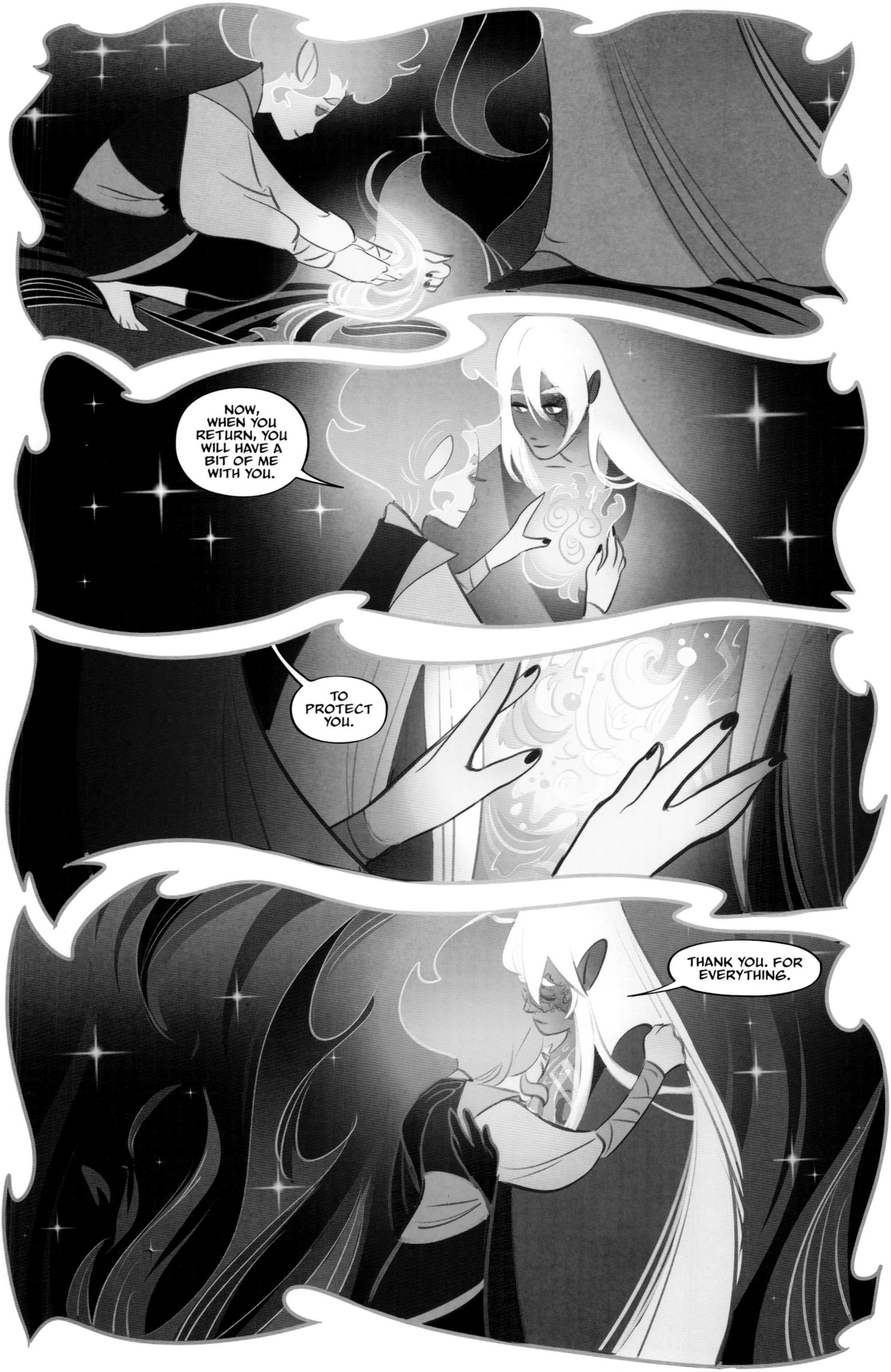
NOW, WHEN YOU RETURN, YOU WILL HAVE A BIT OF ME WITH YOU.
TO PROTECT YOU.
THANK YOU. FOR EVERYTHING.

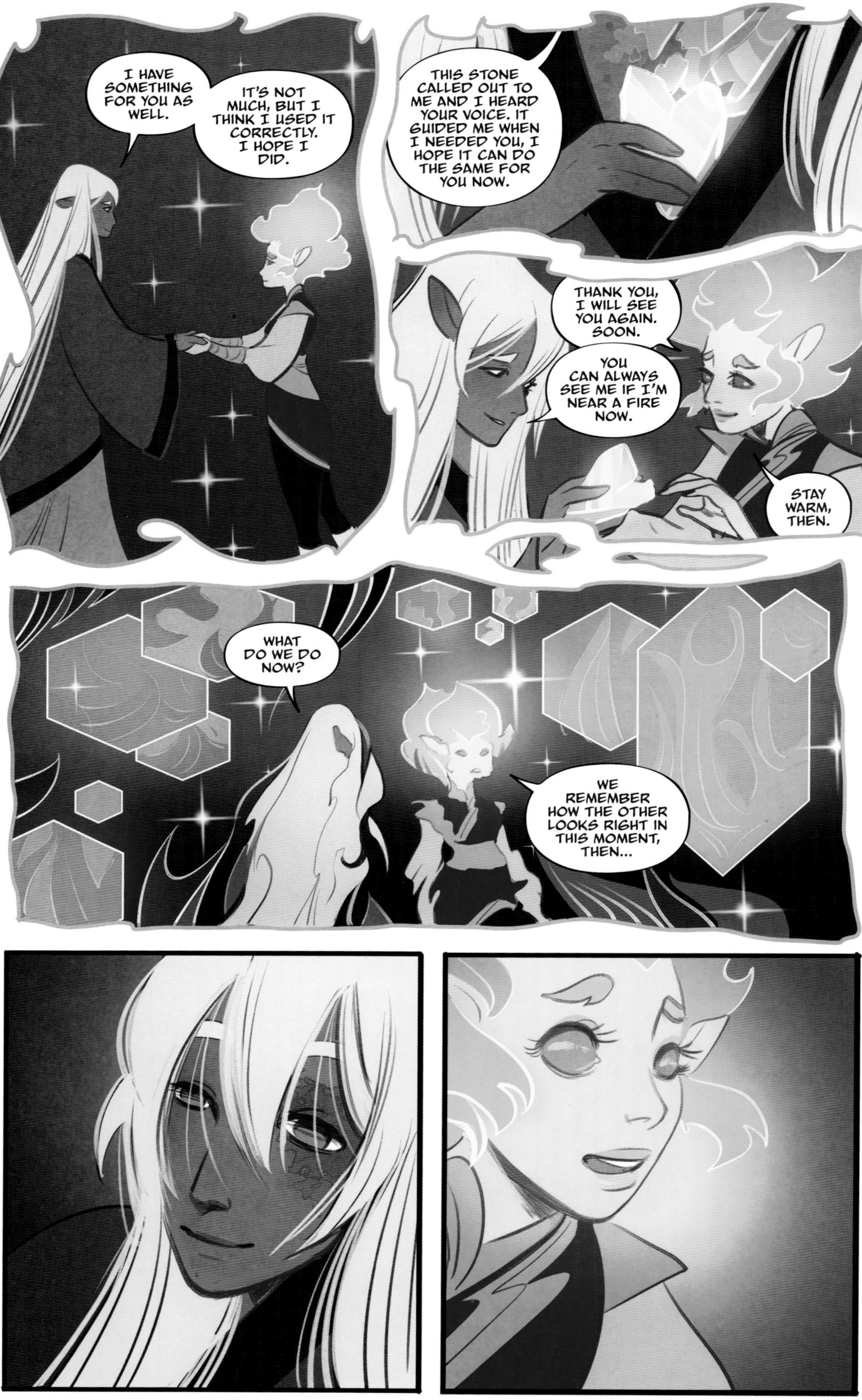
I HAVE SOMETHING FOR YOU AS WELL.
IT'S NOT MUCH, BUT I THINK I USED IT CORRECTLY. I HOPE I DID.
THIS STONE CALLED OUT TO ME AND I HEARD YOUR VOICE. IT GUIDED ME WHEN I NEEDED YOU, I HOPE IT CAN DO THE SAME FOR YOU NOW.
THANK YOU, I WILL SEE YOU AGAIN. SOON.
YOU CAN ALWAYS SEE ME IF I'M NEAR A FIRE NOW.
STAY WARM, THEN.
WHAT DO WE DO NOW?
WE REMEMBER HOW THE OTHER LOOKS RIGHT IN THIS MOMENT, THEN...

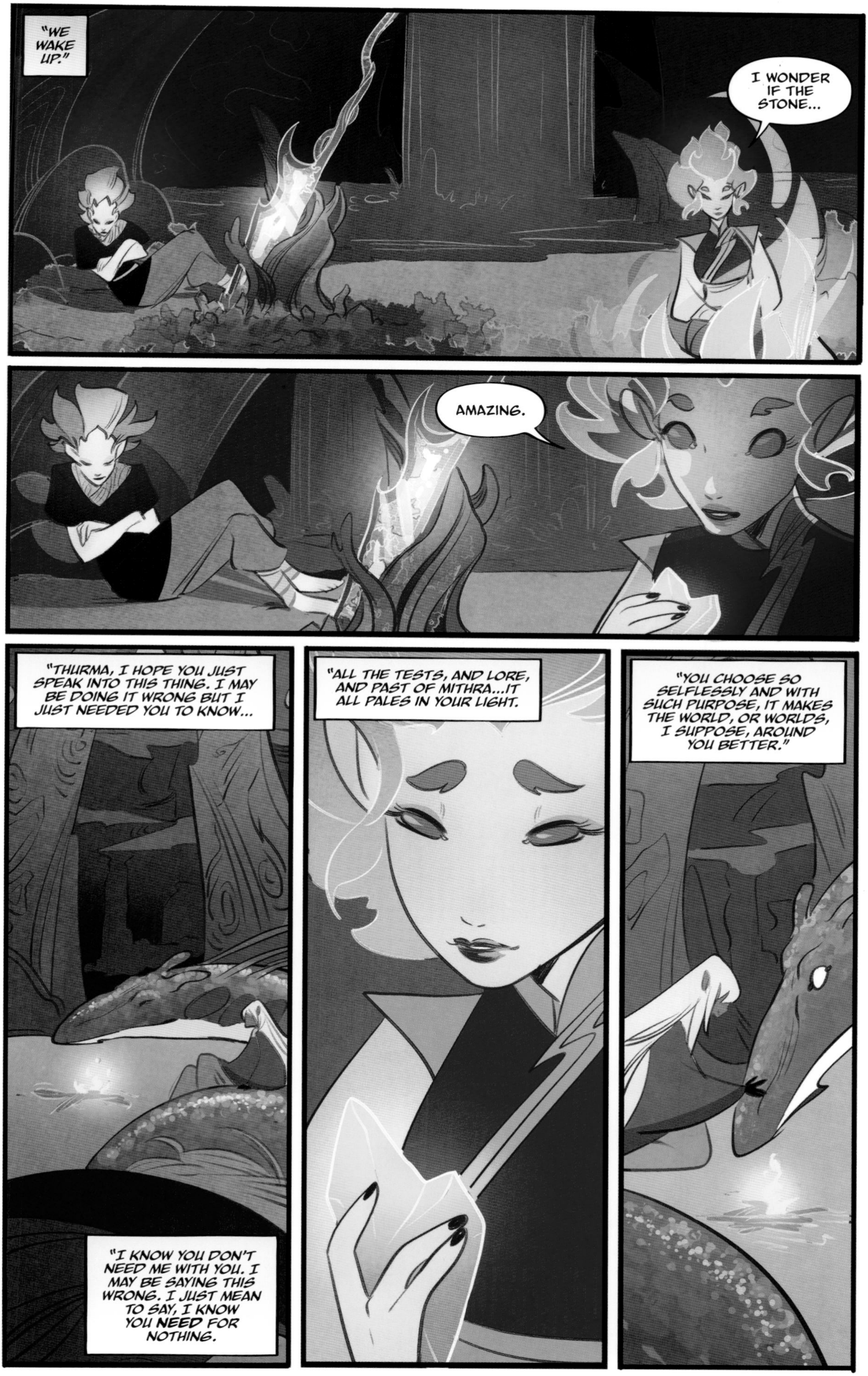
"WE WAKE UP."
I WONDER IF THE STONE...
AMAZING.
"THURMA, I HOPE YOU JUST SPEAK INTO THIS THING. I MAY BE DOING IT WRONG BUT I JUST NEEDED YOU TO KNOW...
"I KNOW YOU DON'T NEED ME WITH YOU. I MAY BE SAYING THIS WRONG. I JUST MEAN TO SAY, I KNOW YOU NEED FOR NOTHING.
"ALL THE TESTS, AND LORE, AND PAST OF MITHRA...IT ALL PALES IN YOUR LIGHT.
"YOU CHOOSE SO SELFLESSLY AND WITH SUCH PURPOSE, IT MAKES THE WORLD, OR WORLDS, I SUPPOSE, AROUND YOU BETTER."

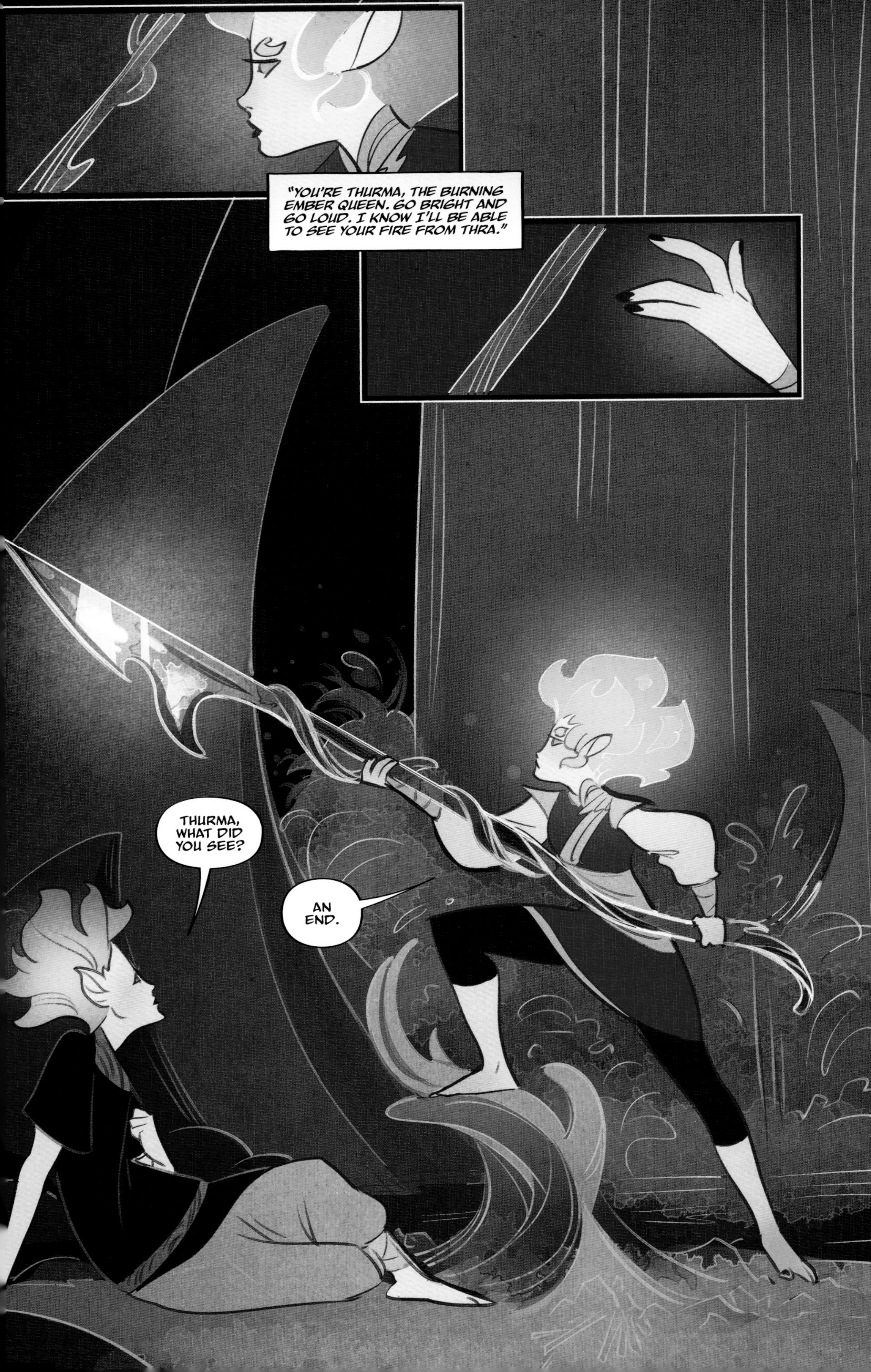
"YOU'RE THURMA, THE BURNING EMBER QUEEN. GO BRIGHT AND GO LOUD. I KNOW I'LL BE ABLE TO SEE YOUR FIRE FROM THRA."
THURMA, WHAT DID YOU SEE?
AN END.

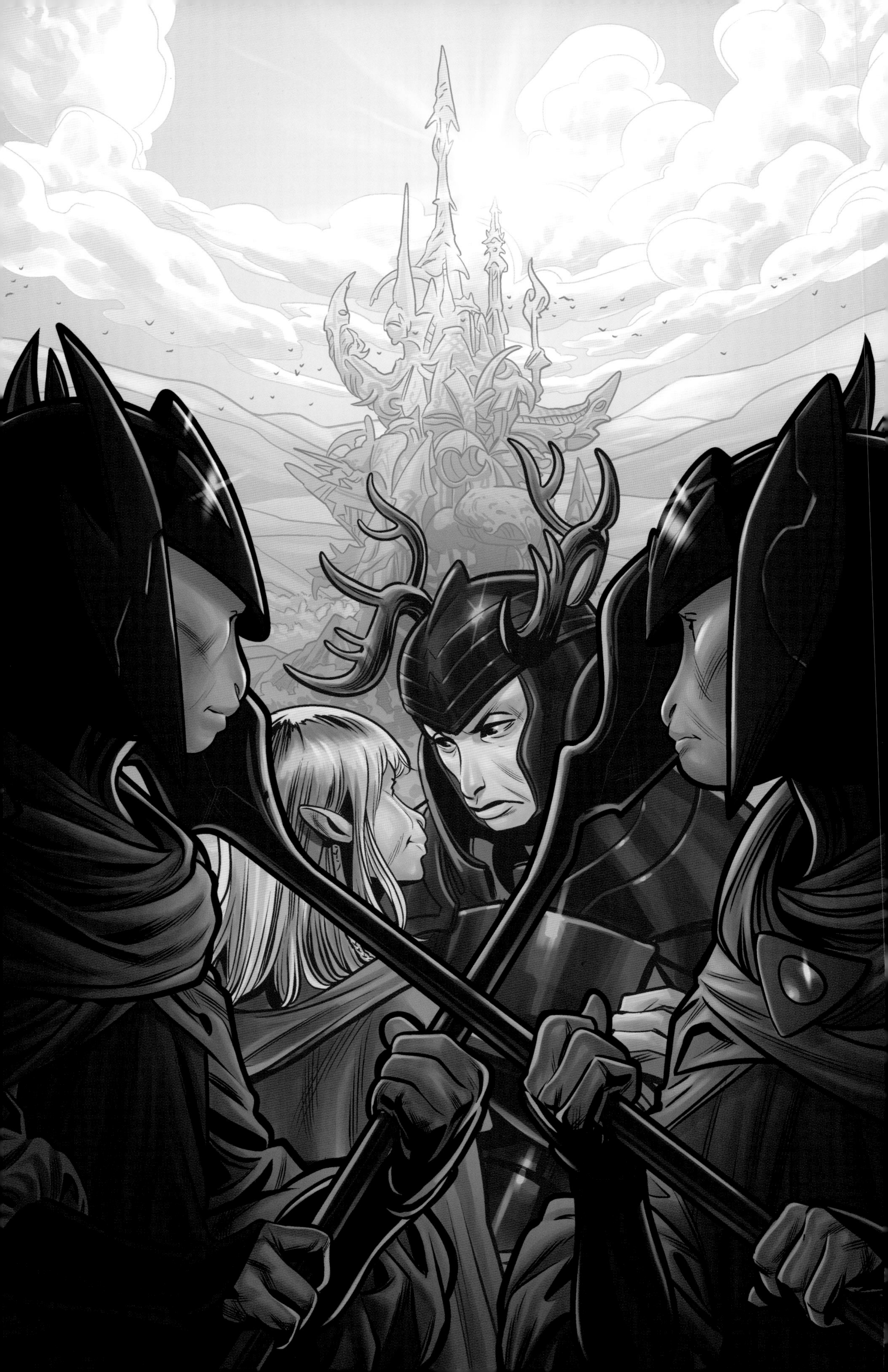

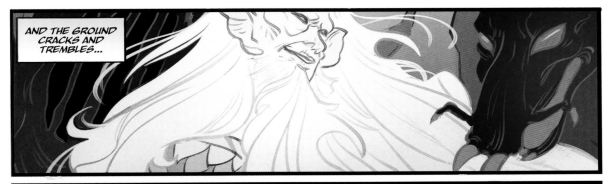

AND THE GROUND CRACKS AND TREMBLES...

AS OUR FIRE RISES FROM THE EMBERS...

A SINGLE SPARK...

FROM WITHIN THE DARK...

BOILS AND BEARS...

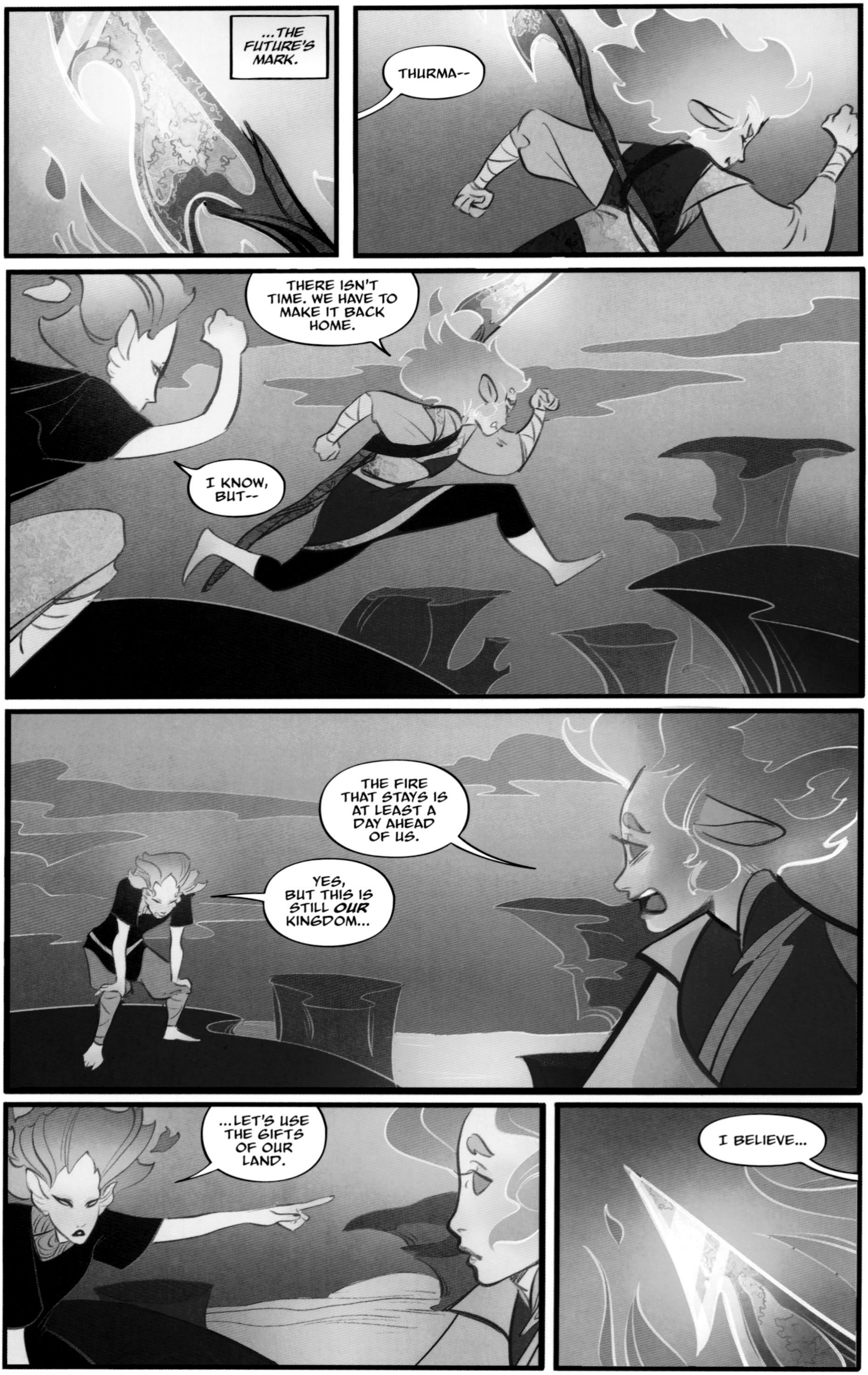
...THE FUTURE'S MARK.
THURMA--
THERE ISN'T TIME. WE HAVE TO MAKE IT BACK HOME.
I KNOW, BUT--
THE FIRE THAT STAYS IS AT LEAST A DAY AHEAD OF US.
YES, BUT THIS IS STILL OUR KINGDOM...
...LET'S USE THE GIFTS OF OUR LAND.
I BELIEVE...

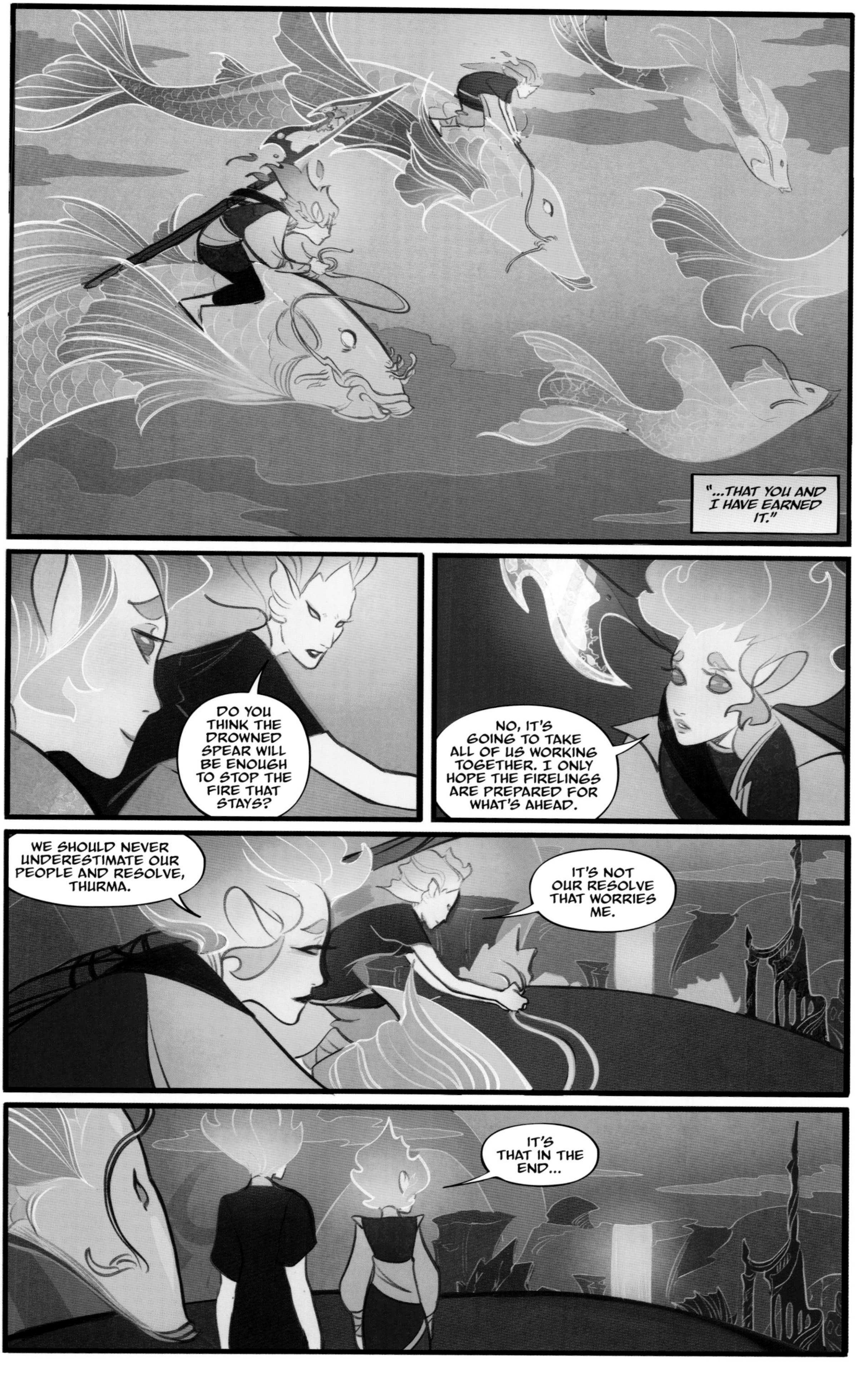
"...THAT YOU AND I HAVE EARNED IT."
DO YOU THINK THE DROWNED SPEAR WILL BE ENOUGH TO STOP THE FIRE THAT STAYS?
NO, IT'S GOING TO TAKE ALL OF US WORKING TOGETHER. I ONLY HOPE THE FIRELINGS ARE PREPARED FOR WHAT'S AHEAD.
WE SHOULD NEVER UNDERESTIMATE OUR PEOPLE AND RESOLVE, THURMA.
IT'S NOT OUR RESOLVE THAT WORRIES ME.
IT'S THAT IN THE END...

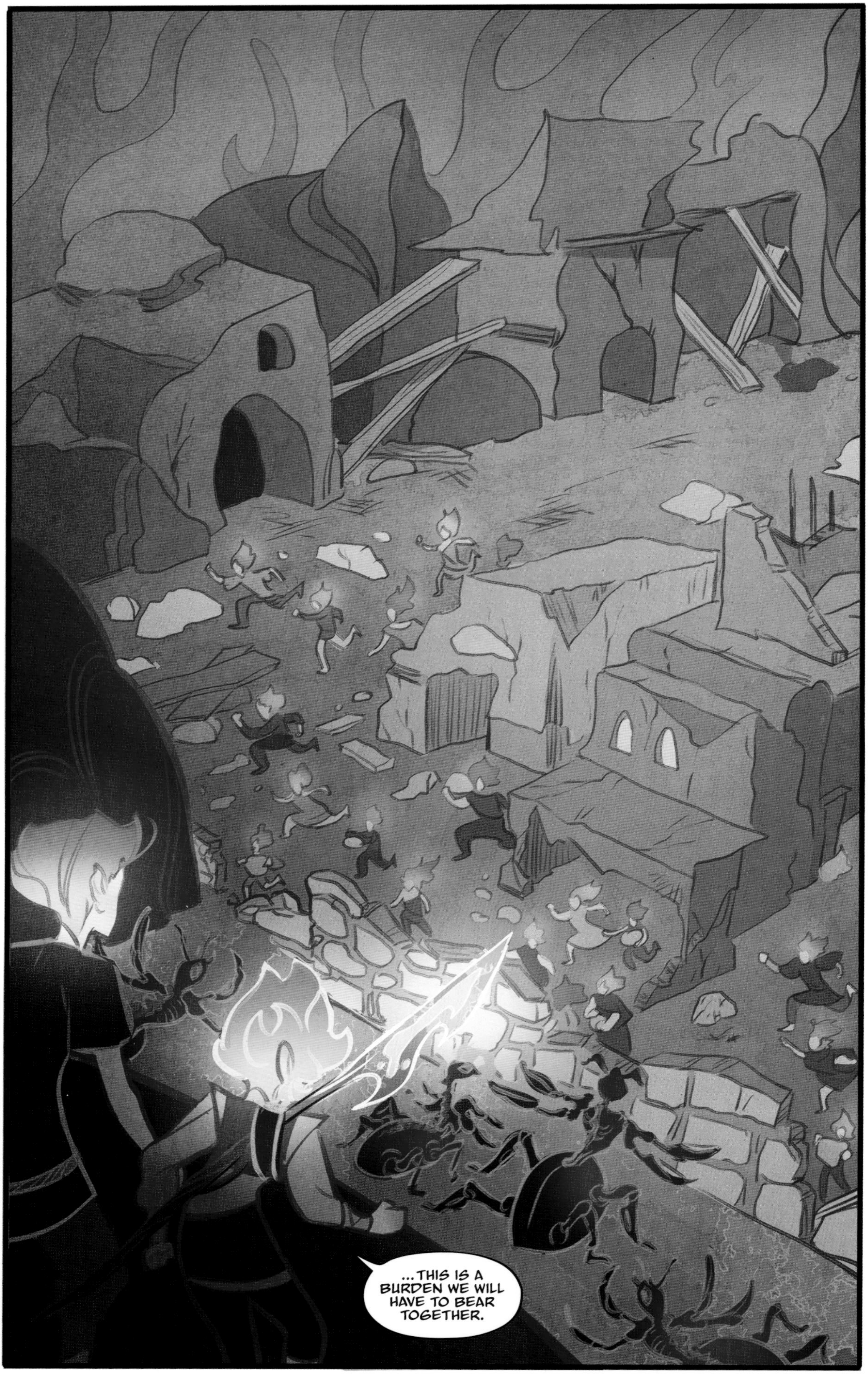
...THIS IS A BURDEN WE WILL HAVE TO BEAR TOGETHER.

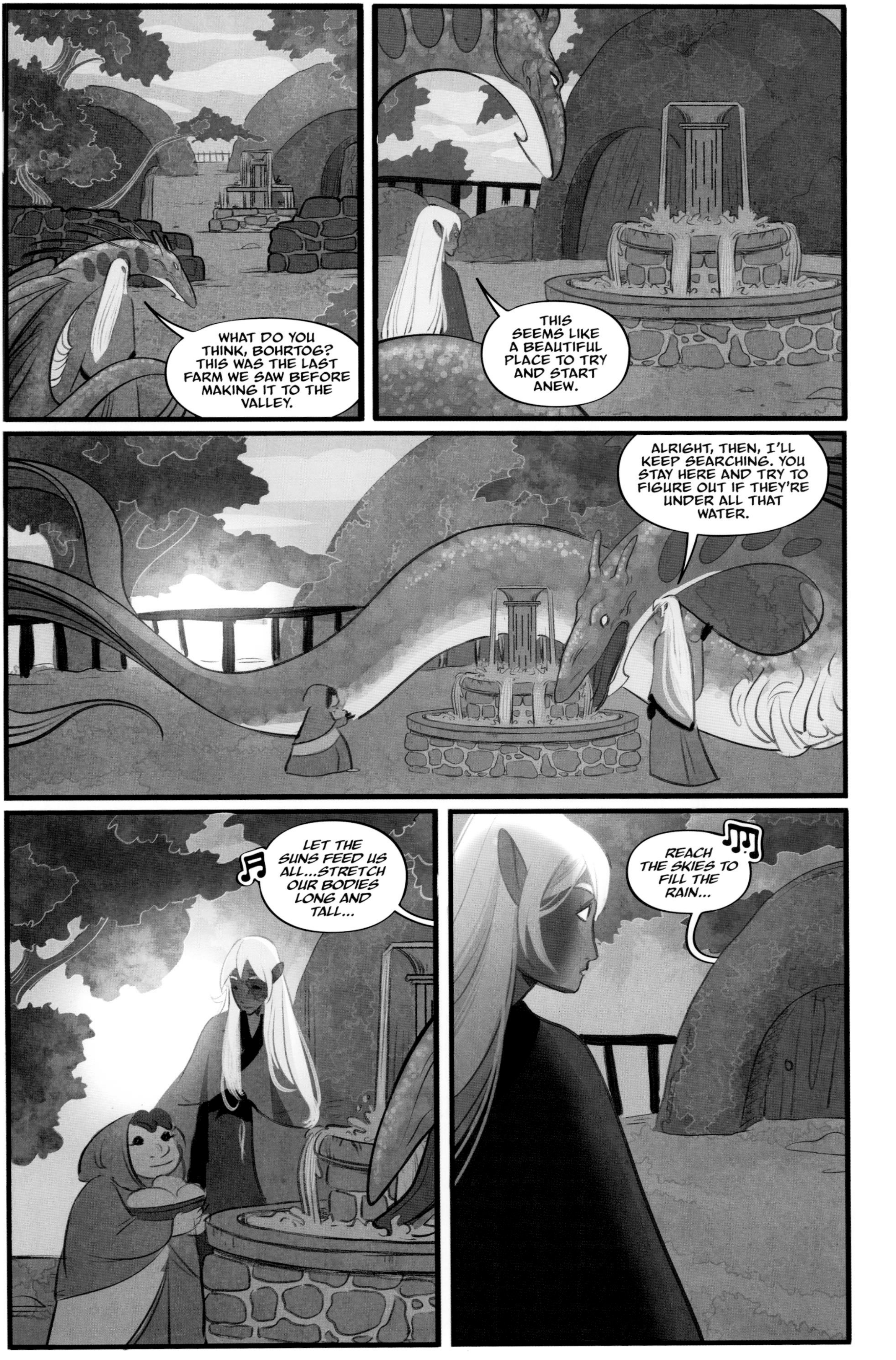
WHAT DO YOU THINK, BOHRTOG? THIS WAS THE LAST FARM WE SAW BEFORE MAKING IT TO THE VALLEY.
THIS SEEMS LIKE A BEAUTIFUL PLACE TO TRY AND START ANEW.
ALRIGHT, THEN, I'LL KEEP SEARCHING. YOU STAY HERE AND TRY TO FIGURE OUT IF THEY'RE UNDER ALL THAT WATER.
LET THE SUNS FEED US ALL...STRETCH OUR BODIES LONG AND TALL...
REACH THE SKIES TO FILL THE RAIN...

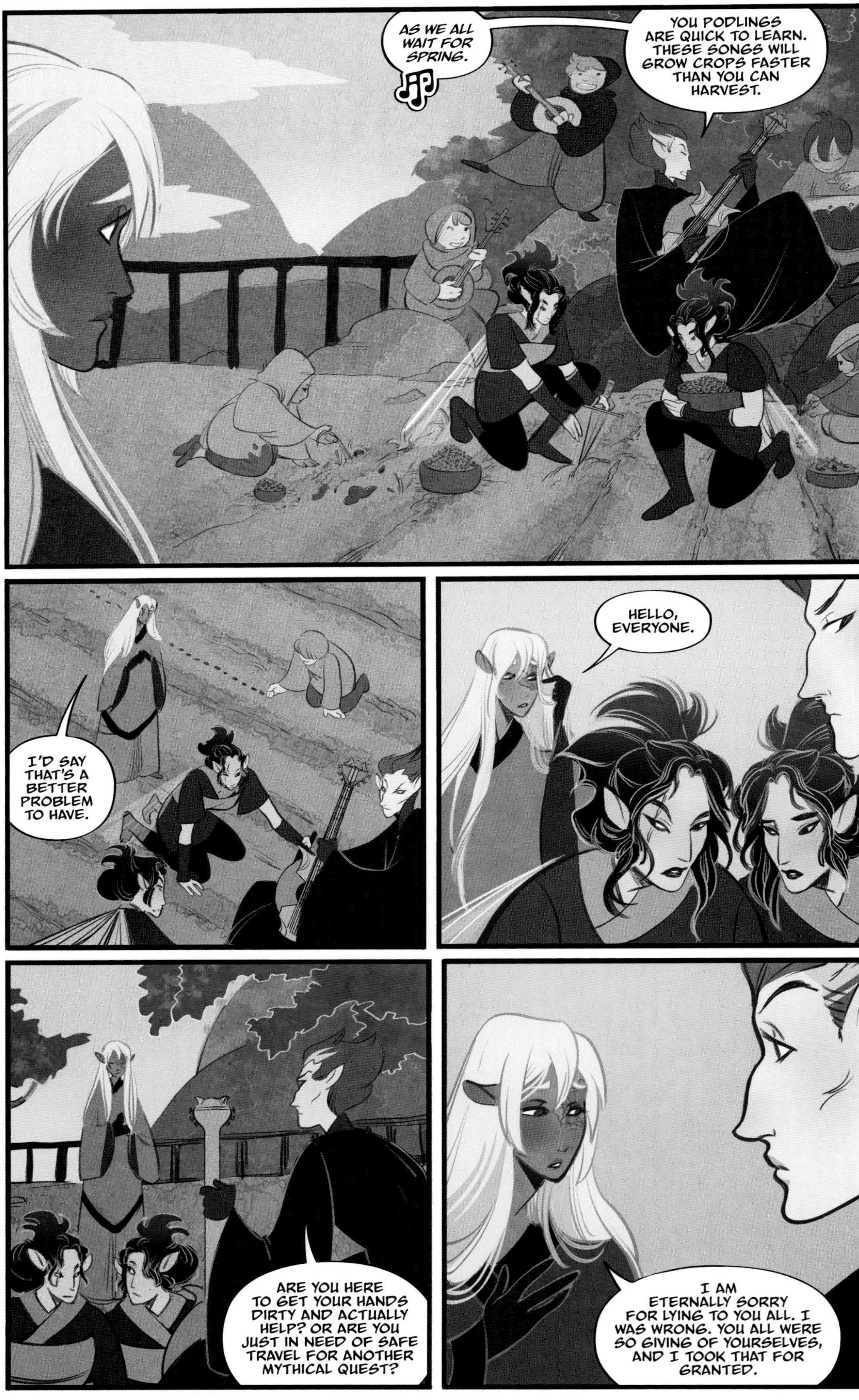
AS WE ALL WAIT FOR SPRING.
YOU PODLINGS ARE QUICK TO LEARN. THESE SONGS WILL GROW CROPS FASTER THAN YOU CAN HARVEST.
I'D SAY THAT'S A BETTER PROBLEM TO HAVE.
HELLO, EVERYONE.
ARE YOU HERE TO GET YOUR HANDS DIRTY AND ACTUALLY HELP? OR ARE YOU JUST IN NEED OF SAFE TRAVEL FOR ANOTHER MYTHICAL QUEST?
I AM ETERNALLY SORRY FOR LYING TO YOU ALL. I WAS WRONG. YOU ALL WERE SO GIVING OF YOURSELVES, AND I TOOK THAT FOR GRANTED.

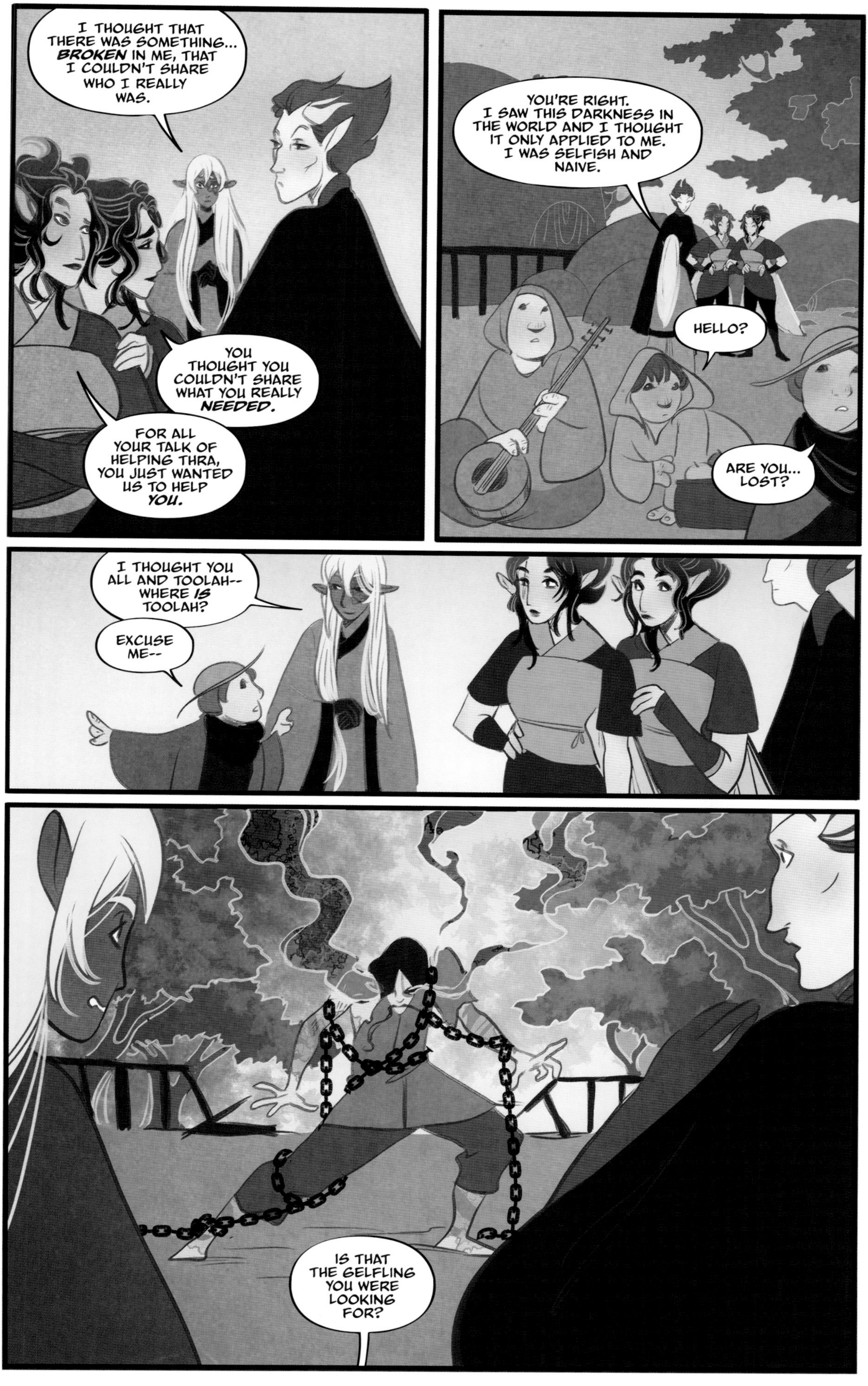
I THOUGHT THAT THERE WAS SOMETHING... **BROKEN** IN ME, THAT I COULDN'T SHARE WHO I REALLY WAS.
YOU THOUGHT YOU COULDN'T SHARE WHAT YOU REALLY **NEEDED.**
FOR ALL YOUR TALK OF HELPING THRA, YOU JUST WANTED US TO HELP **YOU.**
YOU'RE RIGHT. I SAW THIS DARKNESS IN THE WORLD AND I THOUGHT IT ONLY APPLIED TO ME. I WAS SELFISH AND NAIVE.
HELLO?
ARE YOU... LOST?
I THOUGHT YOU ALL AND TOOLAH-- WHERE **IS** TOOLAH?
EXCUSE ME--
IS THAT THE GELFLING YOU WERE LOOKING FOR?

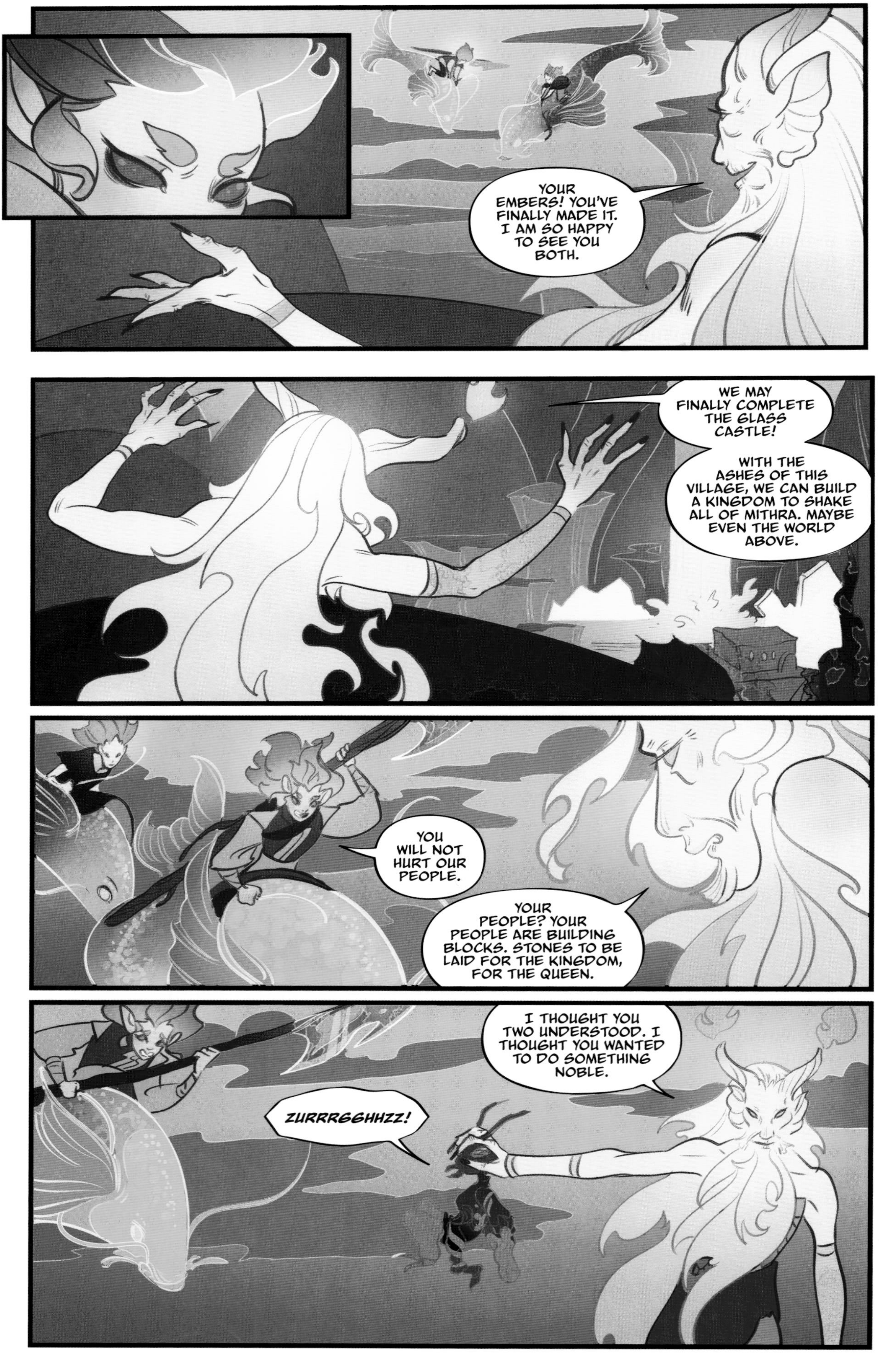
YOUR EMBERS! YOU'VE FINALLY MADE IT. I AM SO HAPPY TO SEE YOU BOTH.
WE MAY FINALLY COMPLETE THE GLASS CASTLE!
WITH THE ASHES OF THIS VILLAGE, WE CAN BUILD A KINGDOM TO SHAKE ALL OF MITHRA. MAYBE EVEN THE WORLD ABOVE.
YOU WILL NOT HURT OUR PEOPLE.
YOUR PEOPLE? YOUR PEOPLE ARE BUILDING BLOCKS. STONES TO BE LAID FOR THE KINGDOM, FOR THE QUEEN.
I THOUGHT YOU TWO UNDERSTOOD. I THOUGHT YOU WANTED TO DO SOMETHING NOBLE.
ZURRRGGHHZZ!

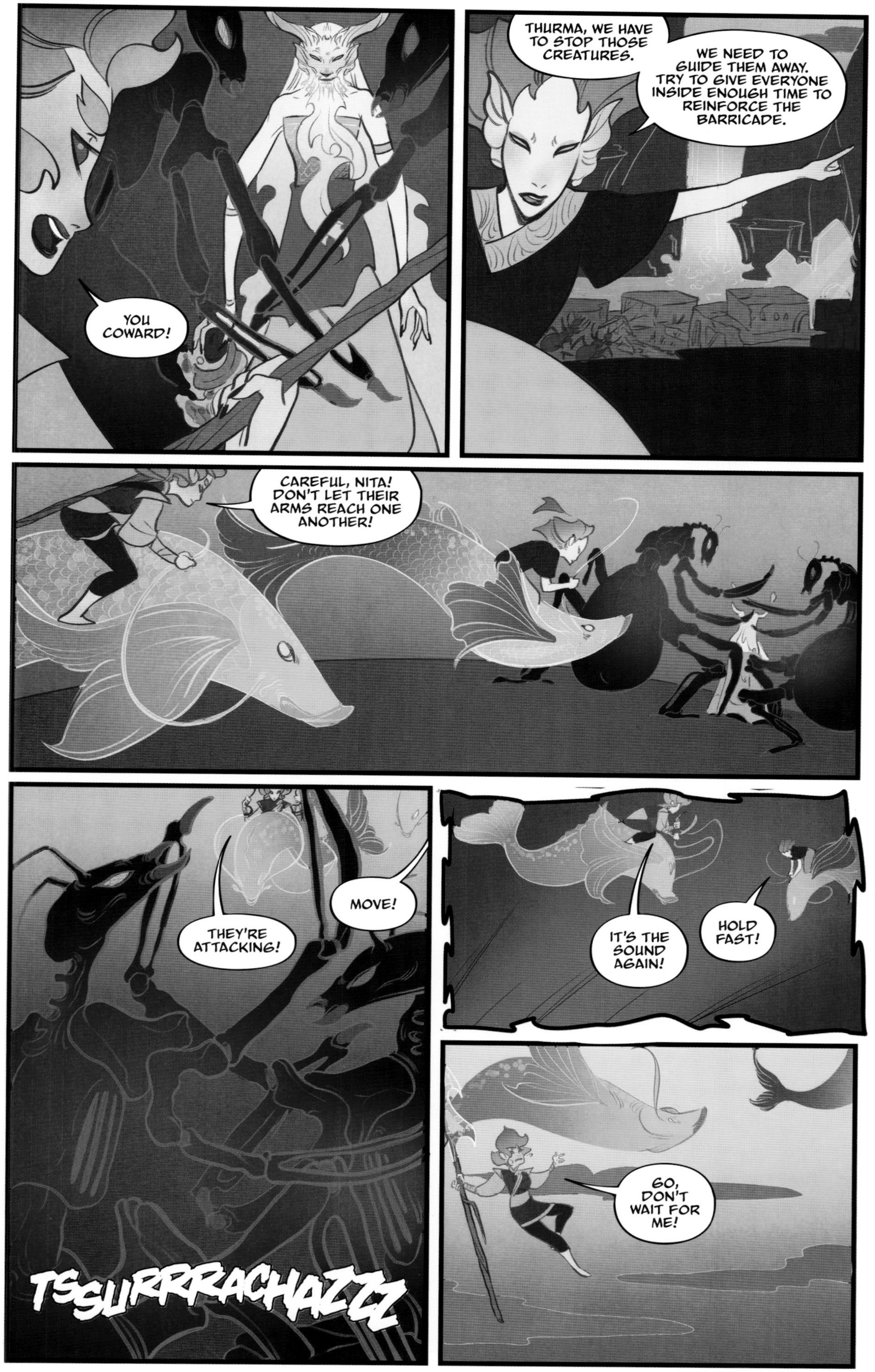
YOU COWARD!
THURMA, WE HAVE TO STOP THOSE CREATURES.
WE NEED TO GUIDE THEM AWAY. TRY TO GIVE EVERYONE INSIDE ENOUGH TIME TO REINFORCE THE BARRICADE.
CAREFUL, NITA! DON'T LET THEIR ARMS REACH ONE ANOTHER!
THEY'RE ATTACKING!
MOVE!
TSSURRRACHAZZZ
IT'S THE SOUND AGAIN!
HOLD FAST!
GO, DON'T WAIT FOR ME!

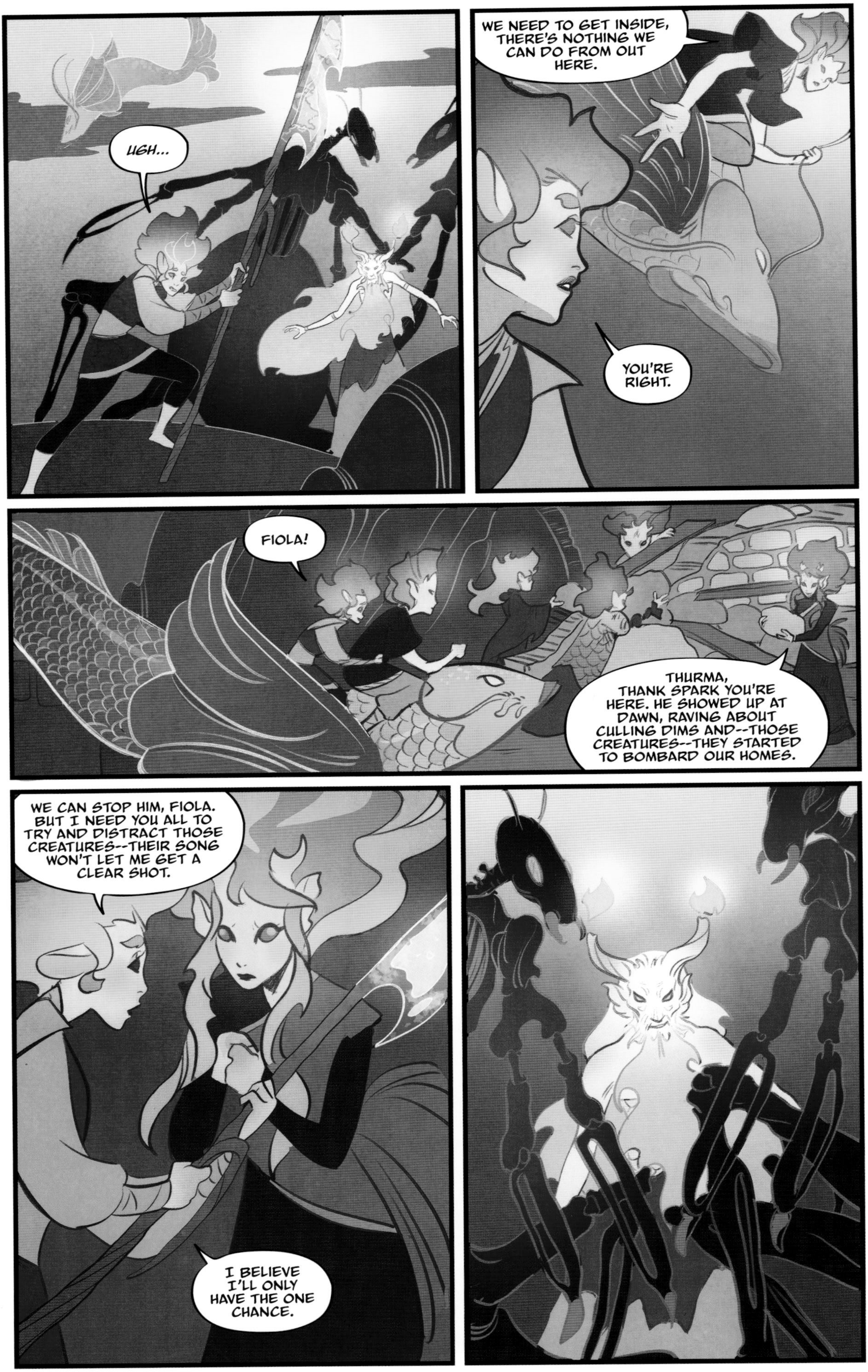
UGH...
WE NEED TO GET INSIDE, THERE'S NOTHING WE CAN DO FROM OUT HERE.
YOU'RE RIGHT.
FIOLA!
THURMA, THANK SPARK YOU'RE HERE. HE SHOWED UP AT DAWN, RAVING ABOUT CULLING DIMS AND--THOSE CREATURES--THEY STARTED TO BOMBARD OUR HOMES.
WE CAN STOP HIM, FIOLA. BUT I NEED YOU ALL TO TRY AND DISTRACT THOSE CREATURES--THEIR SONG WON'T LET ME GET A CLEAR SHOT.
I BELIEVE I'LL ONLY HAVE THE ONE CHANCE.

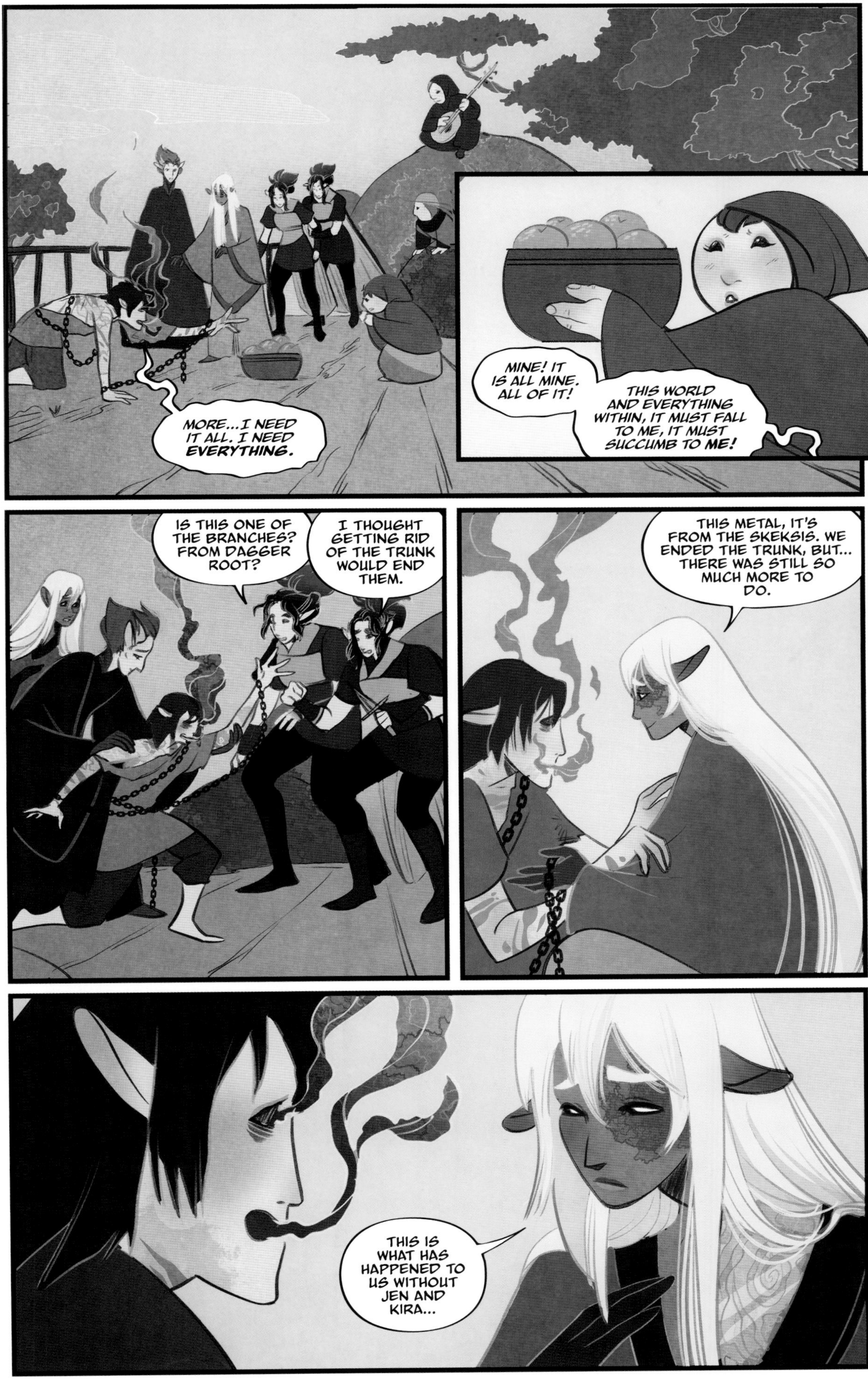
MORE... I NEED IT ALL. I NEED EVERYTHING.
MINE! IT IS ALL MINE. ALL OF IT!
THIS WORLD AND EVERYTHING WITHIN, IT MUST FALL TO ME, IT MUST SUCCUMB TO ME!
IS THIS ONE OF THE BRANCHES? FROM DAGGER ROOT?
I THOUGHT GETTING RID OF THE TRUNK WOULD END THEM.
THIS METAL, IT'S FROM THE SKEKSIS. WE ENDED THE TRUNK, BUT... THERE WAS STILL SO MUCH MORE TO DO.
THIS IS WHAT HAS HAPPENED TO US WITHOUT JEN AND KIRA...

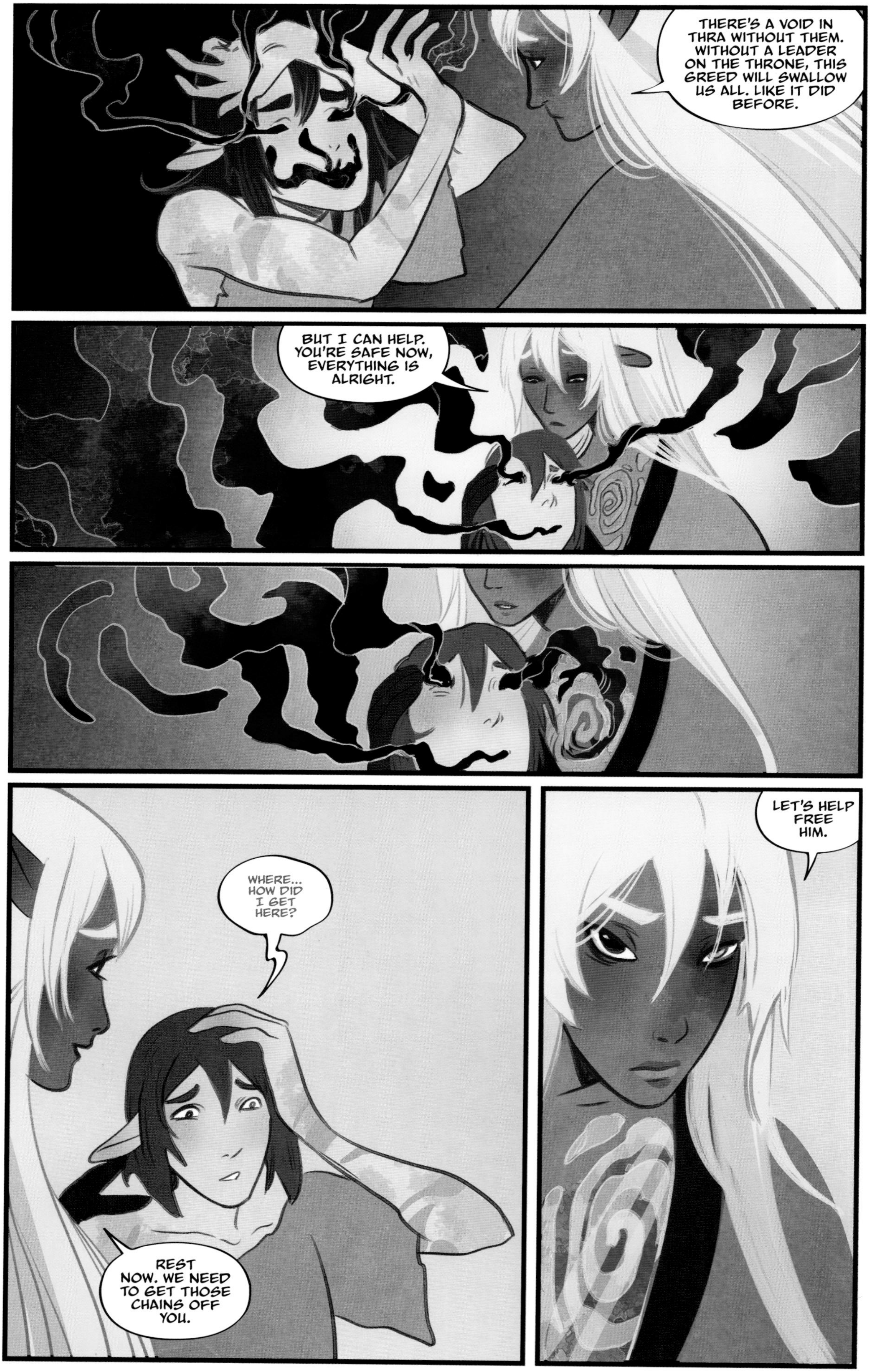
THERE'S A VOID IN THRA WITHOUT THEM. WITHOUT A LEADER ON THE THRONE, THIS GREED WILL SWALLOW US ALL. LIKE IT DID BEFORE.
BUT I CAN HELP. YOU'RE SAFE NOW, EVERYTHING IS ALRIGHT.
WHERE... HOW DID I GET HERE?
REST NOW. WE NEED TO GET THOSE CHAINS OFF YOU.
LET'S HELP FREE HIM.

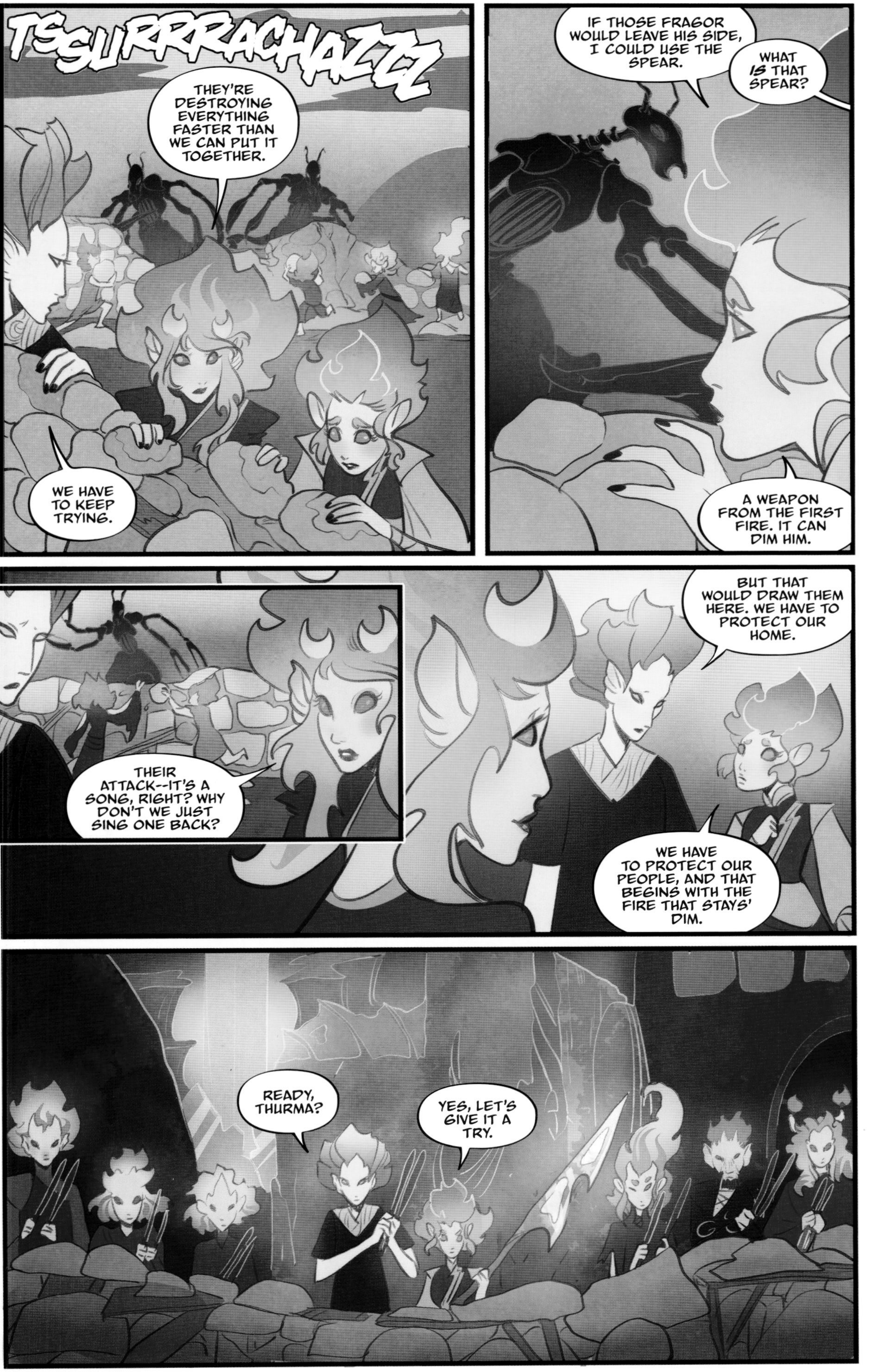
TSSURRRACHAZZZ
THEY'RE DESTROYING EVERYTHING FASTER THAN WE CAN PUT IT TOGETHER.
WE HAVE TO KEEP TRYING.
IF THOSE FRAGOR WOULD LEAVE HIS SIDE, I COULD USE THE SPEAR.
WHAT *IS* THAT SPEAR?
A WEAPON FROM THE FIRST FIRE. IT CAN DIM HIM.
THEIR ATTACK--IT'S A SONG, RIGHT? WHY DON'T WE JUST SING ONE BACK?
BUT THAT WOULD DRAW THEM HERE. WE HAVE TO PROTECT OUR HOME.
WE HAVE TO PROTECT OUR PEOPLE, AND THAT BEGINS WITH THE FIRE THAT STAYS' DIM.
READY, THURMA?
YES, LET'S GIVE IT A TRY.

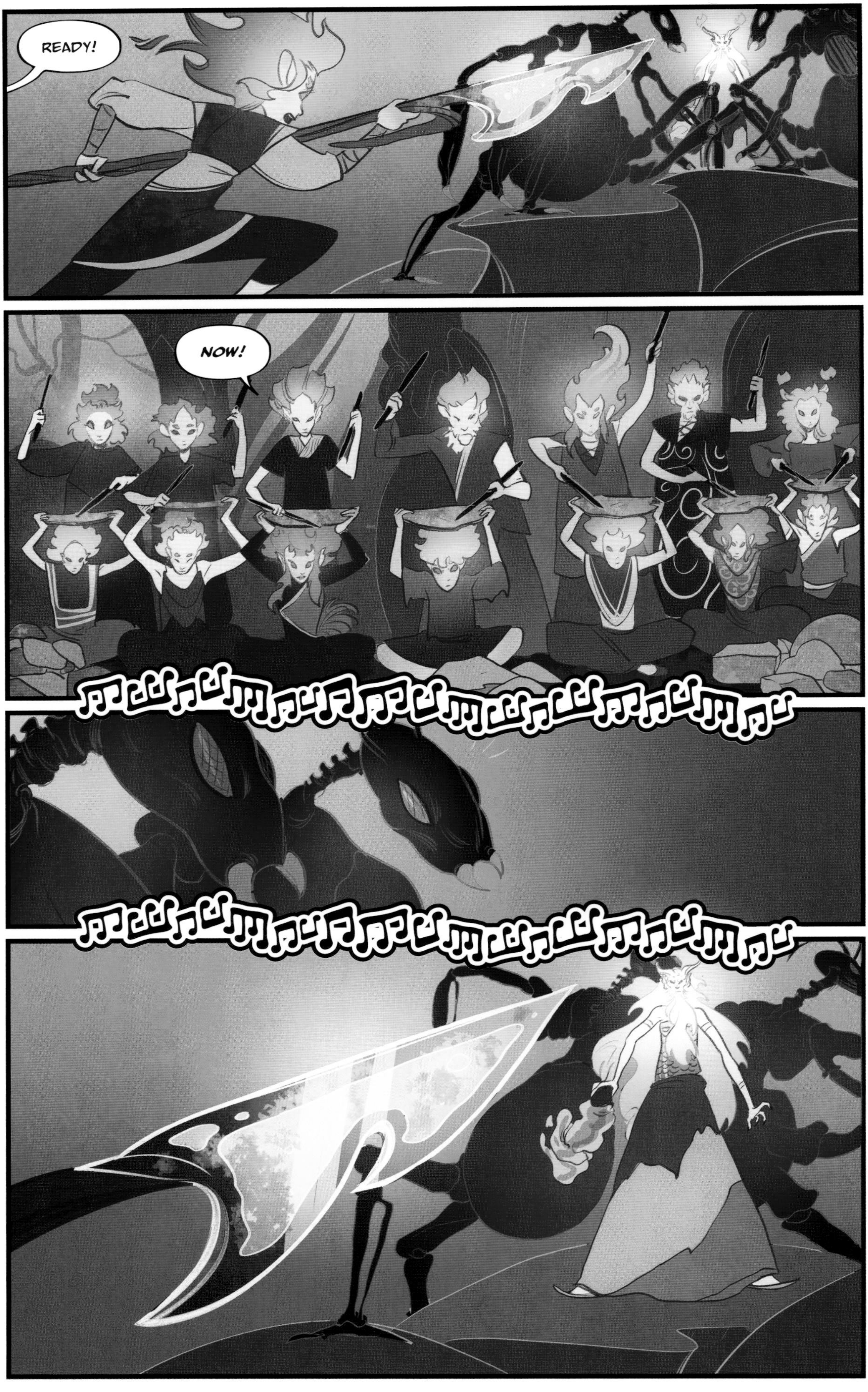
READY!
NOW!

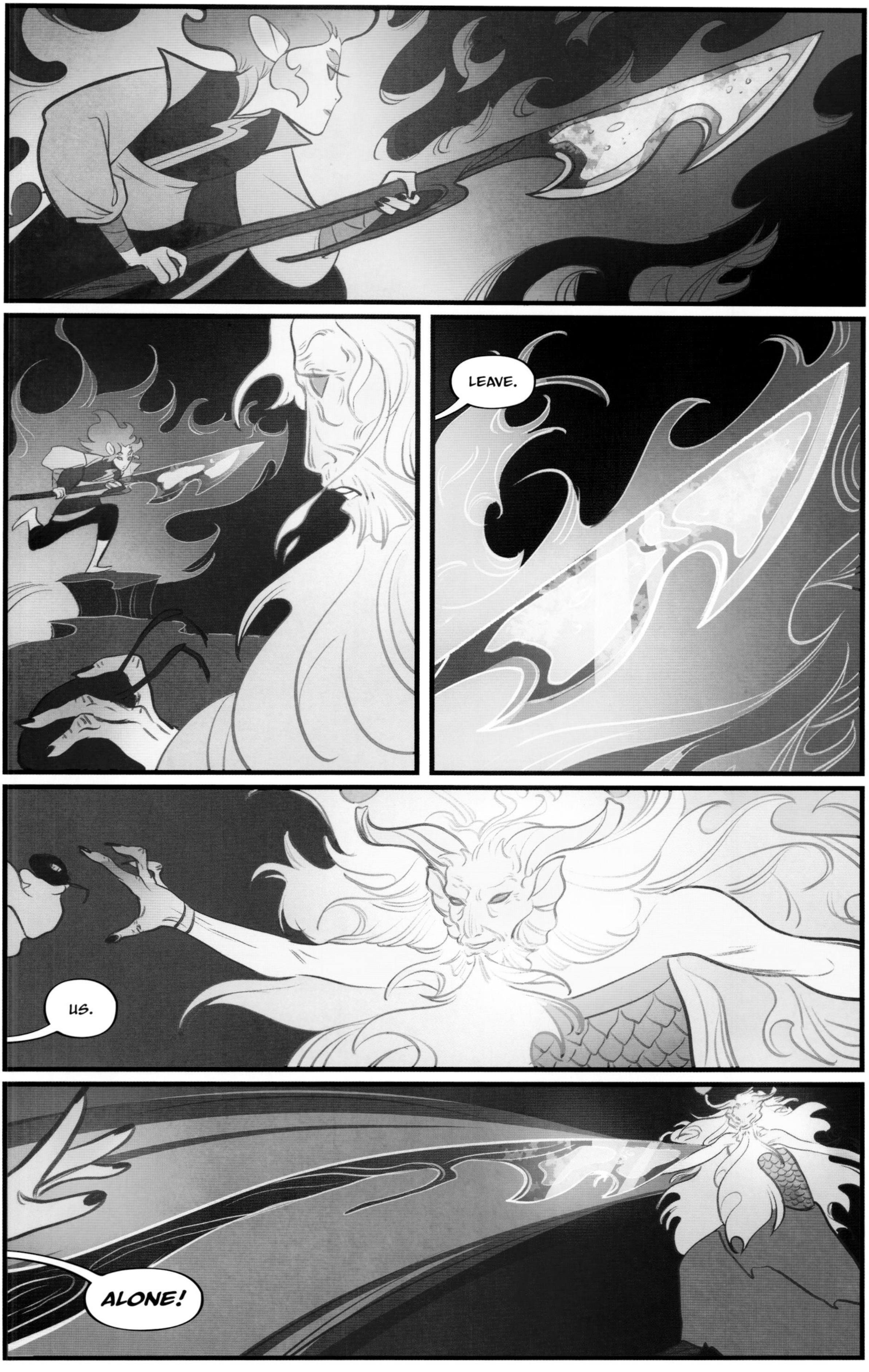
LEAVE.
US.
ALONE!

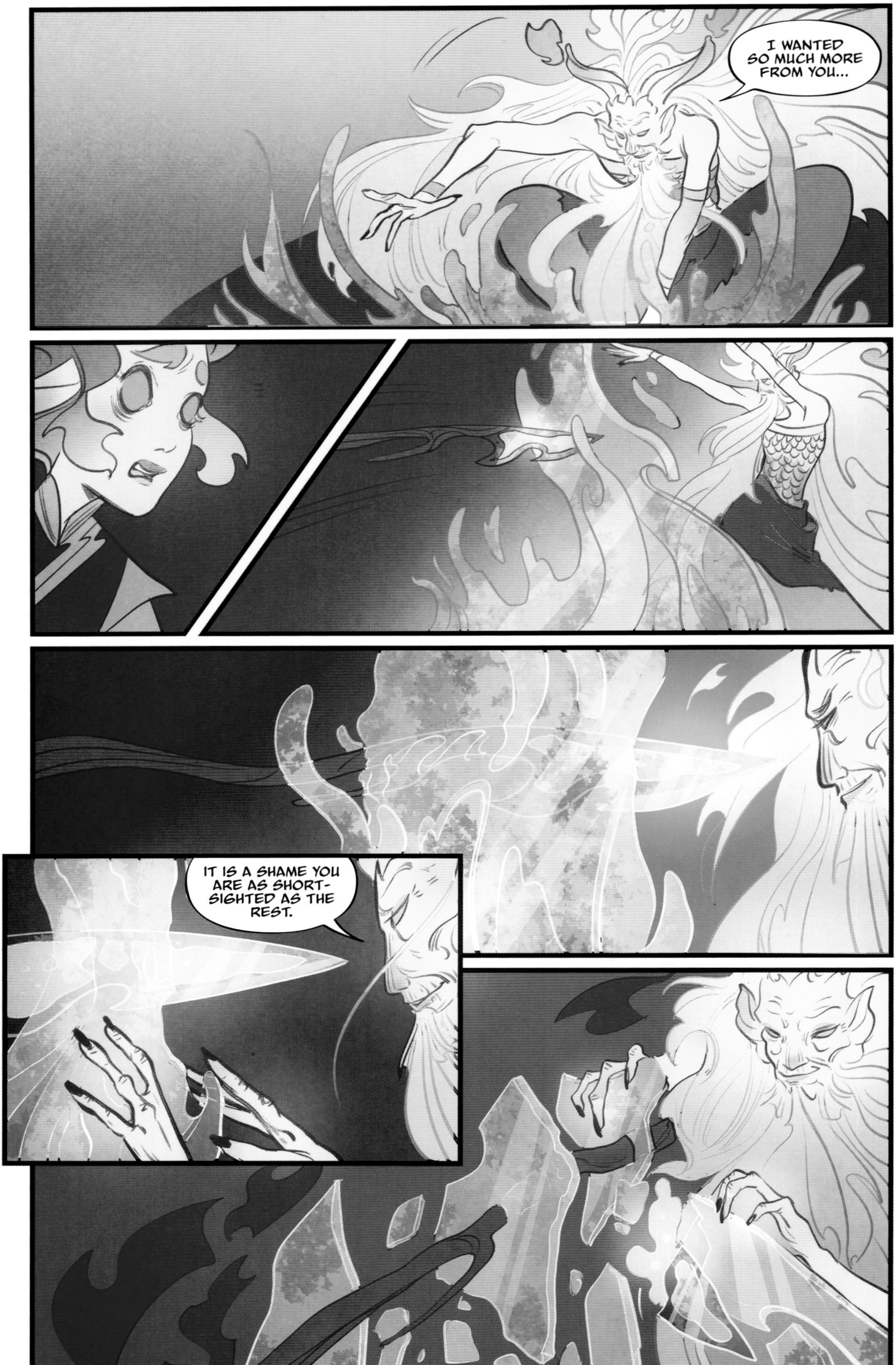
I WANTED SO MUCH MORE FROM YOU...
IT IS A SHAME YOU ARE AS SHORT-SIGHTED AS THE REST.

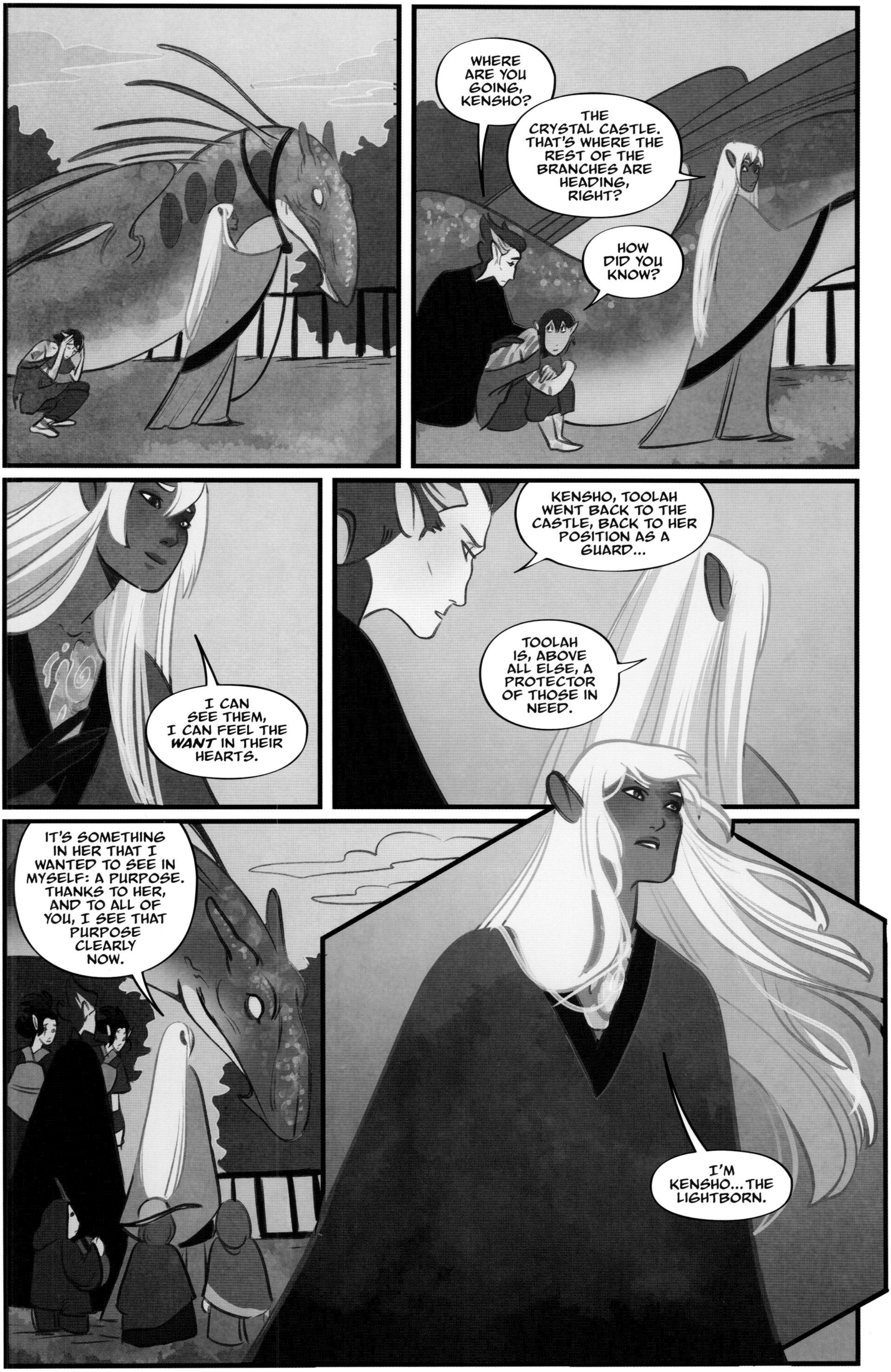
WHERE ARE YOU GOING, KENSHO?
THE CRYSTAL CASTLE. THAT'S WHERE THE REST OF THE BRANCHES ARE HEADING, RIGHT?
HOW DID YOU KNOW?
I CAN SEE THEM, I CAN FEEL THE *WANT* IN THEIR HEARTS.
KENSHO, TOOLAH WENT BACK TO THE CASTLE, BACK TO HER POSITION AS A GUARD...
TOOLAH IS, ABOVE ALL ELSE, A PROTECTOR OF THOSE IN NEED.
IT'S SOMETHING IN HER THAT I WANTED TO SEE IN MYSELF: A PURPOSE. THANKS TO HER, AND TO ALL OF YOU, I SEE THAT PURPOSE CLEARLY NOW.
I'M KENSHO... THE LIGHTBORN.

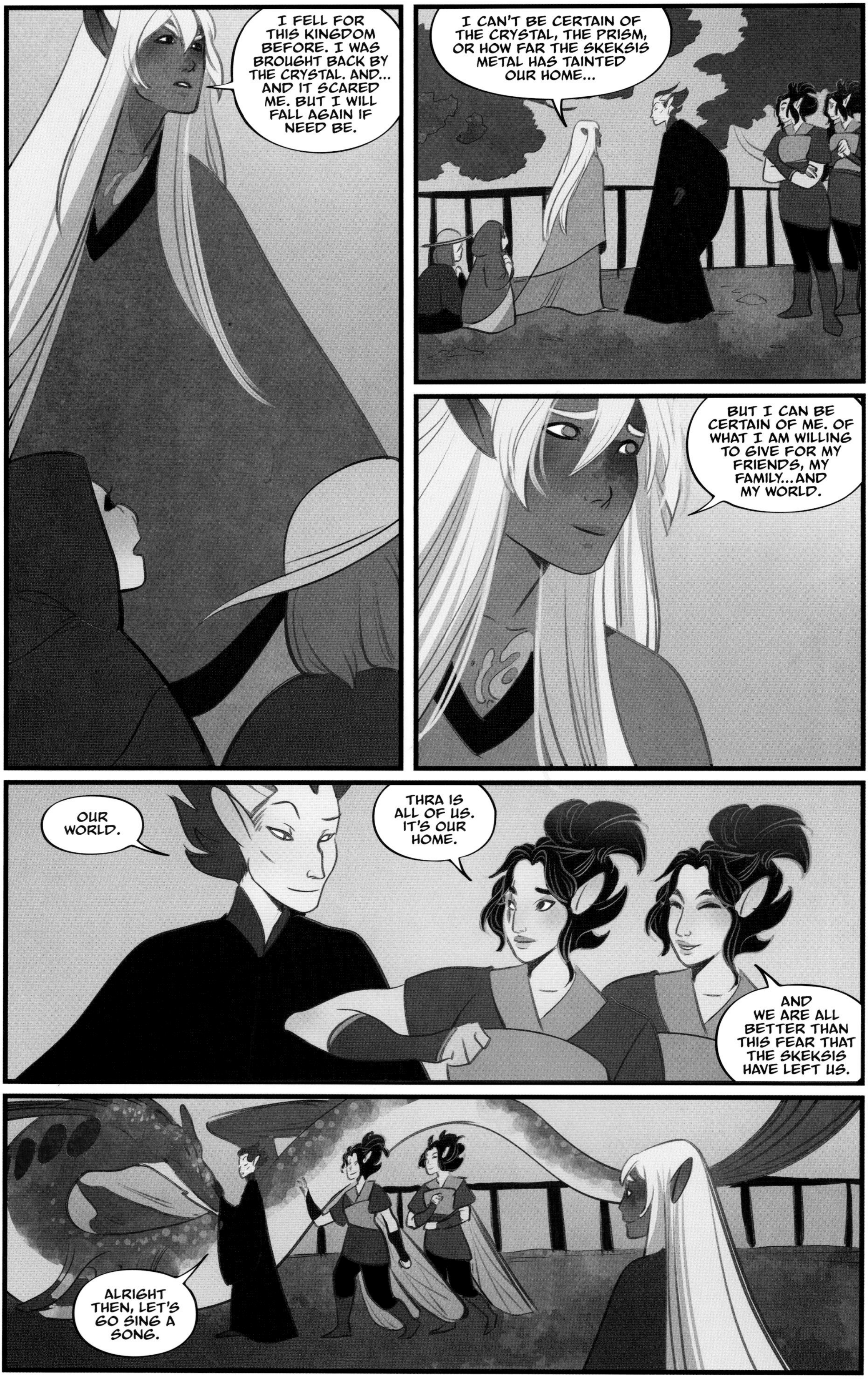
I FELL FOR THIS KINGDOM BEFORE. I WAS BROUGHT BACK BY THE CRYSTAL. AND... AND IT SCARED ME. BUT I WILL FALL AGAIN IF NEED BE.
I CAN'T BE CERTAIN OF THE CRYSTAL, THE PRISM, OR HOW FAR THE SKEKSIS METAL HAS TAINTED OUR HOME...
BUT I CAN BE CERTAIN OF ME. OF WHAT I AM WILLING TO GIVE FOR MY FRIENDS, MY FAMILY...AND MY WORLD.
OUR WORLD.
THRA IS ALL OF US. IT'S OUR HOME.
AND WE ARE ALL BETTER THAN THIS FEAR THAT THE SKEKSIS HAVE LEFT US.
ALRIGHT THEN, LET'S GO SING A SONG.

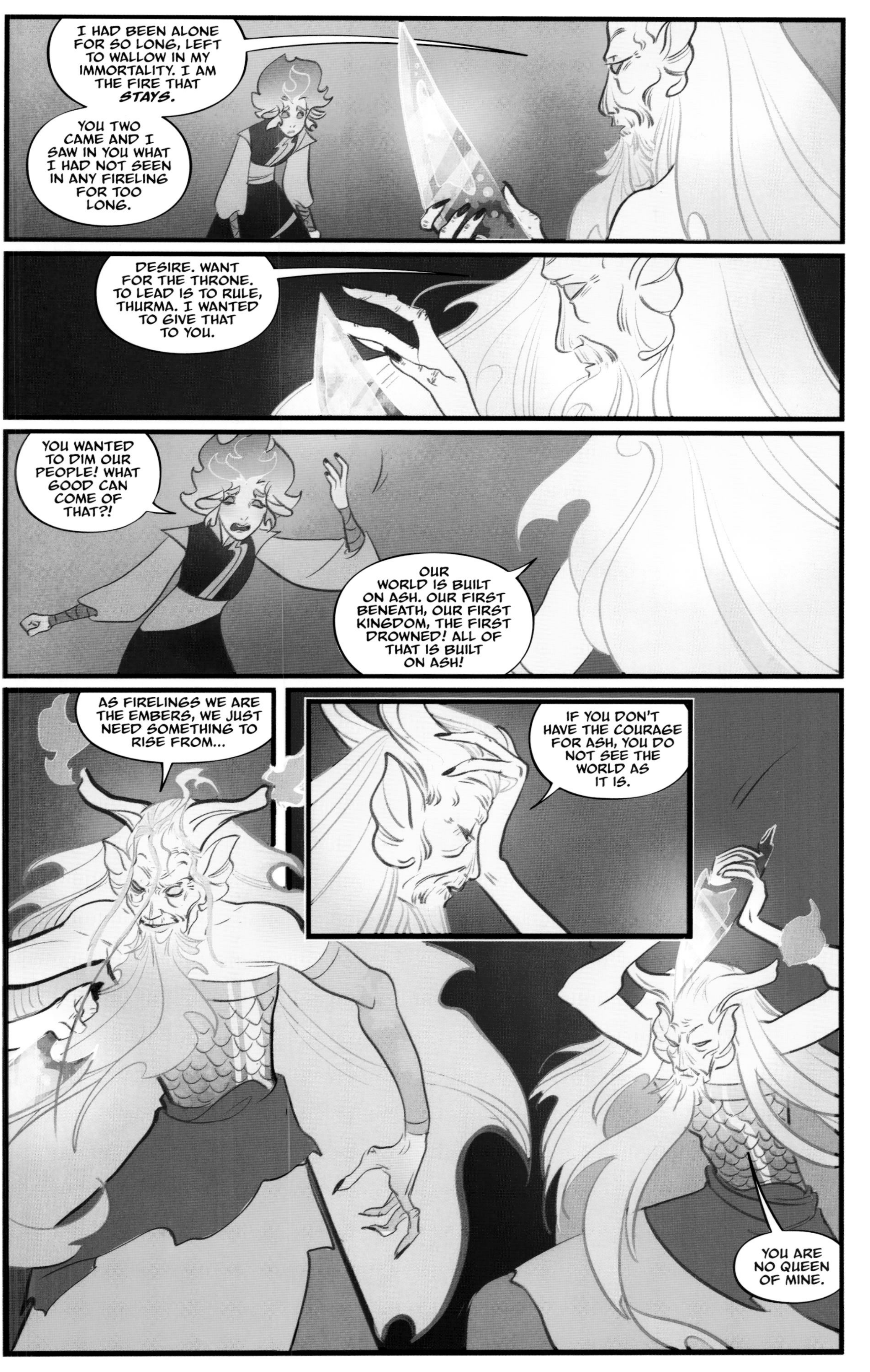
I HAD BEEN ALONE FOR SO LONG, LEFT TO WALLOW IN MY IMMORTALITY. I AM THE FIRE THAT *STAYS.*
YOU TWO CAME AND I SAW IN YOU WHAT I HAD NOT SEEN IN ANY FIRELING FOR TOO LONG.
DESIRE. WANT FOR THE THRONE. TO LEAD IS TO RULE, THURMA. I WANTED TO GIVE THAT TO YOU.
YOU WANTED TO DIM OUR PEOPLE! WHAT GOOD CAN COME OF THAT?!
OUR WORLD IS BUILT ON ASH. OUR FIRST BENEATH, OUR FIRST KINGDOM, THE FIRST DROWNED! ALL OF THAT IS BUILT ON ASH!
AS FIRELINGS WE ARE THE EMBERS, WE JUST NEED SOMETHING TO RISE FROM...
IF YOU DON'T HAVE THE COURAGE FOR ASH, YOU DO NOT SEE THE WORLD AS IT IS.
YOU ARE NO QUEEN OF MINE.

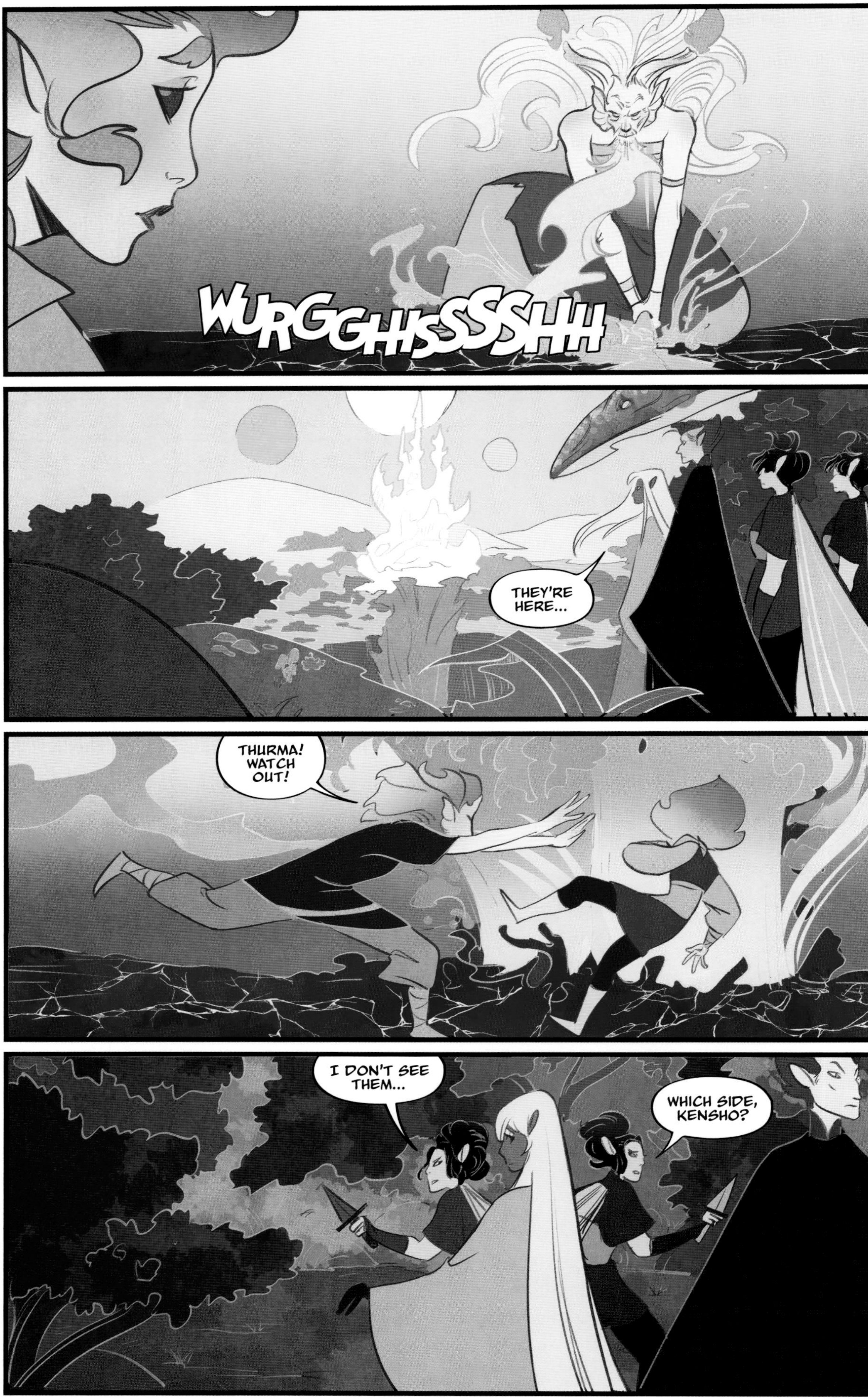
WURGGHISSSSHH
THEY'RE HERE...
THURMA! WATCH OUT!
I DON'T SEE THEM...
WHICH SIDE, KENSHO?

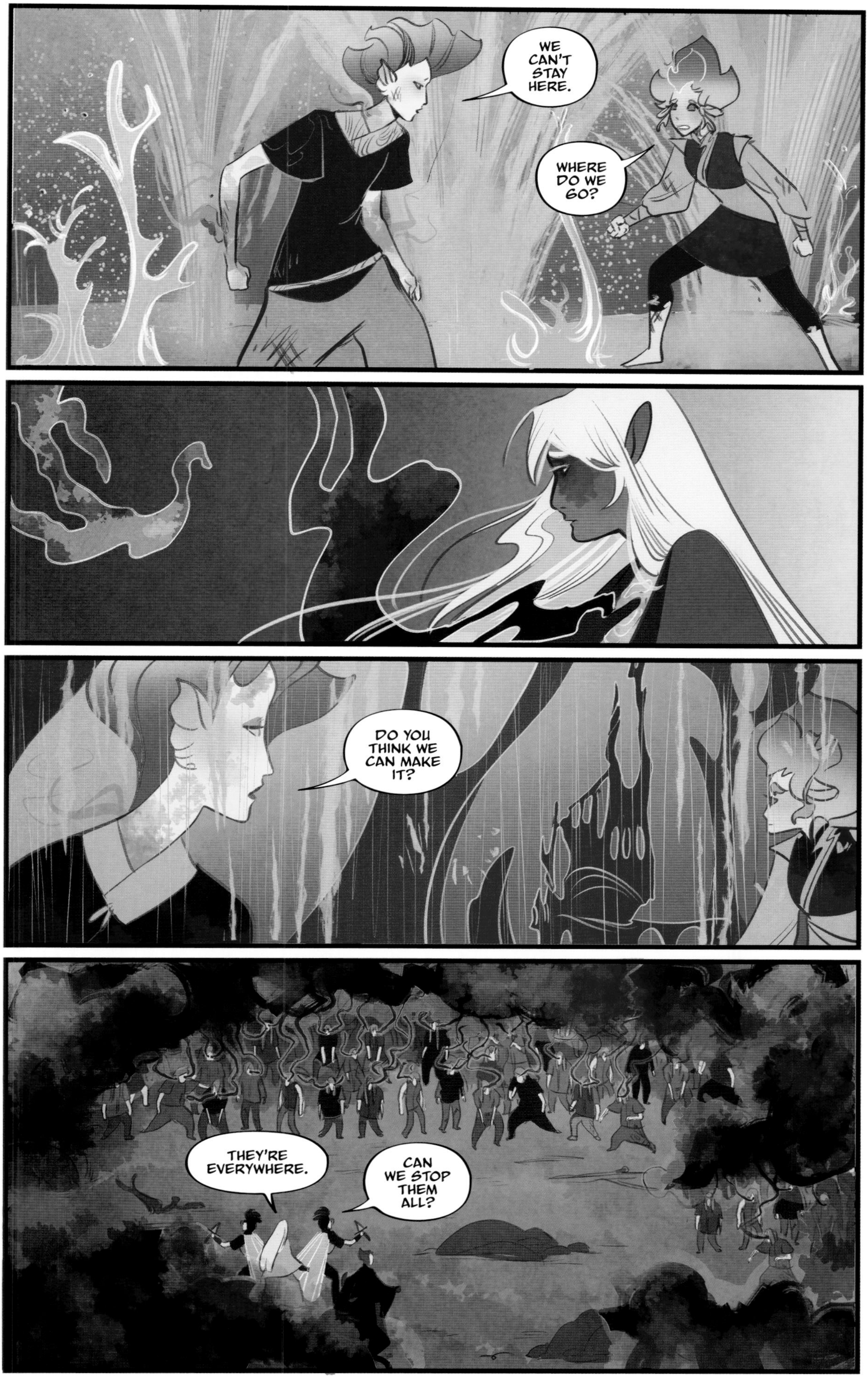
WE CAN'T STAY HERE.
WHERE DO WE GO?
DO YOU THINK WE CAN MAKE IT?
THEY'RE EVERYWHERE.
CAN WE STOP THEM ALL?

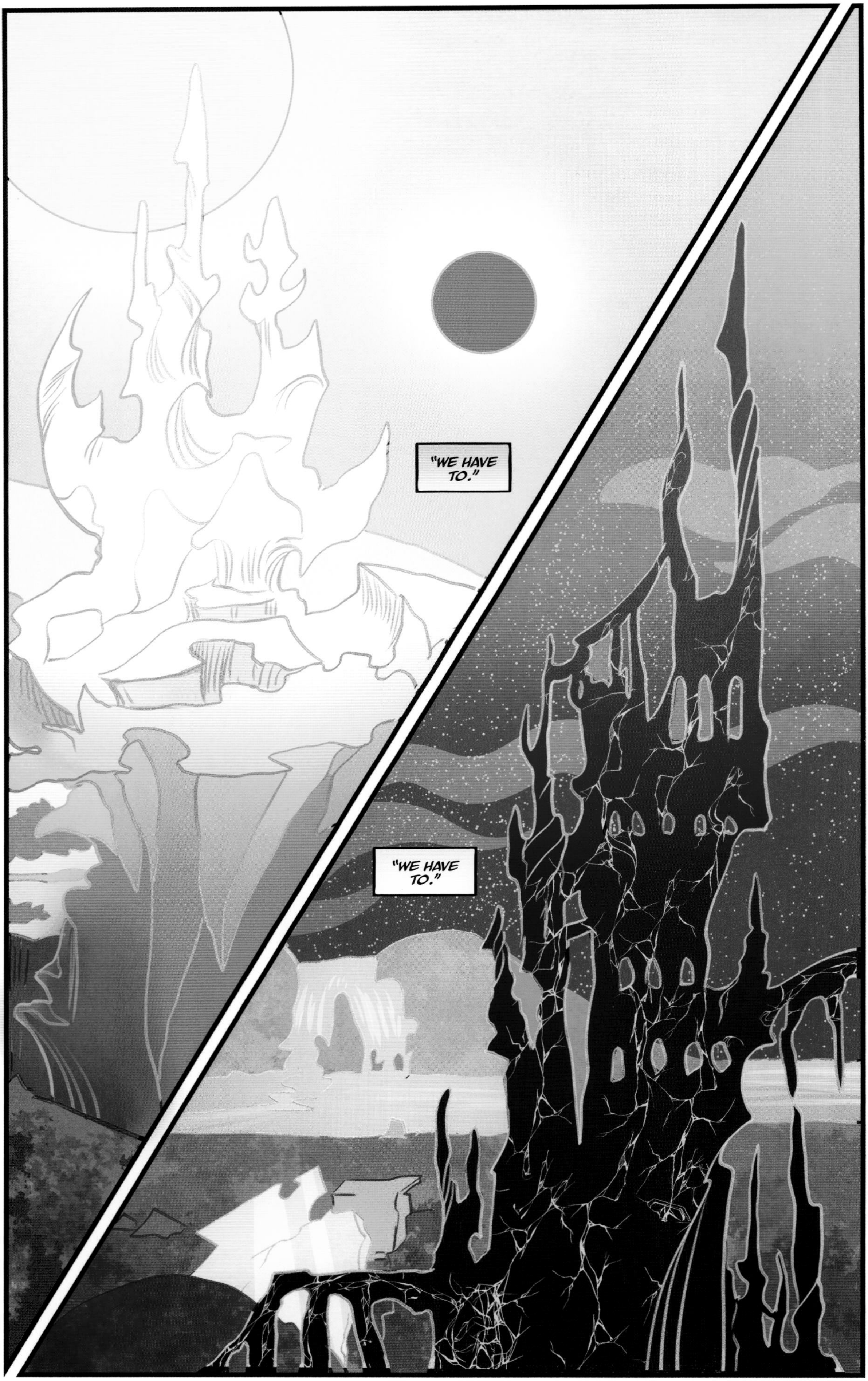
"WE HAVE TO."
"WE HAVE TO."

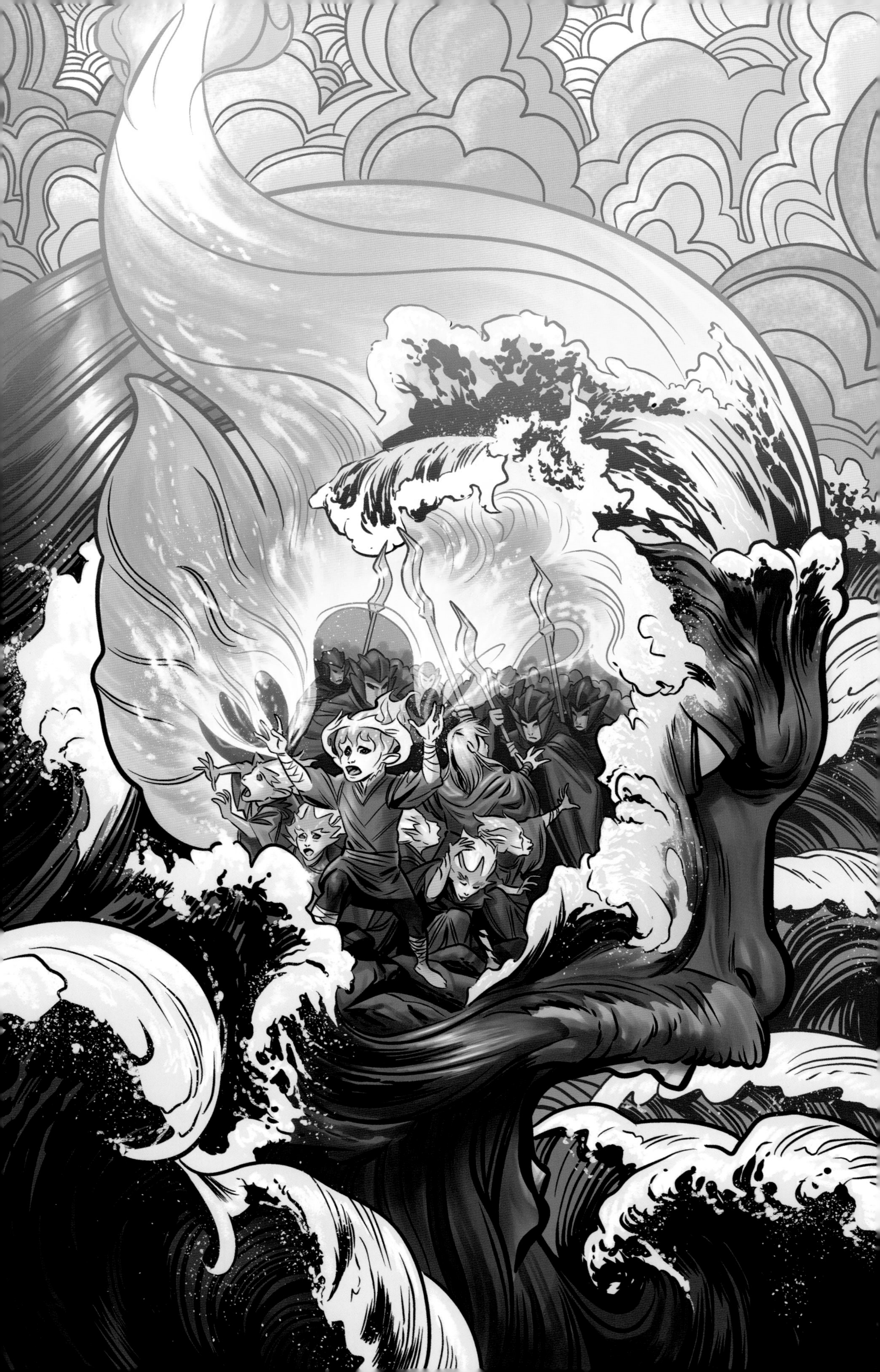

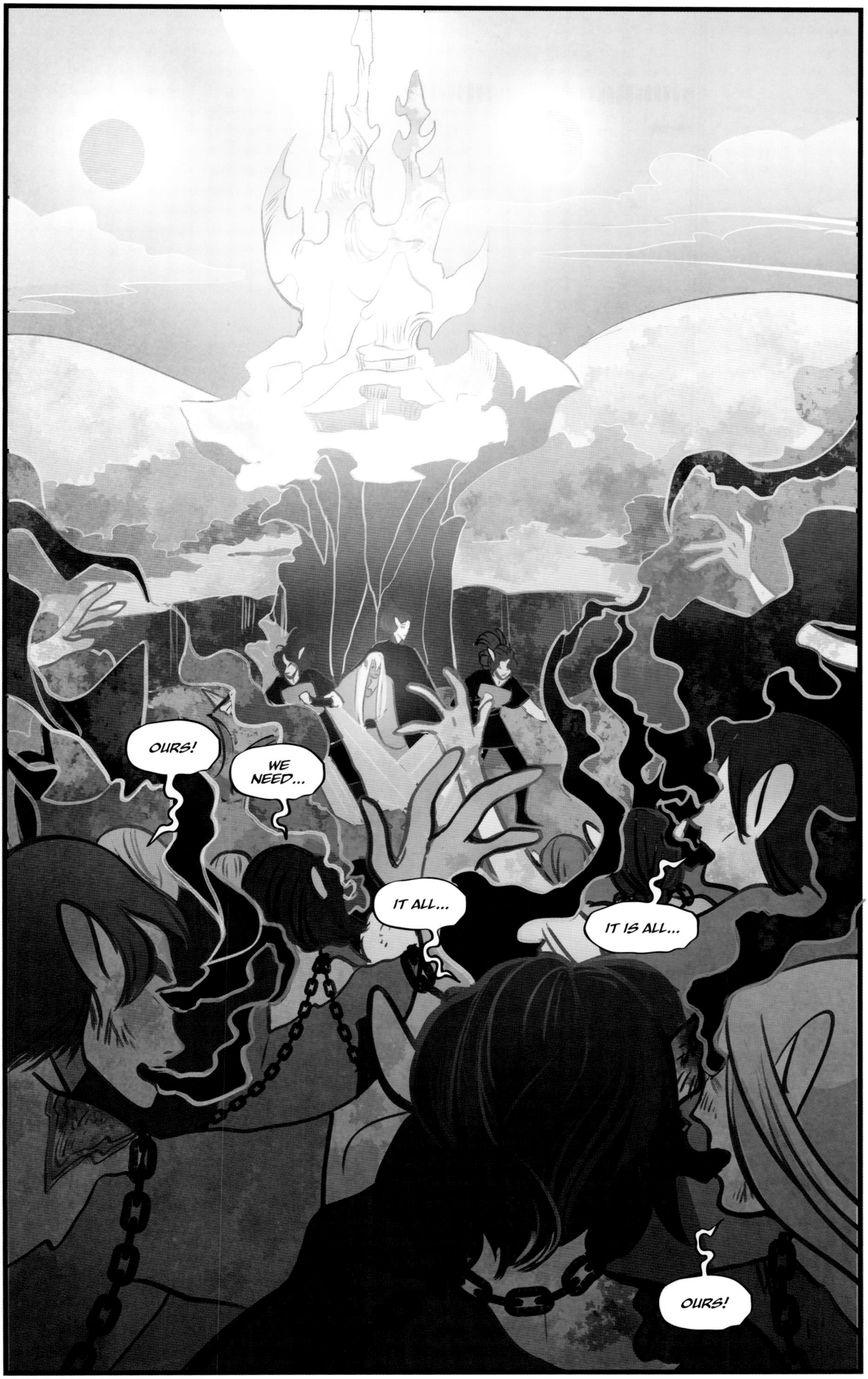
OURS!
WE NEED...
IT ALL...
IT IS ALL...
OURS!

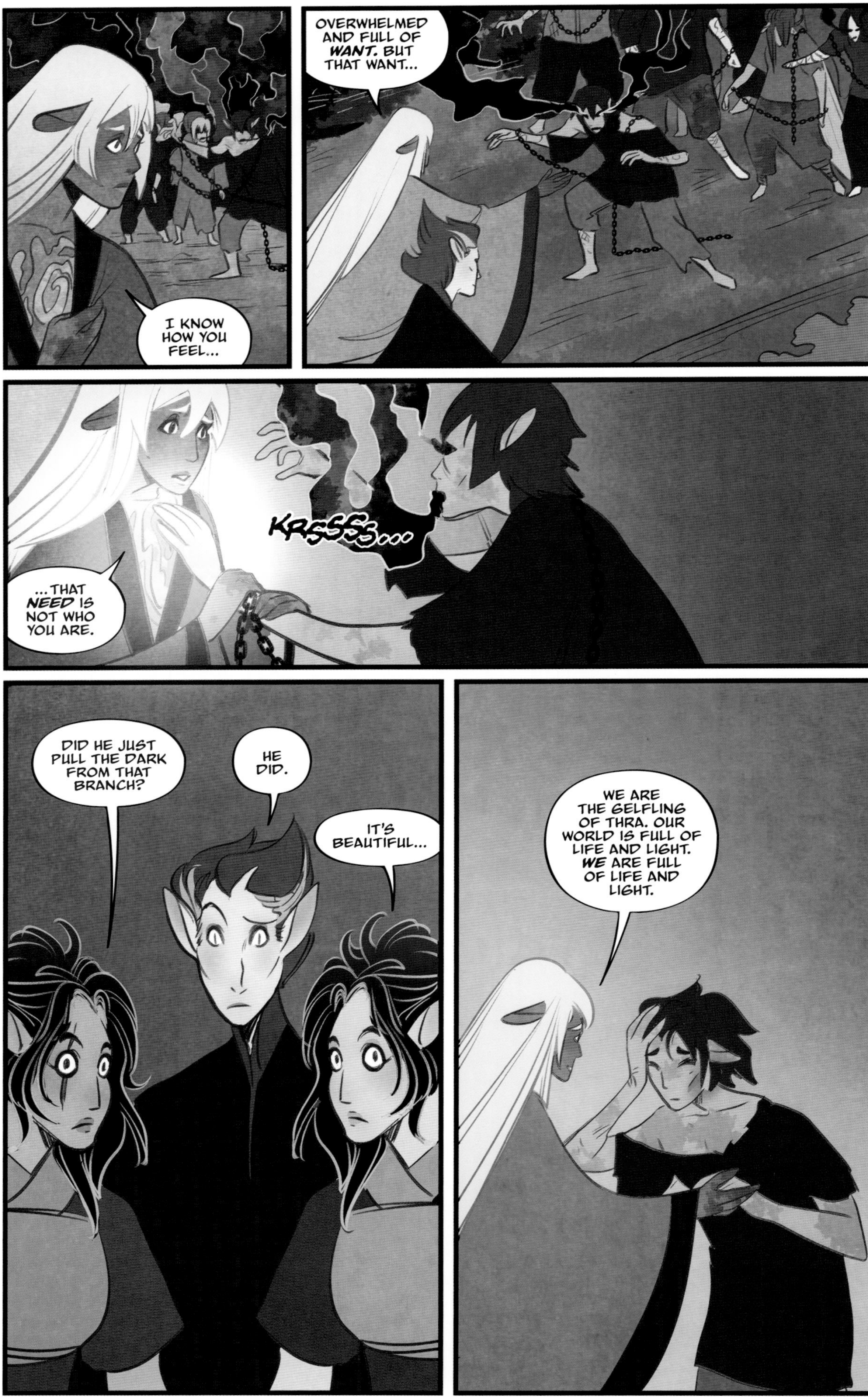
I KNOW HOW YOU FEEL...
OVERWHELMED AND FULL OF WANT. BUT THAT WANT...
...THAT NEED IS NOT WHO YOU ARE.
KRSSSS...
DID HE JUST PULL THE DARK FROM THAT BRANCH?
HE DID.
IT'S BEAUTIFUL...
WE ARE THE GELFLING OF THRA. OUR WORLD IS FULL OF LIFE AND LIGHT. WE ARE FULL OF LIFE AND LIGHT.

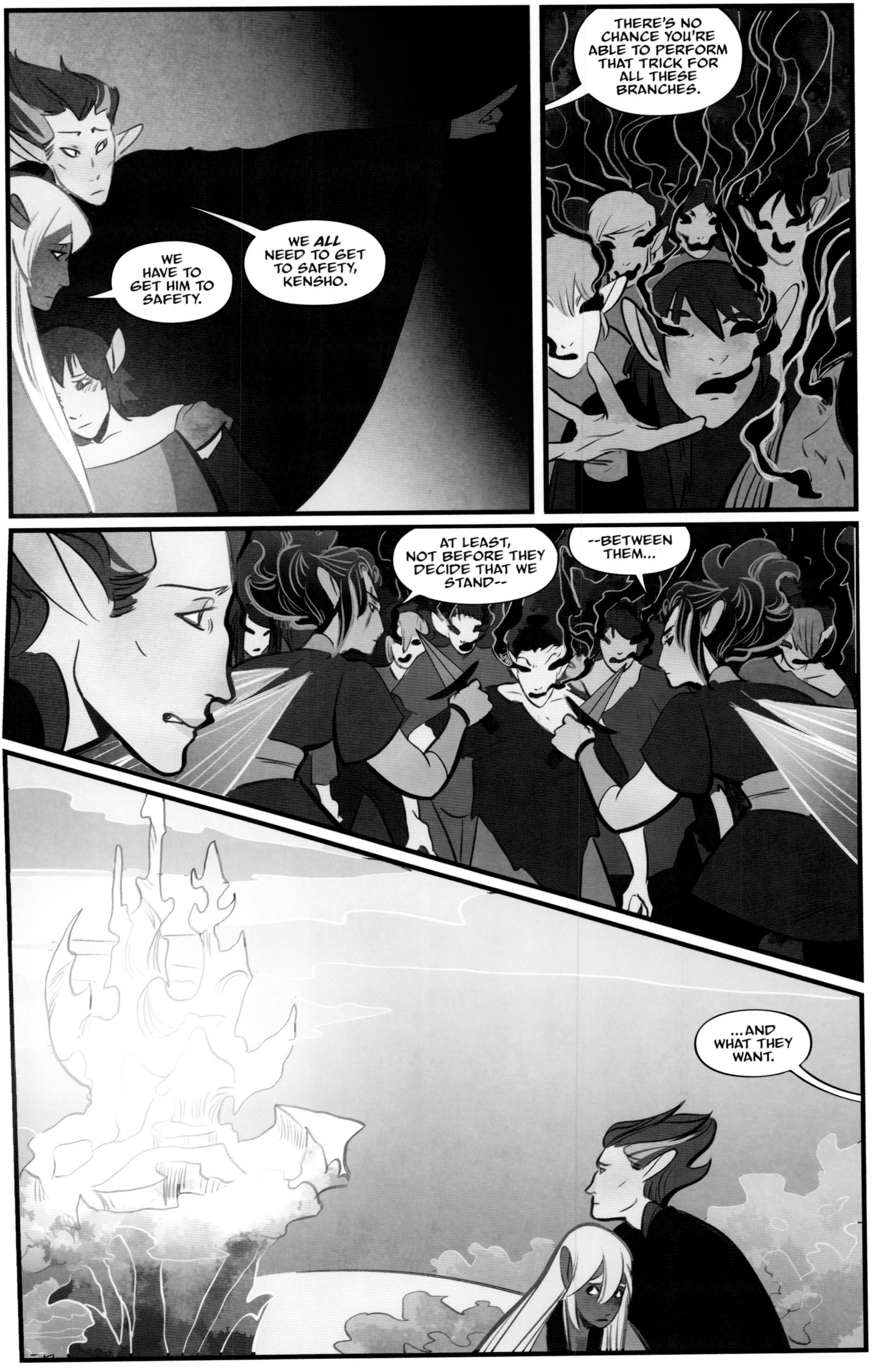
WE HAVE TO GET HIM TO SAFETY.
WE ALL NEED TO GET TO SAFETY, KENSHO.
THERE'S NO CHANCE YOU'RE ABLE TO PERFORM THAT TRICK FOR ALL THESE BRANCHES.
AT LEAST, NOT BEFORE THEY DECIDE THAT WE STAND--
--BETWEEN THEM...
...AND WHAT THEY WANT.

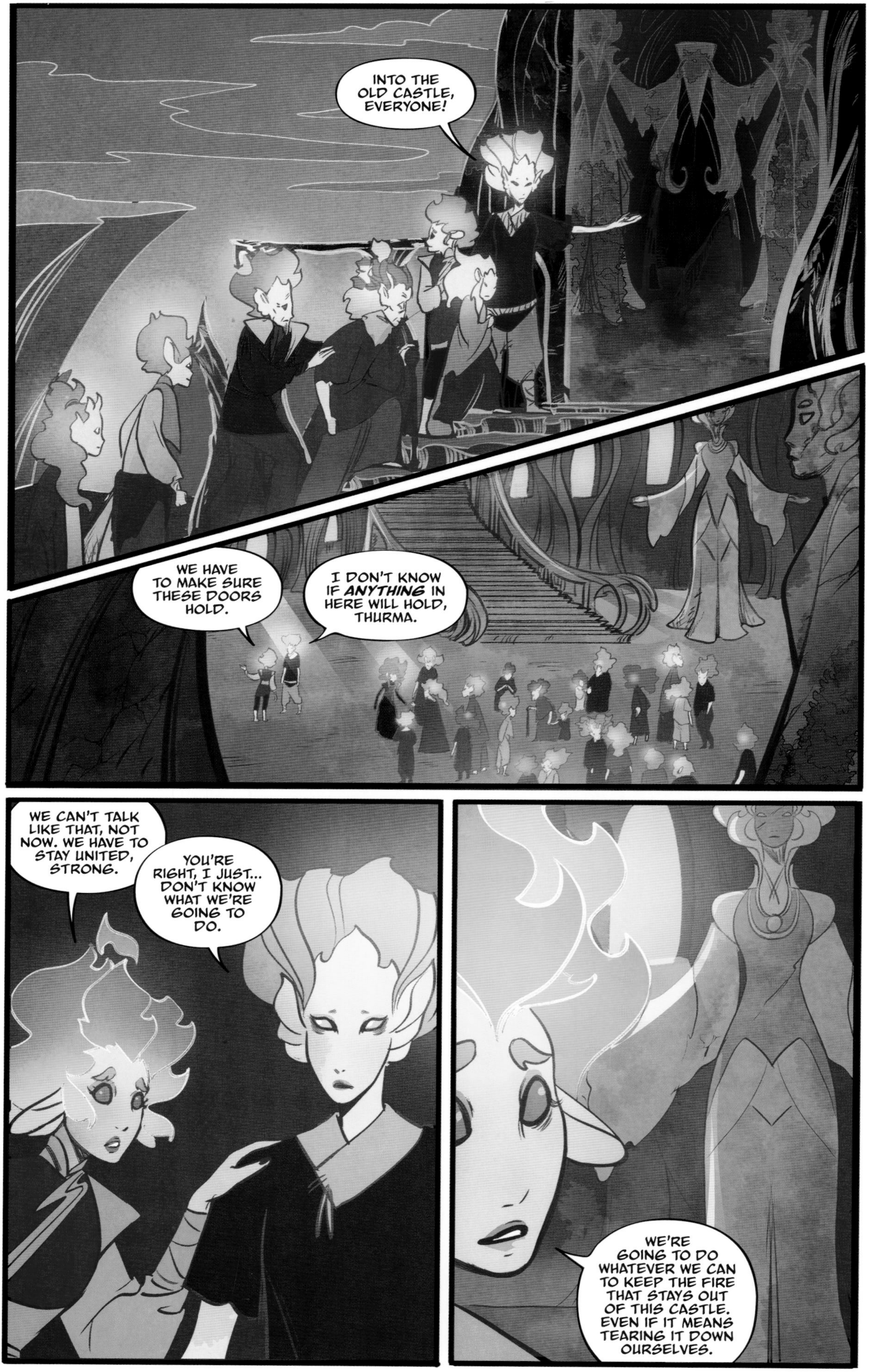
INTO THE OLD CASTLE, EVERYONE!
WE HAVE TO MAKE SURE THESE DOORS HOLD.
I DON'T KNOW IF *ANYTHING* IN HERE WILL HOLD, THURMA.
WE CAN'T TALK LIKE THAT, NOT NOW. WE HAVE TO STAY UNITED, STRONG.
YOU'RE RIGHT, I JUST... DON'T KNOW WHAT WE'RE GOING TO DO.
WE'RE GOING TO DO WHATEVER WE CAN TO KEEP THE FIRE THAT STAYS OUT OF THIS CASTLE. EVEN IF IT MEANS TEARING IT DOWN OURSELVES.

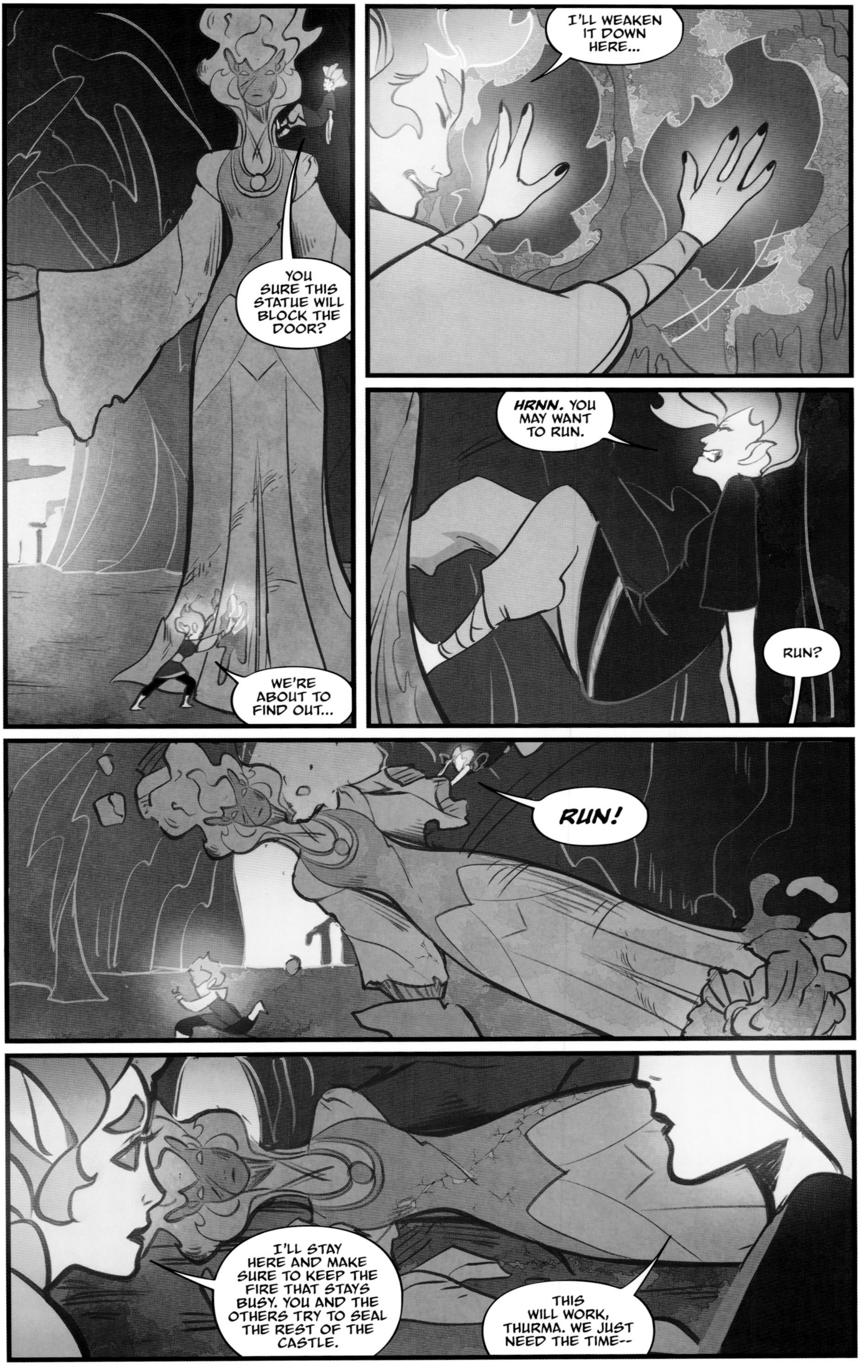
YOU SURE THIS STATUE WILL BLOCK THE DOOR?
WE'RE ABOUT TO FIND OUT...
I'LL WEAKEN IT DOWN HERE...
HRNN. YOU MAY WANT TO RUN.
RUN?
RUN!
I'LL STAY HERE AND MAKE SURE TO KEEP THE FIRE THAT STAYS BUSY. YOU AND THE OTHERS TRY TO SEAL THE REST OF THE CASTLE.
THIS WILL WORK, THURMA. WE JUST NEED THE TIME--

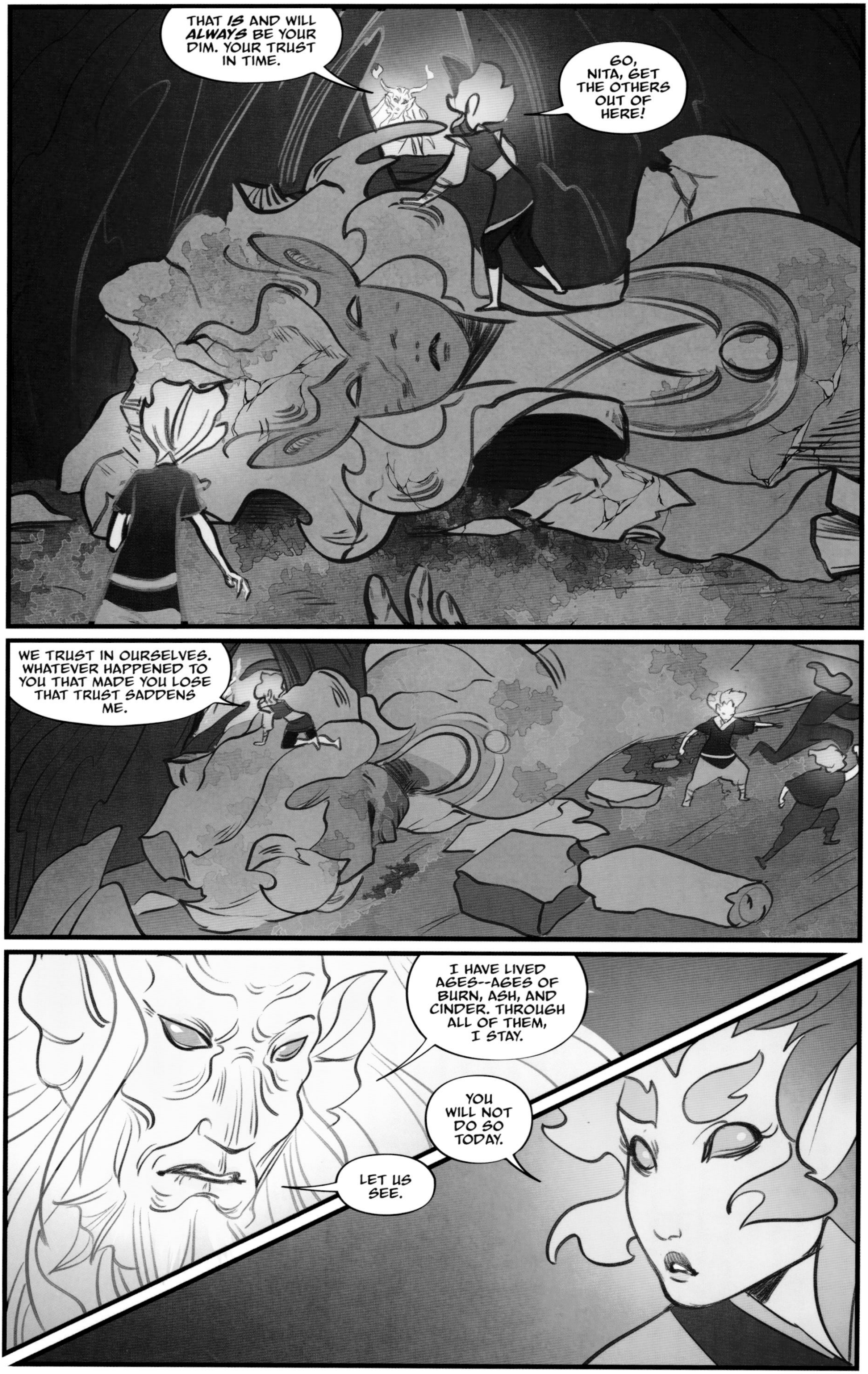
THAT *IS* AND WILL **ALWAYS** BE YOUR DIM. YOUR TRUST IN TIME.
GO, NITA, GET THE OTHERS OUT OF HERE!
WE TRUST IN OURSELVES. WHATEVER HAPPENED TO YOU THAT MADE YOU LOSE THAT TRUST SADDENS ME.
I HAVE LIVED AGES--AGES OF BURN, ASH, AND CINDER. THROUGH ALL OF THEM, I STAY.
YOU WILL NOT DO SO TODAY.
LET US SEE.

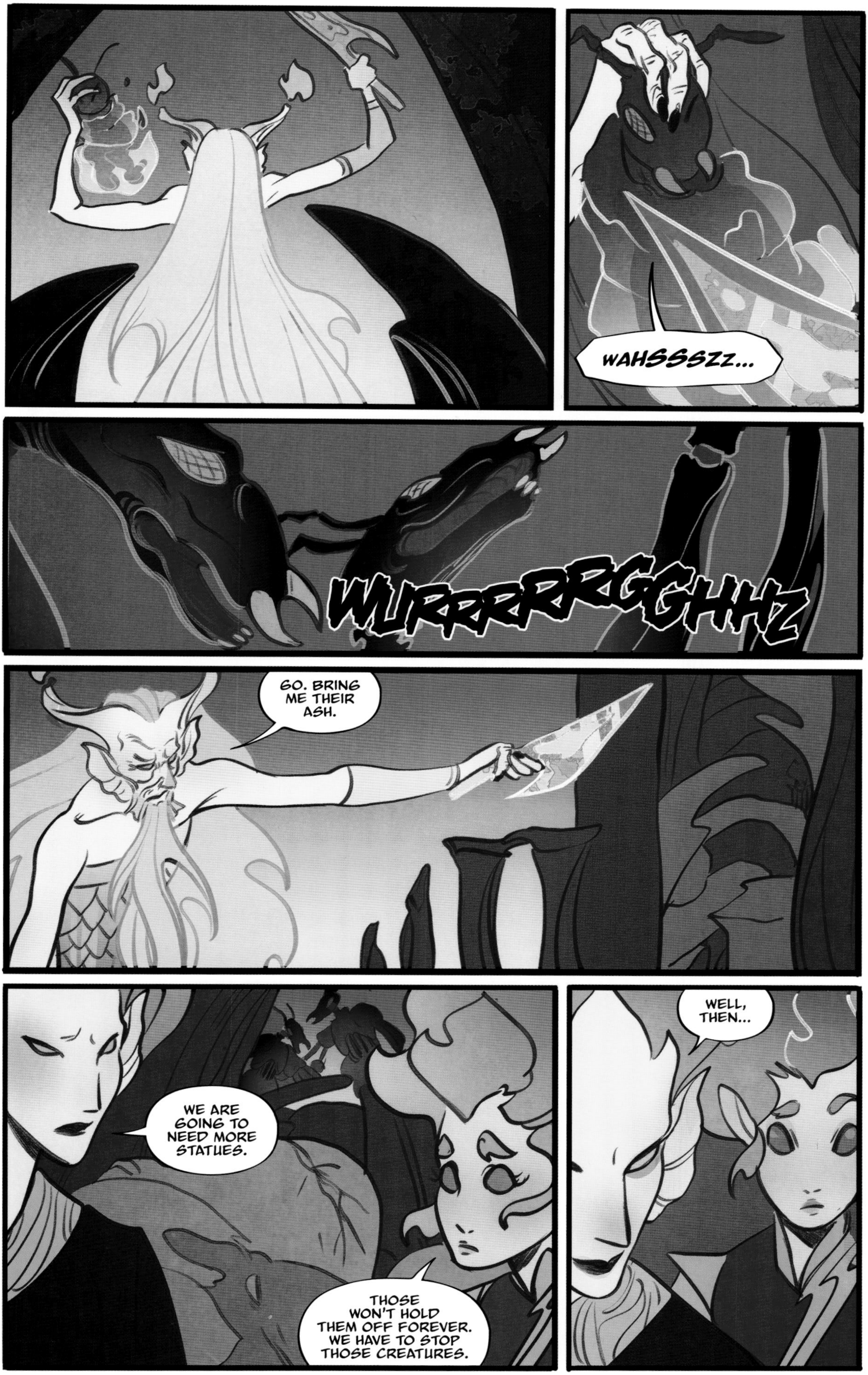
WAHSSSZZ...
WURRRRRRGGHHZ
GO. BRING ME THEIR ASH.
WE ARE GOING TO NEED MORE STATUES.
THOSE WON'T HOLD THEM OFF FOREVER. WE HAVE TO STOP THOSE CREATURES.
WELL, THEN...

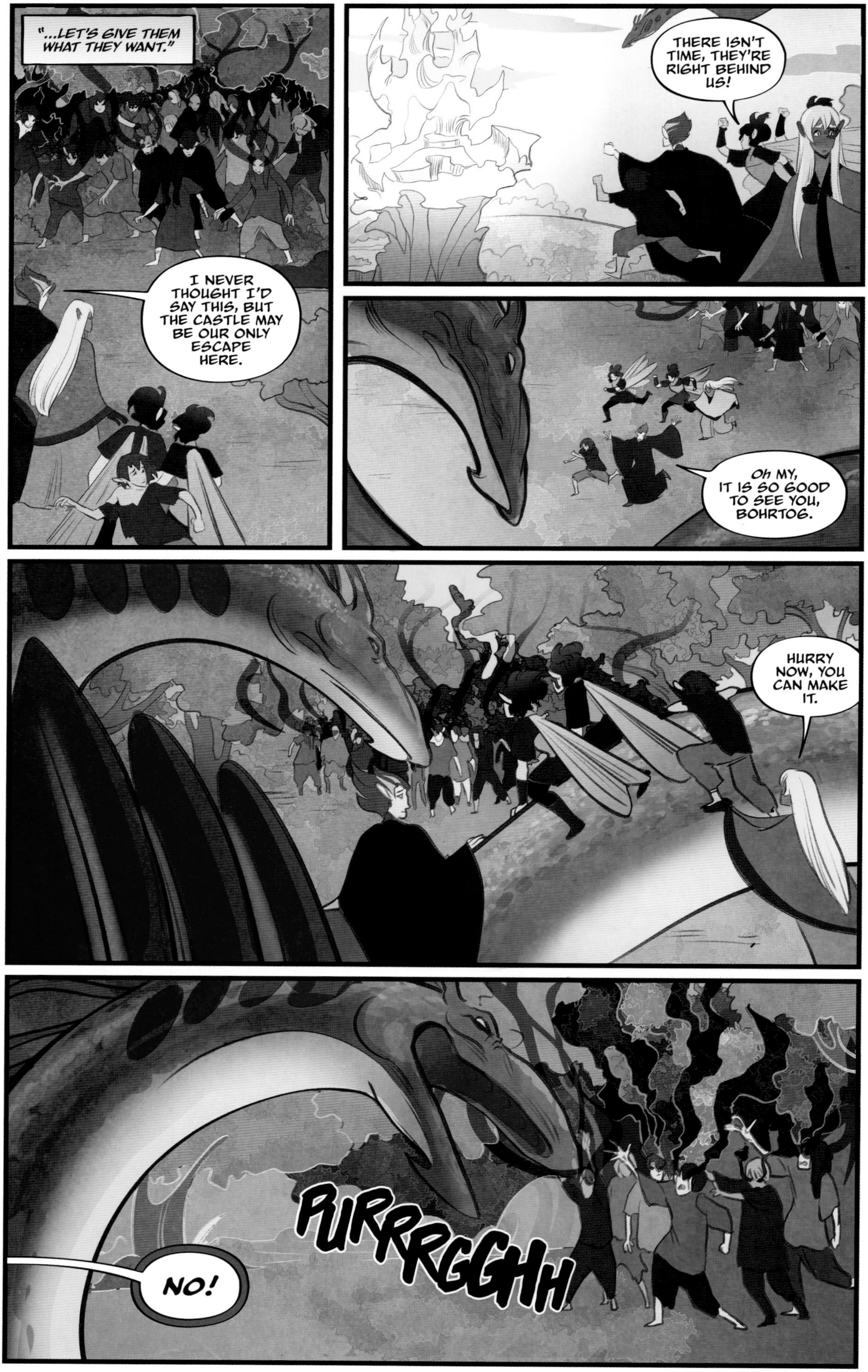
"...LET'S GIVE THEM WHAT THEY WANT."
I NEVER THOUGHT I'D SAY THIS, BUT THE CASTLE MAY BE OUR ONLY ESCAPE HERE.
THERE ISN'T TIME, THEY'RE RIGHT BEHIND US!
OH MY, IT IS SO GOOD TO SEE YOU, BOHRTOG.
HURRY NOW, YOU CAN MAKE IT.
PURRRGGHH
NO!

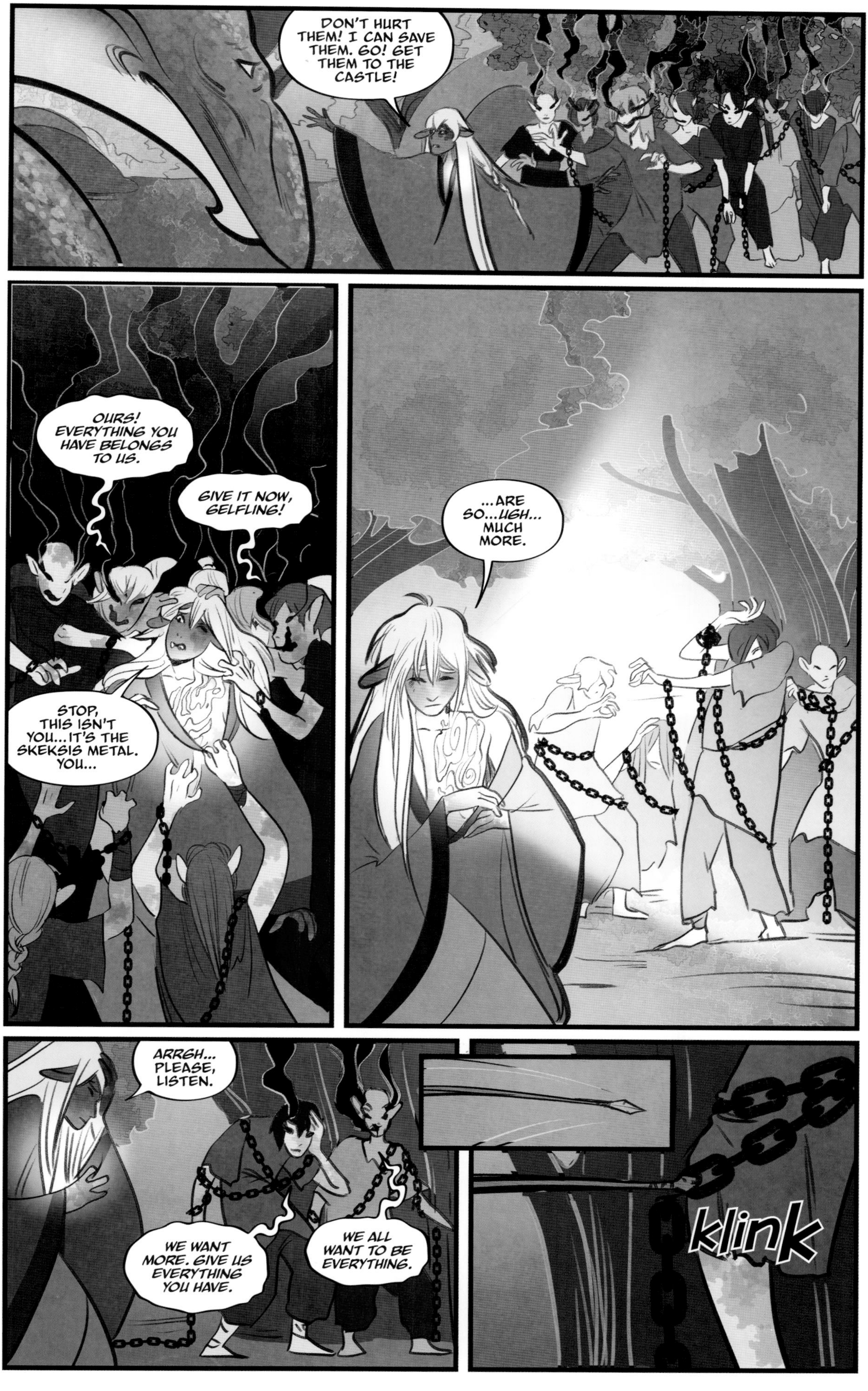
DON'T HURT THEM! I CAN SAVE THEM. GO! GET THEM TO THE CASTLE!
OURS! EVERYTHING YOU HAVE BELONGS TO US.
GIVE IT NOW, GELFLING!
STOP, THIS ISN'T YOU...IT'S THE SKEKSIS METAL. YOU...
...ARE SO...UGH... MUCH MORE.
ARRGH... PLEASE, LISTEN.
WE WANT MORE. GIVE US EVERYTHING YOU HAVE.
WE ALL WANT TO BE EVERYTHING.
klink

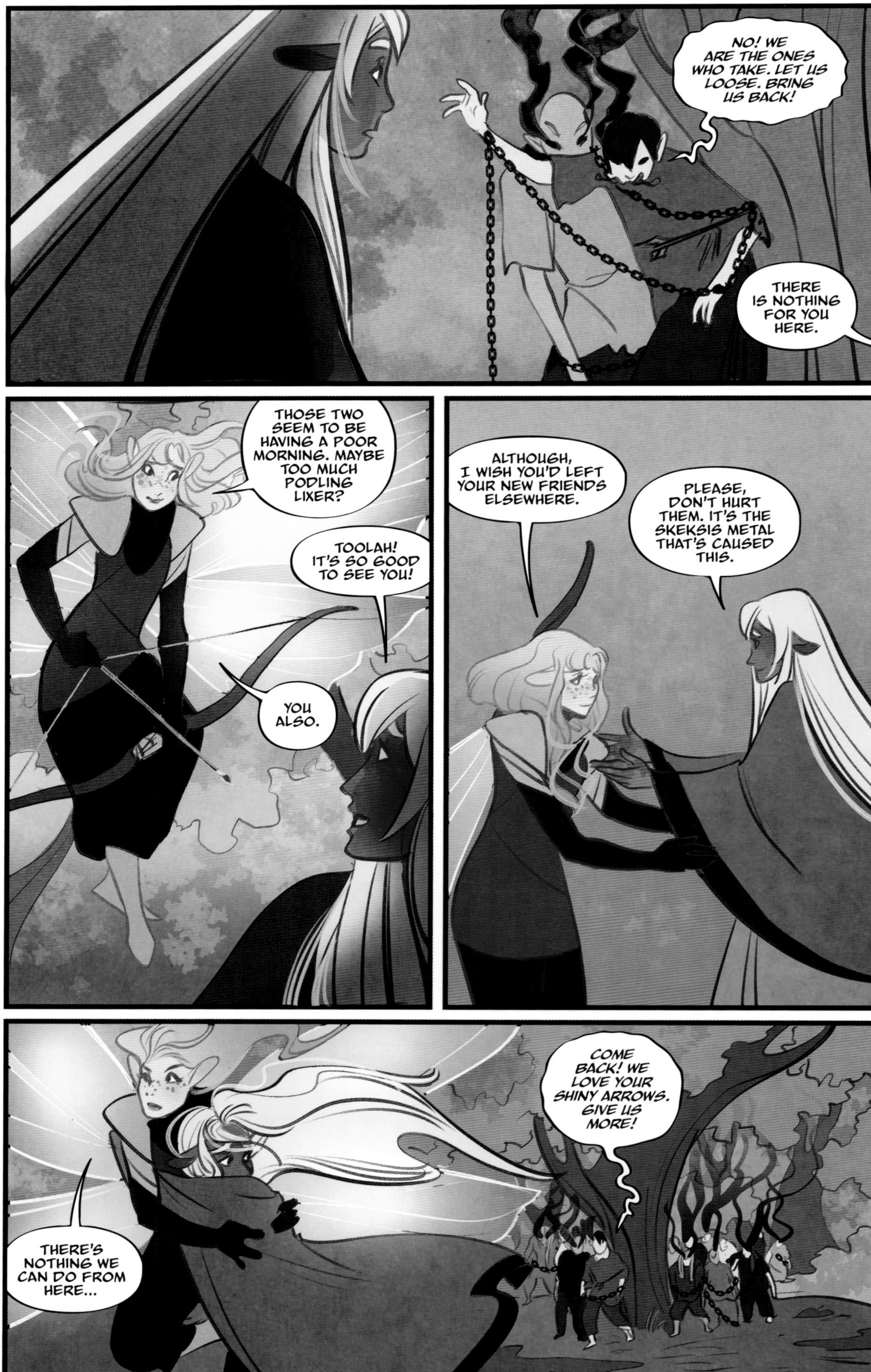
NO! WE ARE THE ONES WHO TAKE. LET US LOOSE. BRING US BACK!
THERE IS NOTHING FOR YOU HERE.
THOSE TWO SEEM TO BE HAVING A POOR MORNING. MAYBE TOO MUCH PODLING LIXER?
TOOLAH! IT'S SO GOOD TO SEE YOU!
YOU ALSO.
ALTHOUGH, I WISH YOU'D LEFT YOUR NEW FRIENDS ELSEWHERE.
PLEASE, DON'T HURT THEM. IT'S THE SKEKSIS METAL THAT'S CAUSED THIS.
COME BACK! WE LOVE YOUR SHINY ARROWS. GIVE US MORE!
THERE'S NOTHING WE CAN DO FROM HERE...

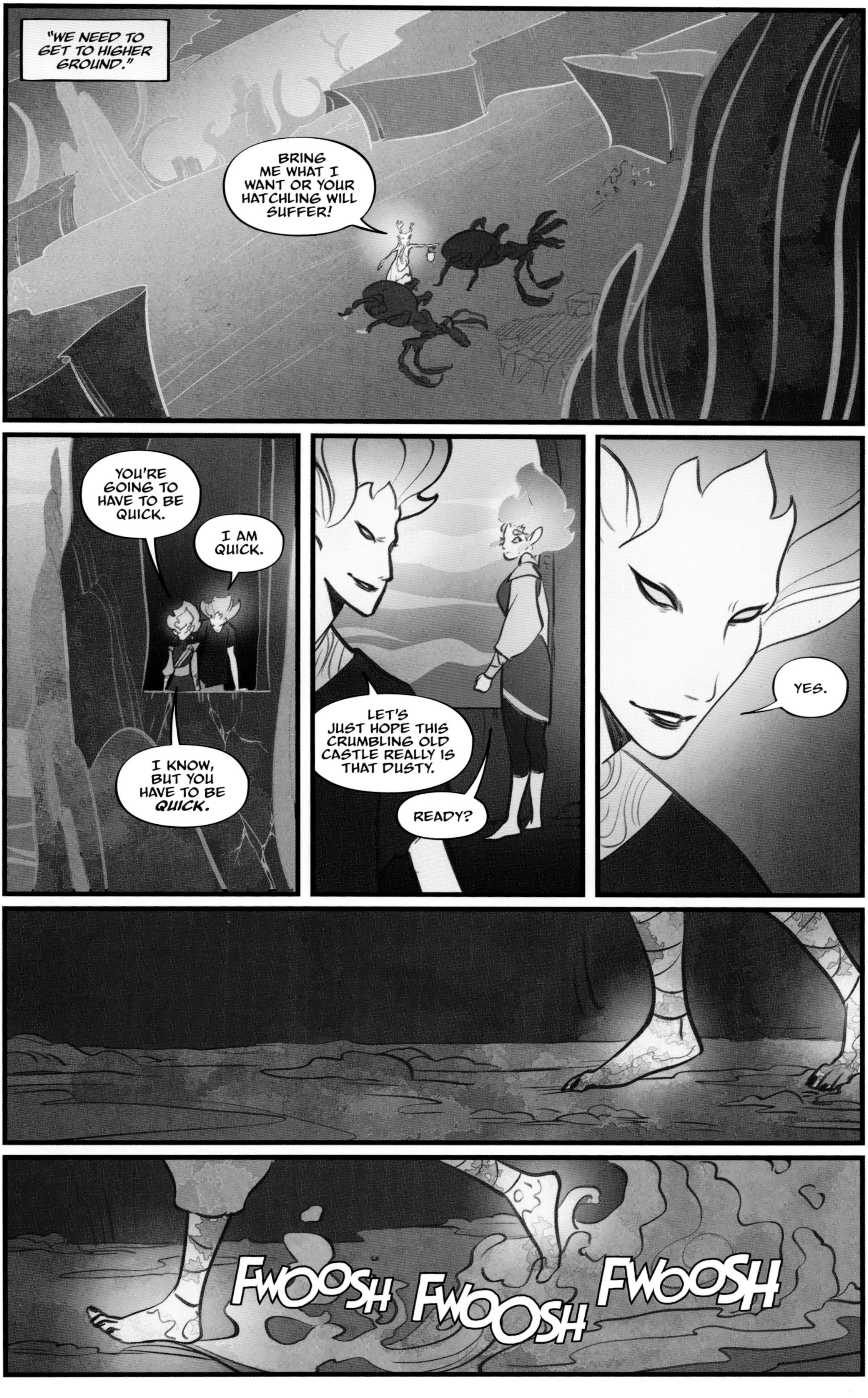
"WE NEED TO GET TO HIGHER GROUND."
BRING ME WHAT I WANT OR YOUR HATCHLING WILL SUFFER!
YOU'RE GOING TO HAVE TO BE QUICK.
I AM QUICK.
I KNOW, BUT YOU HAVE TO BE QUICK.
LET'S JUST HOPE THIS CRUMBLING OLD CASTLE REALLY IS THAT DUSTY.
READY?
YES.
FWOOSH FWOOSH FWOOSH

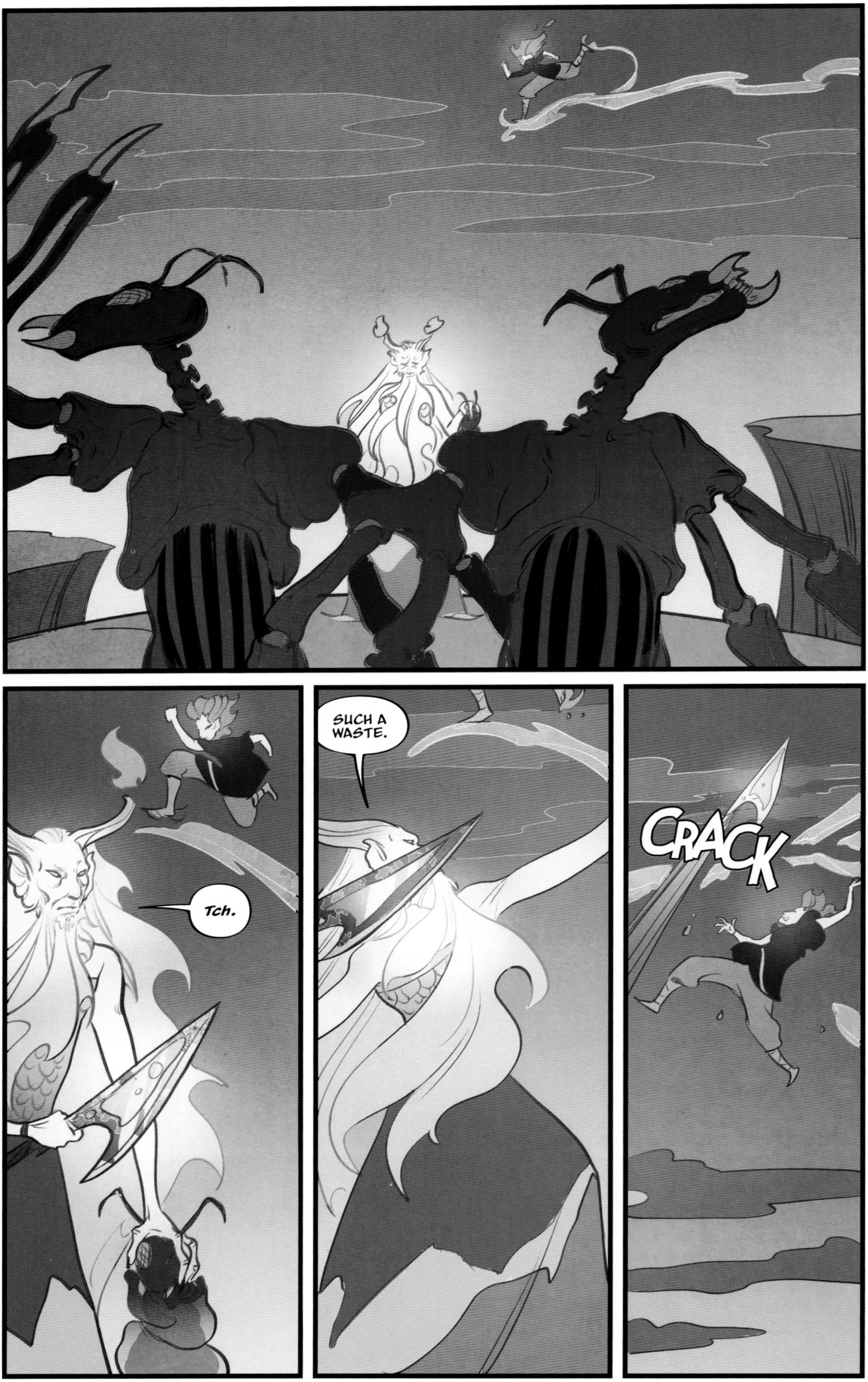
Tch.
SUCH A WASTE.
CRACK

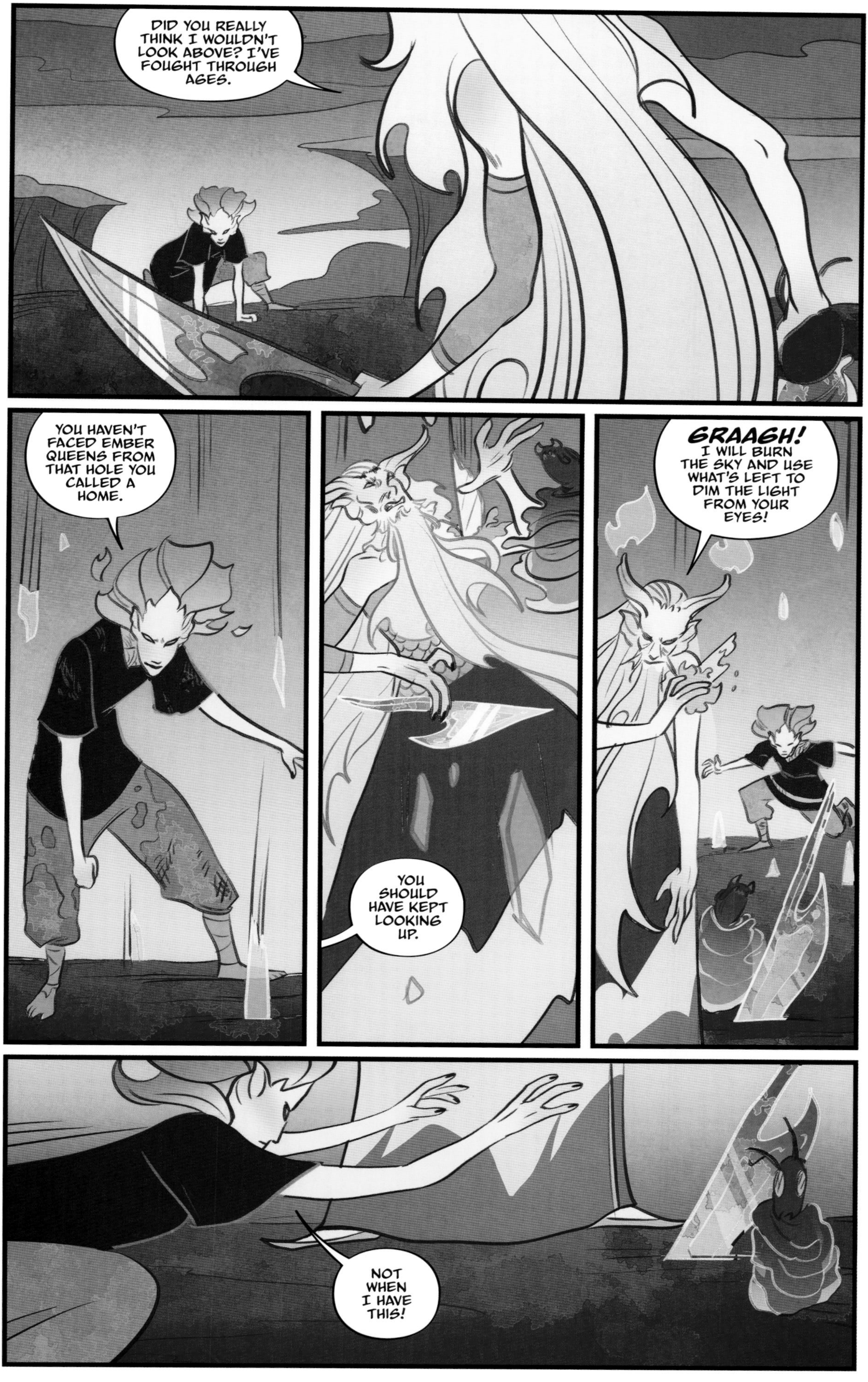
DID YOU REALLY THINK I WOULDN'T LOOK ABOVE? I'VE FOUGHT THROUGH AGES.
YOU HAVEN'T FACED EMBER QUEENS FROM THAT HOLE YOU CALLED A HOME.
YOU SHOULD HAVE KEPT LOOKING UP.
GRAAGH! I WILL BURN THE SKY AND USE WHAT'S LEFT TO DIM THE LIGHT FROM YOUR EYES!
NOT WHEN I HAVE THIS!

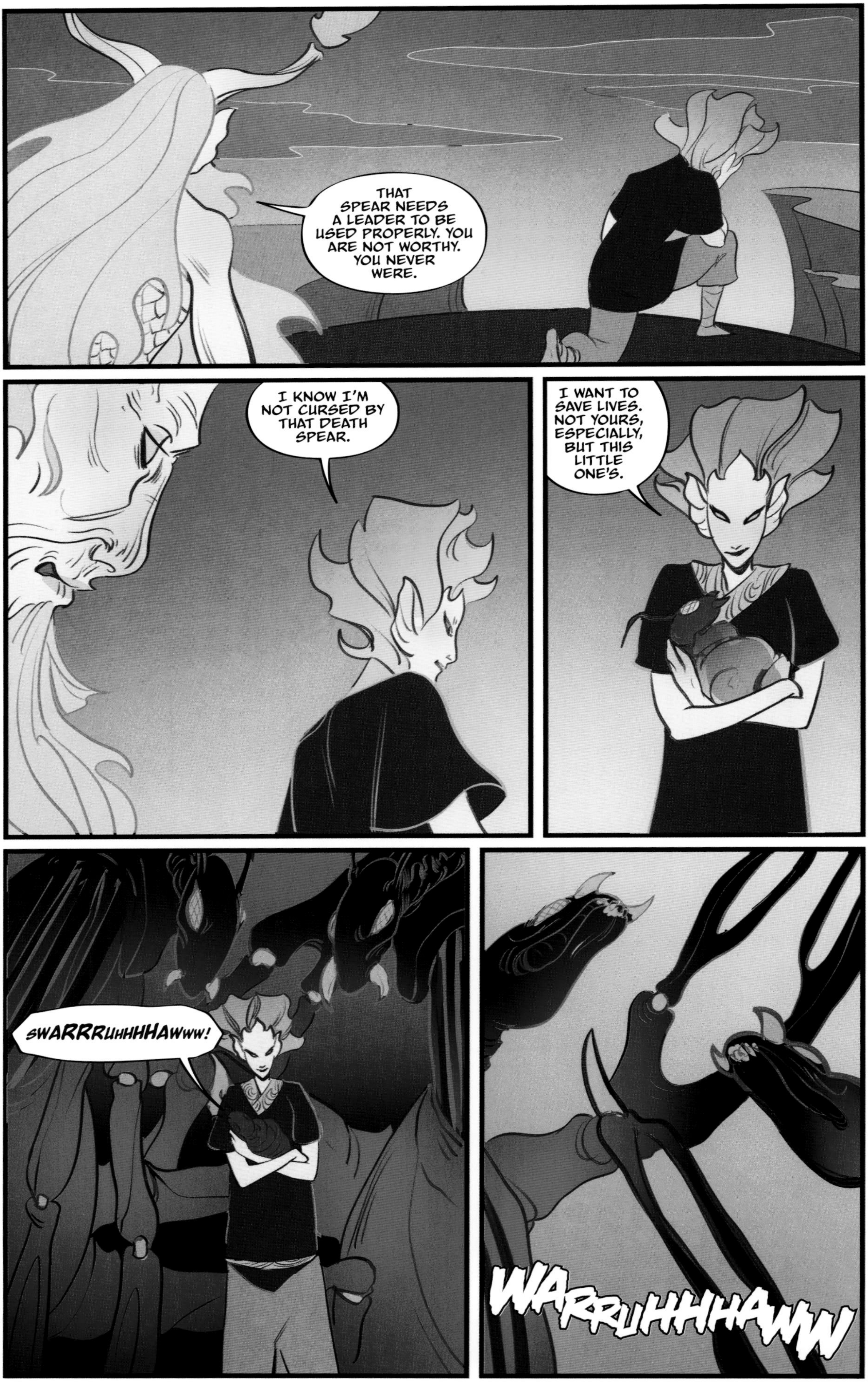
THAT SPEAR NEEDS A LEADER TO BE USED PROPERLY. YOU ARE NOT WORTHY. YOU NEVER WERE.
I KNOW I'M NOT CURSED BY THAT DEATH SPEAR.
I WANT TO SAVE LIVES. NOT YOURS, ESPECIALLY, BUT THIS LITTLE ONE'S.
SWARRRUHHHHAWWW!
WARRRUHHHHAWW

ALL OF YOU, WE'RE GOING TO NEED YOUR HELP.

HELP? *YOU* HAVE BROUGHT THIS HERE. YOU STOLE FROM THE CASTLE AND HAVE NOW PUT IT UNDER SIEGE!

I WASN'T THE ONE WHO BROUGHT THEM HERE. THEY CAME FOR THE OFFERINGS YOU STOCKED AWAY FROM THE PODLINGS AND GELFLING OF THRA.

THEY'VE BEEN DRIVEN MAD BY SKEKSIS ARTIFACTS AND THEIR GREED. IF WE CAN REMOVE THEIR DARKNESS AND THE METAL--

NONSENSE. YOU ARE NOT AND HAVE NEVER BEEN OUR TRUE LEADER. YOU LACK THE WINGS OF A GELFLING CROWN AND WE'LL HEAR NONE OF YOUR ORDERS.

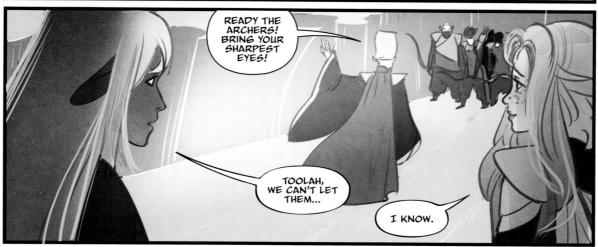

READY THE ARCHERS! BRING YOUR SHARPEST EYES!

TOOLAH, WE CAN'T LET THEM...

I KNOW.

FIRST OFF, IT'S OBVIOUS TO EVERY ARCHER HERE THAT *I* HAVE THE SHARPEST EYES.

AND I NEED YOU ALL TO STAND DOWN.

I KNOW KENSHO HERE HAS LET US-- *ALL* OF US--DOWN IN THE PAST.

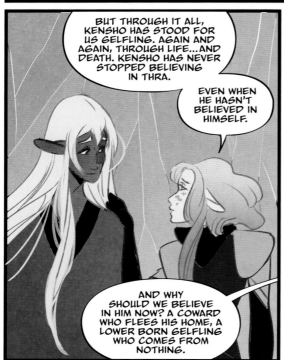

BUT THROUGH IT ALL, KENSHO HAS STOOD FOR US GELFLING. AGAIN AND AGAIN, THROUGH LIFE...AND DEATH. KENSHO HAS NEVER STOPPED BELIEVING IN THRA.

EVEN WHEN HE HASN'T BELIEVED IN HIMSELF.

AND WHY SHOULD WE BELIEVE IN HIM NOW? A COWARD WHO FLEES HIS HOME, A LOWER BORN GELFLING WHO COMES FROM NOTHING.

BECAUSE YOU HAVE TRIED TO CONVINCE US THAT WHERE WE'RE BORN IMPACTS *WHO* WE ARE.

ALL OF US ARE BORN TO THE CRYSTAL, WHETHER INSIDE YOUR CASTLE WALLS OR NOT.

THAT'S IT...

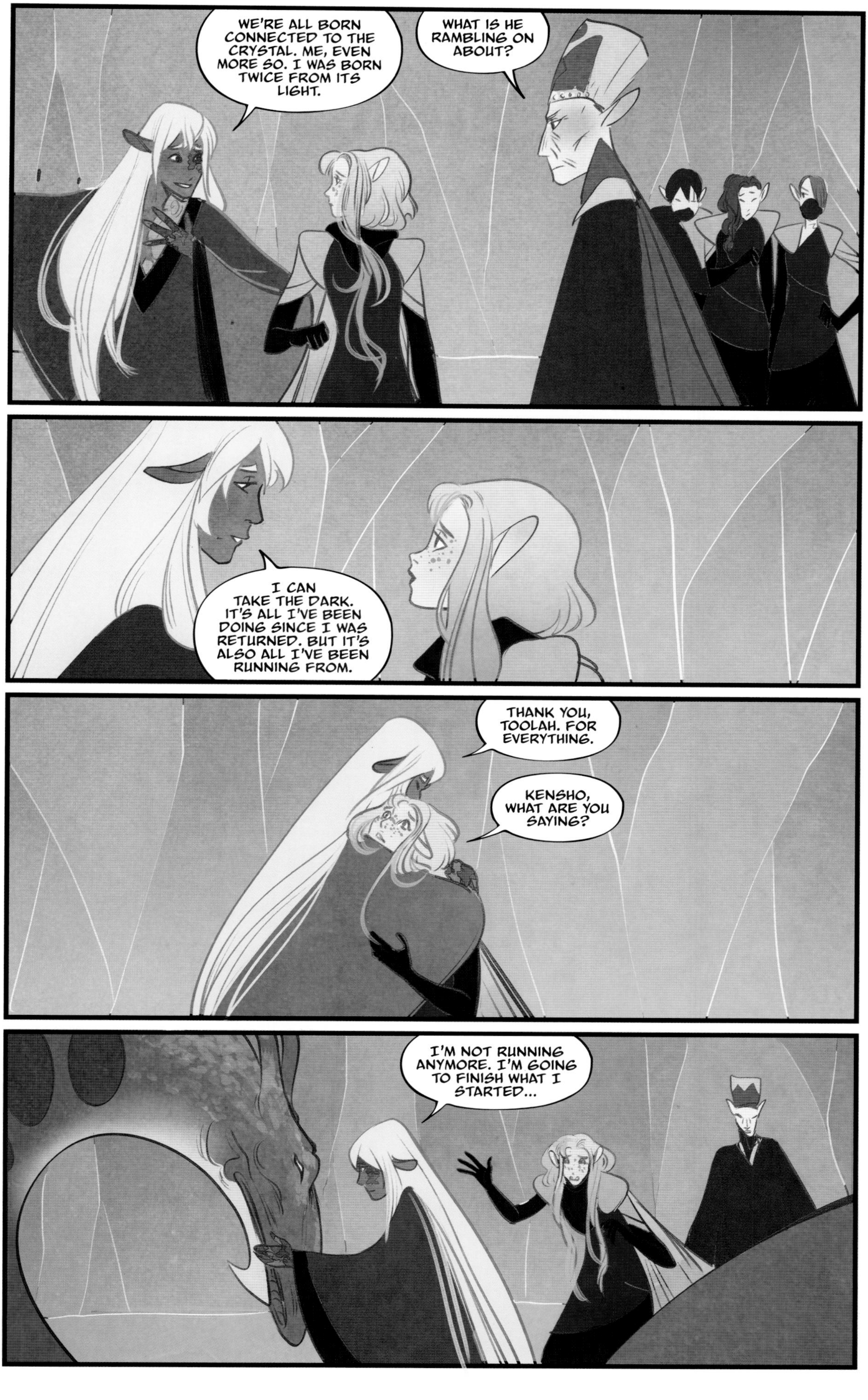
WE'RE ALL BORN CONNECTED TO THE CRYSTAL. ME, EVEN MORE SO. I WAS BORN TWICE FROM ITS LIGHT.
WHAT IS HE RAMBLING ON ABOUT?
I CAN TAKE THE DARK. IT'S ALL I'VE BEEN DOING SINCE I WAS RETURNED. BUT IT'S ALSO ALL I'VE BEEN RUNNING FROM.
THANK YOU, TOOLAH. FOR EVERYTHING.
KENSHO, WHAT ARE YOU SAYING?
I'M NOT RUNNING ANYMORE. I'M GOING TO FINISH WHAT I STARTED...

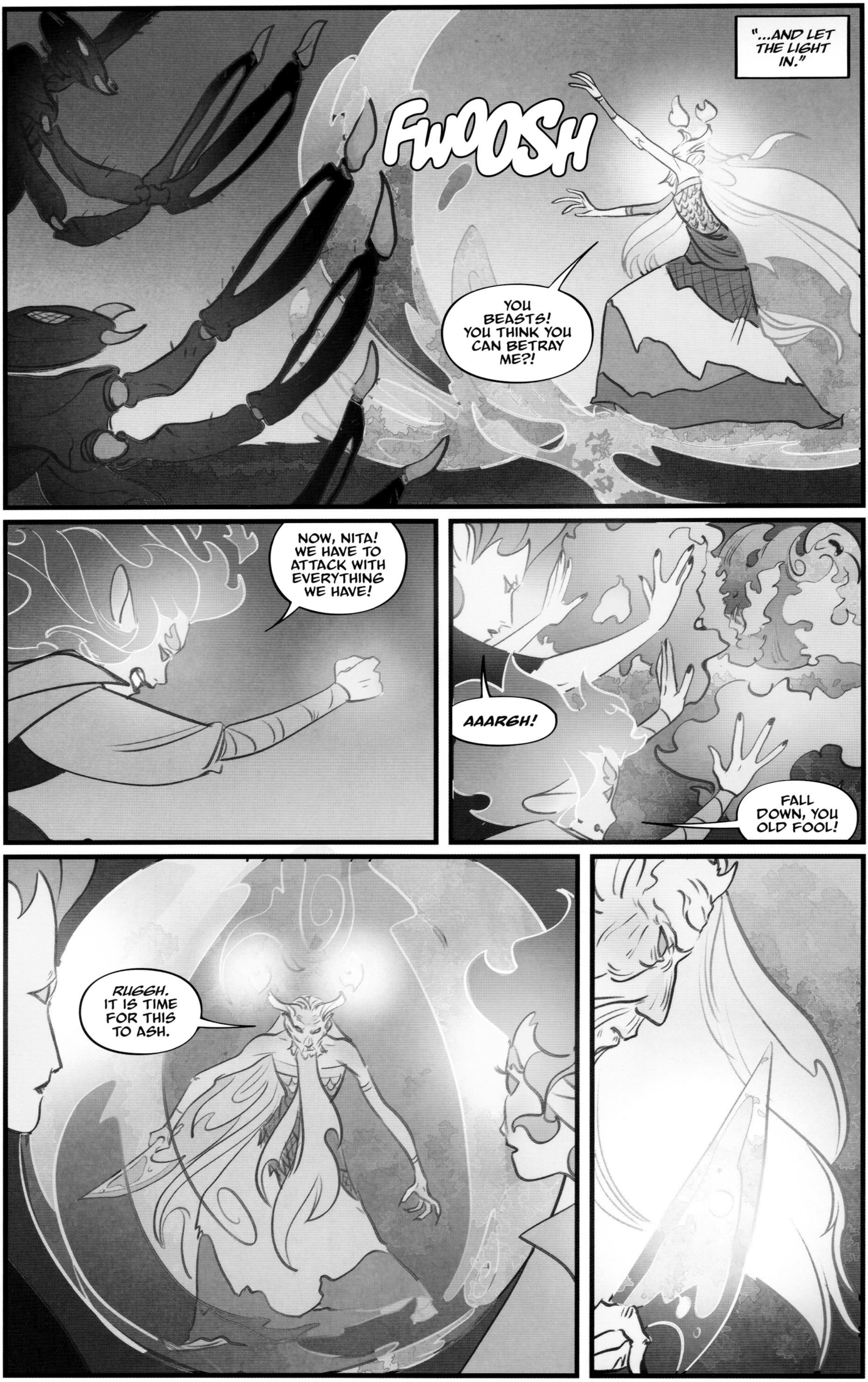
"...AND LET THE LIGHT IN."
FWOOSH
YOU BEASTS! YOU THINK YOU CAN BETRAY ME?!
NOW, NITA! WE HAVE TO ATTACK WITH EVERYTHING WE HAVE!
AAARGH!
FALL DOWN, YOU OLD FOOL!
RUGGH. IT IS TIME FOR THIS TO ASH.

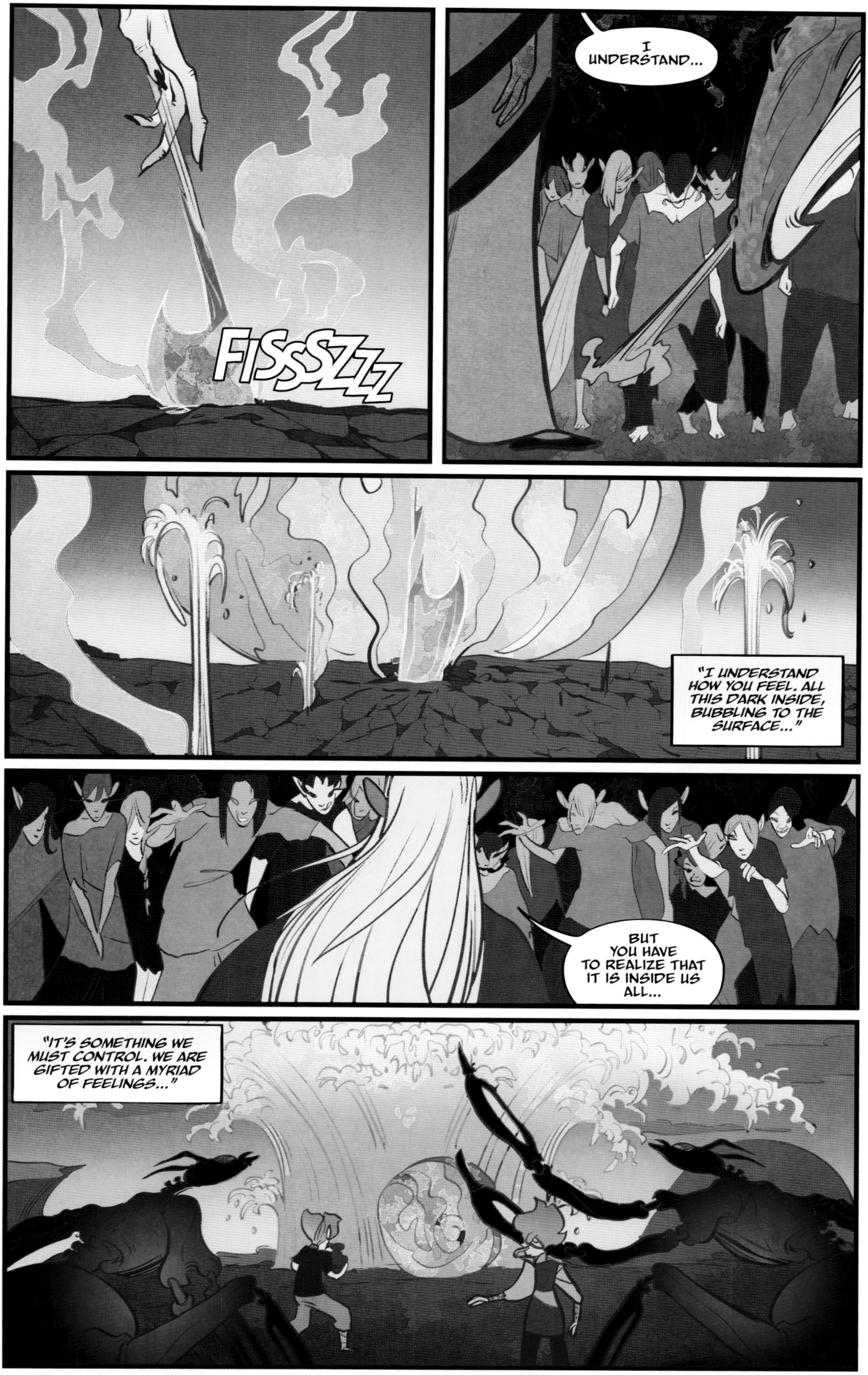
FISSSZZZ
I UNDERSTAND...
"I UNDERSTAND HOW YOU FEEL. ALL THIS DARK INSIDE, BUBBLING TO THE SURFACE..."
BUT YOU HAVE TO REALIZE THAT IT IS INSIDE US ALL...
"IT'S SOMETHING WE MUST CONTROL. WE ARE GIFTED WITH A MYRIAD OF FEELINGS..."

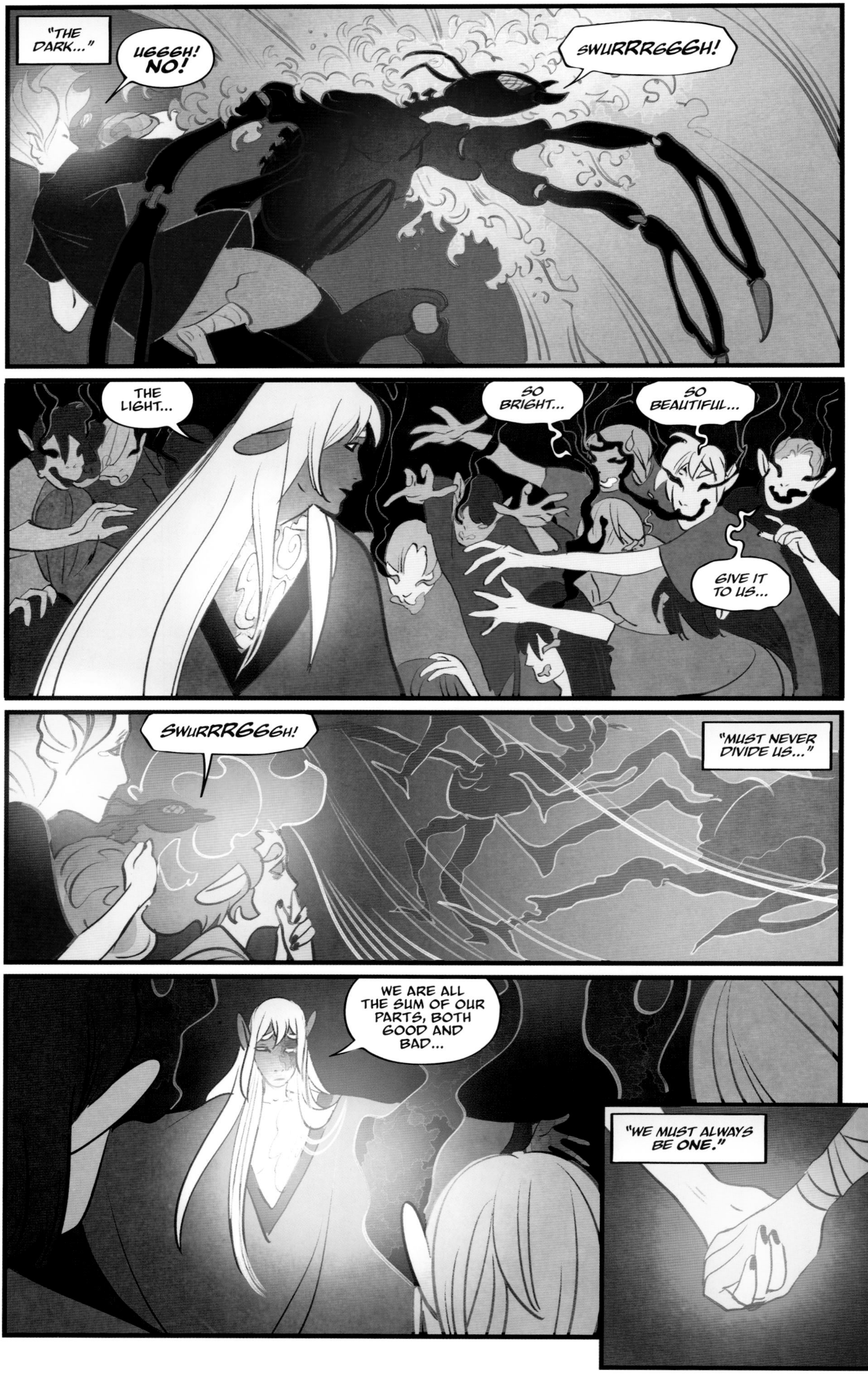
"THE DARK..."
UGGGH! NO!
SWURRRGGGH!
THE LIGHT...
SO BRIGHT...
SO BEAUTIFUL...
GIVE IT TO US...
SWURRRGGGGH!
"MUST NEVER DIVIDE US..."
WE ARE ALL THE SUM OF OUR PARTS, BOTH GOOD AND BAD...
"WE MUST ALWAYS BE ONE."

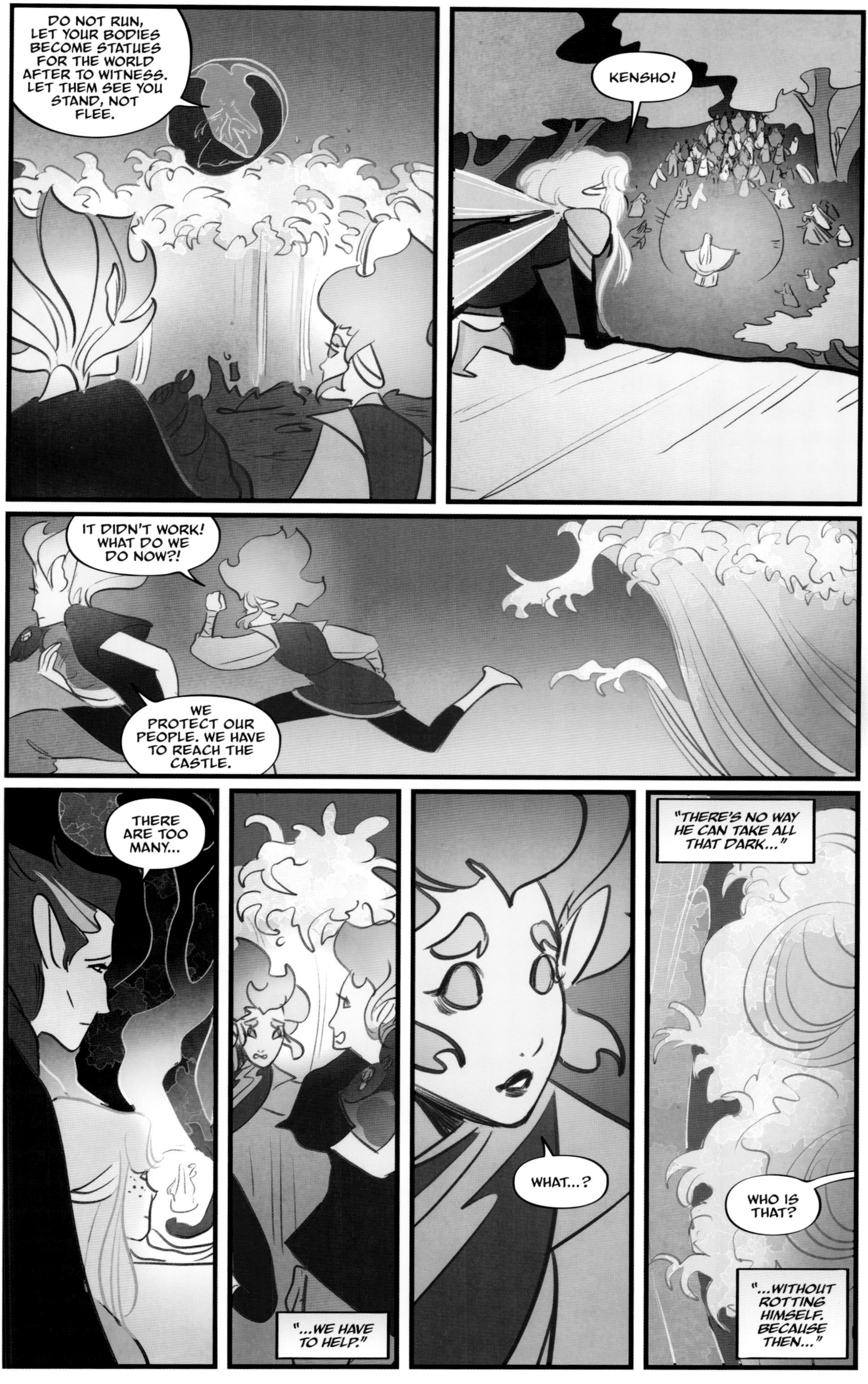
DO NOT RUN, LET YOUR BODIES BECOME STATUES FOR THE WORLD AFTER TO WITNESS. LET THEM SEE YOU STAND, NOT FLEE.
KENSHO!
IT DIDN'T WORK! WHAT DO WE DO NOW?!
WE PROTECT OUR PEOPLE. WE HAVE TO REACH THE CASTLE.
THERE ARE TOO MANY...
"...WE HAVE TO HELP."
WHAT...?
"THERE'S NO WAY HE CAN TAKE ALL THAT DARK..."
WHO IS THAT?
"...WITHOUT ROTTING HIMSELF. BECAUSE THEN..."

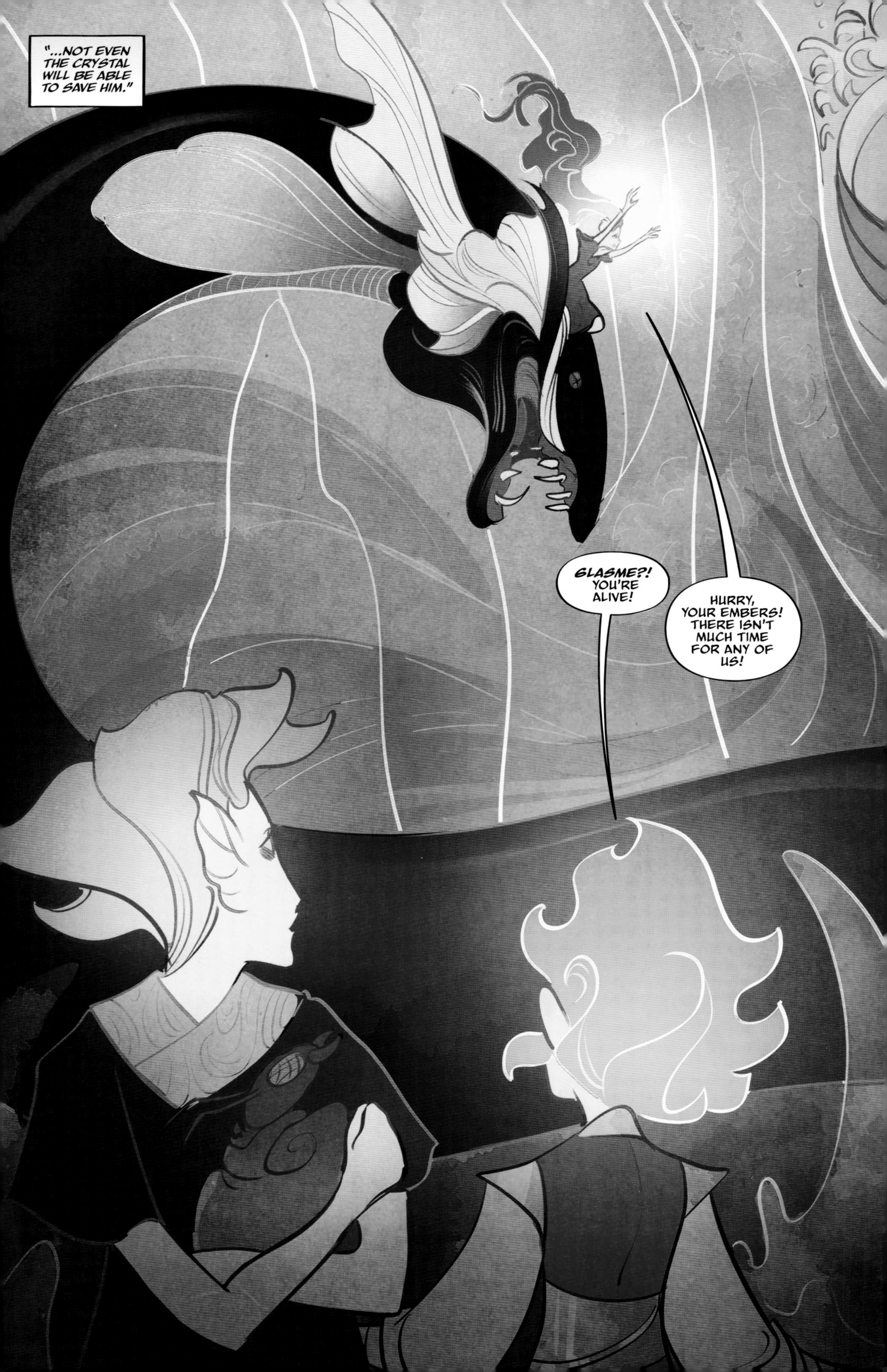
"...NOT EVEN THE CRYSTAL WILL BE ABLE TO SAVE HIM."
GLASME?! YOU'RE ALIVE!
HURRY, YOUR EMBERS! THERE ISN'T MUCH TIME FOR ANY OF US!

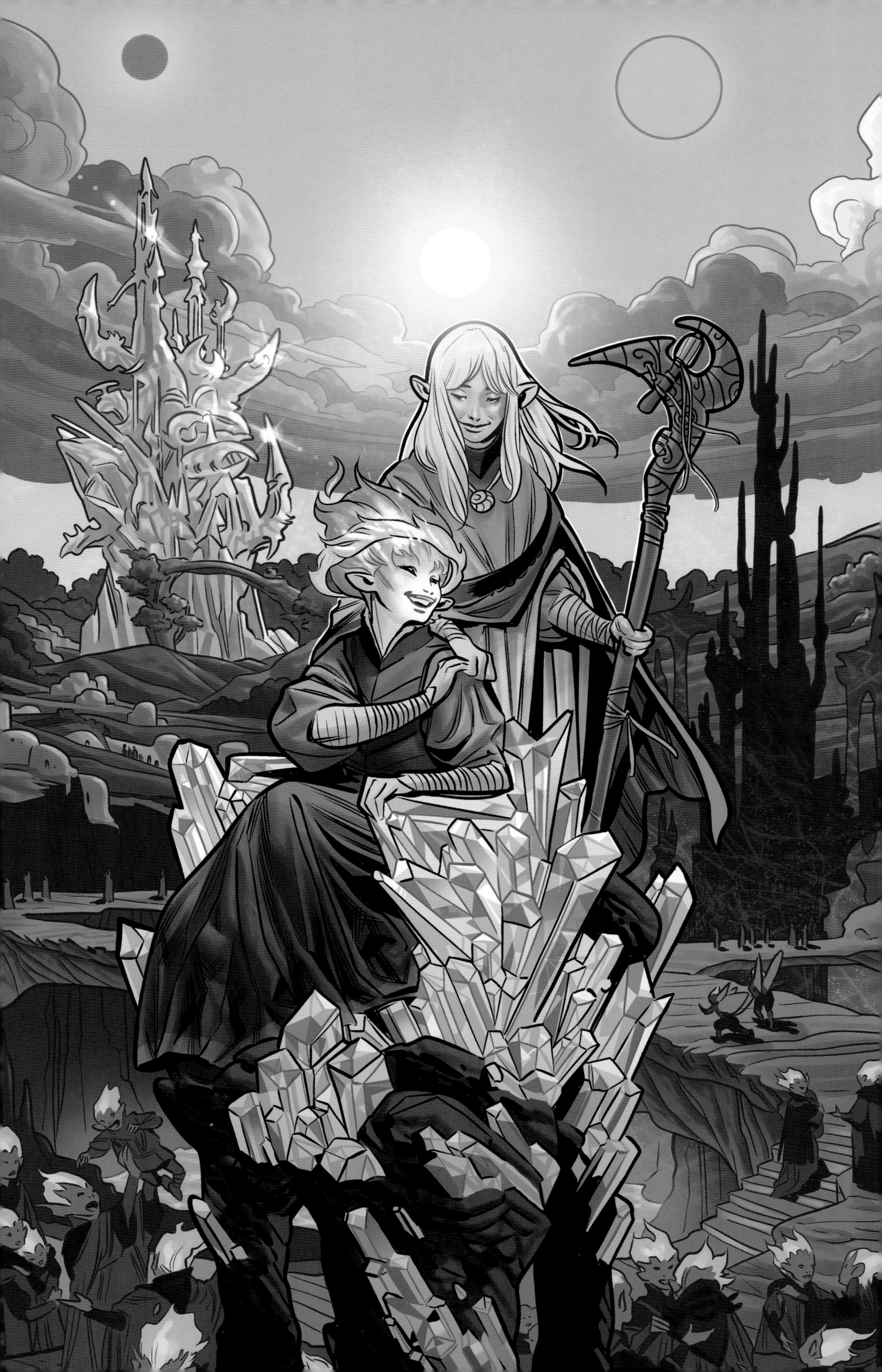

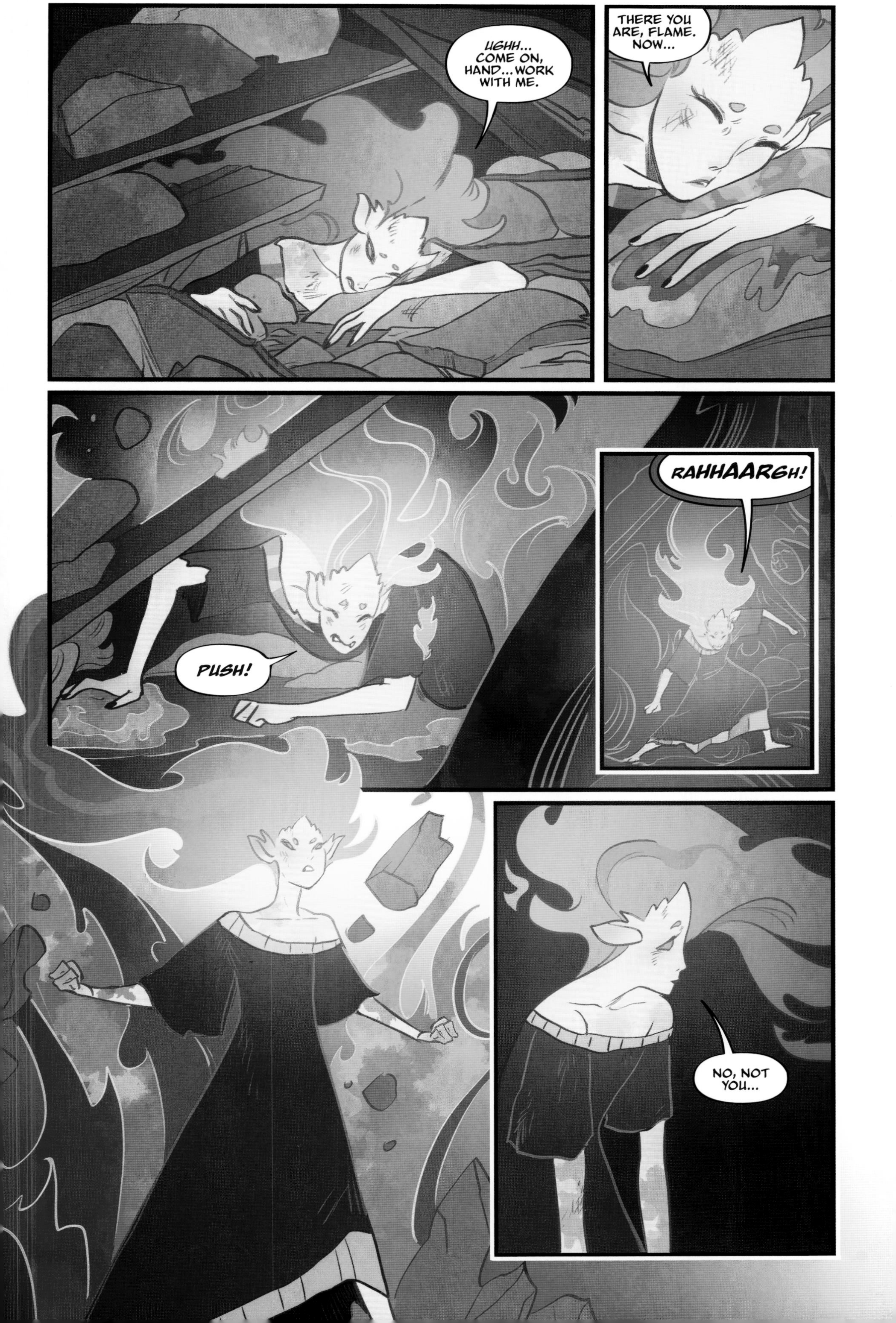
UGHH... COME ON, HAND...WORK WITH ME.
THERE YOU ARE, FLAME. NOW...
PUSH!
RAHHAARGH!
NO, NOT YOU...

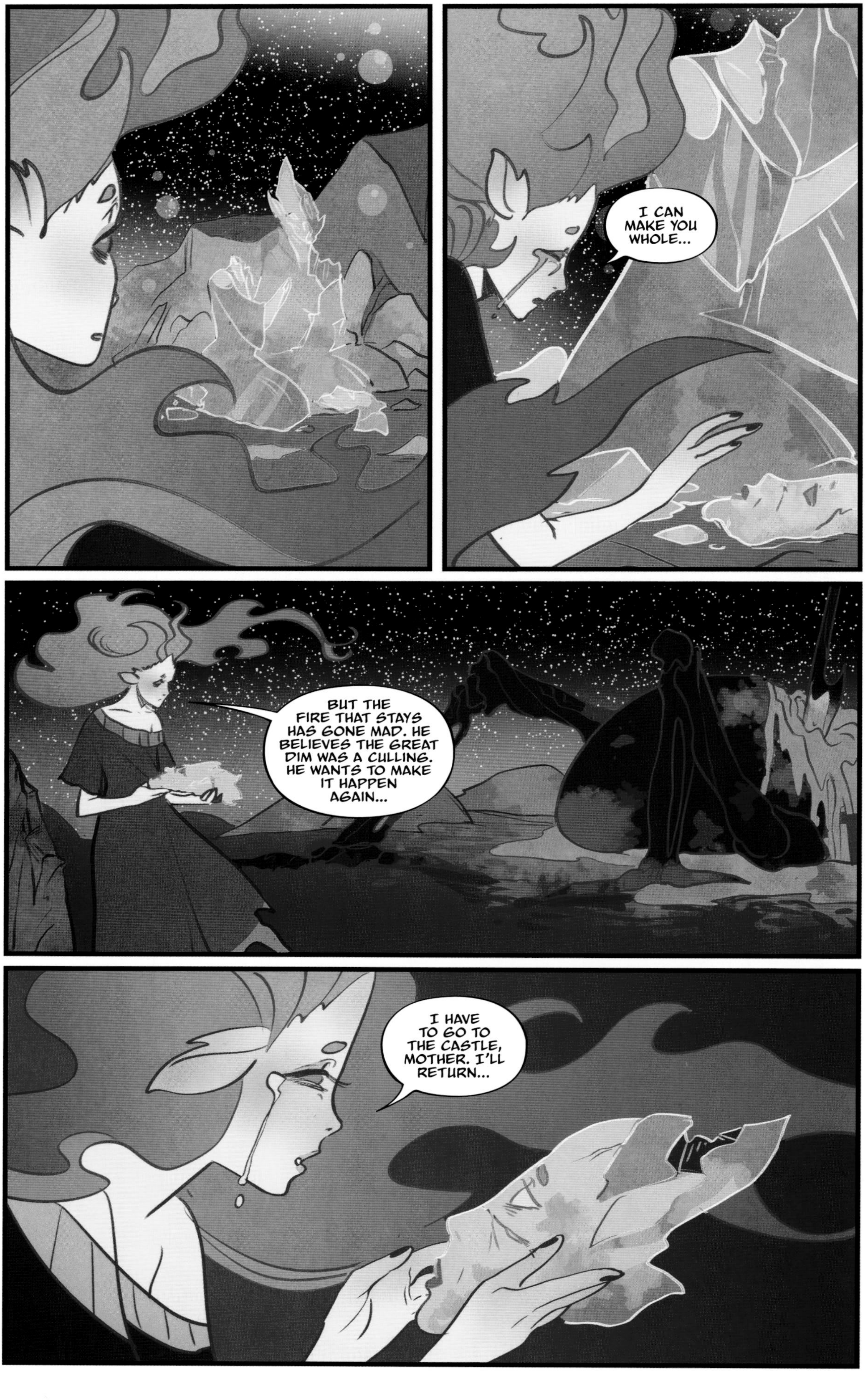
I CAN MAKE YOU WHOLE...
BUT THE FIRE THAT STAYS HAS GONE MAD. HE BELIEVES THE GREAT DIM WAS A CULLING. HE WANTS TO MAKE IT HAPPEN AGAIN...
I HAVE TO GO TO THE CASTLE, MOTHER. I'LL RETURN...

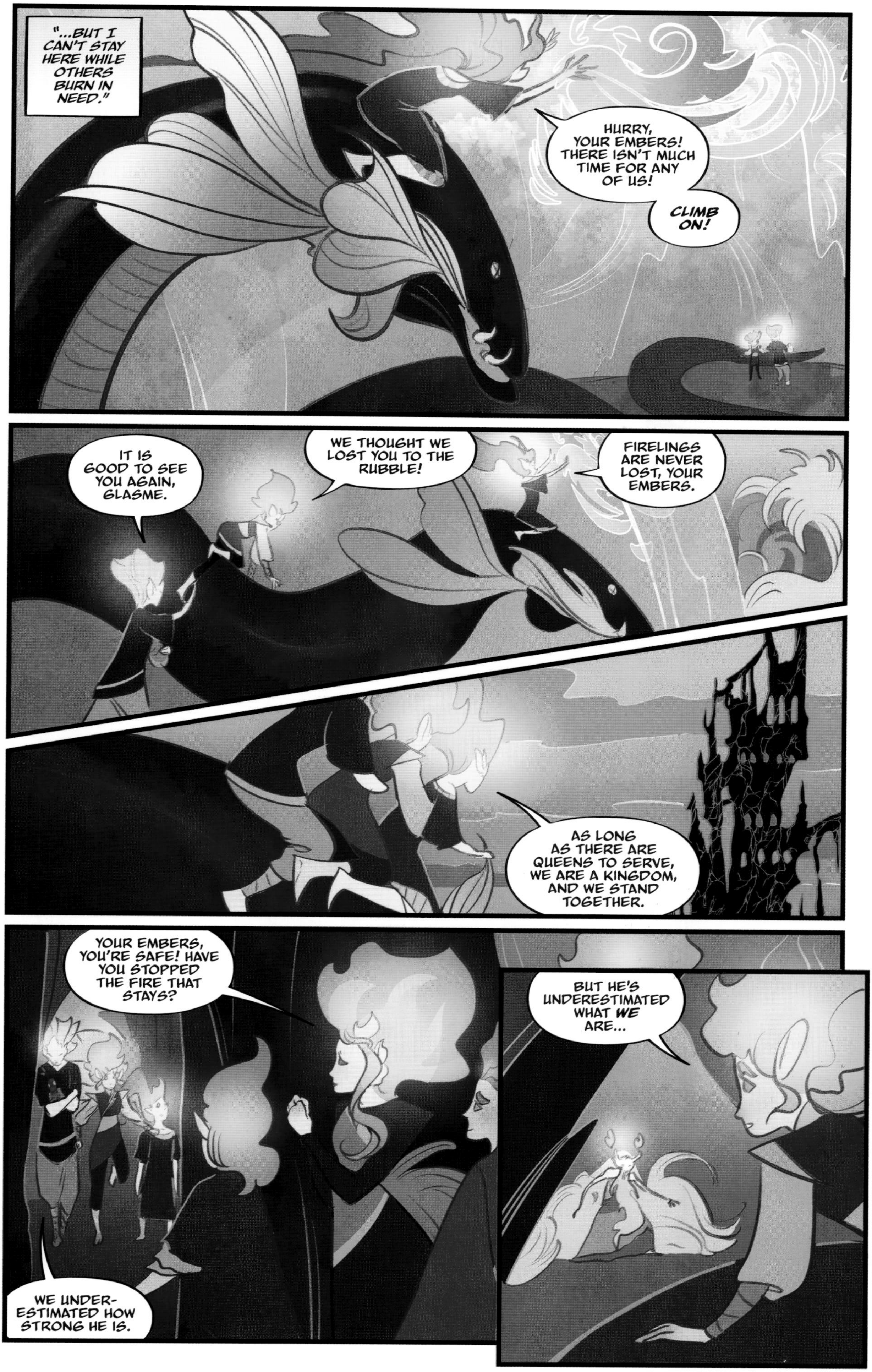
"...BUT I CAN'T STAY HERE WHILE OTHERS BURN IN NEED."
HURRY, YOUR EMBERS! THERE ISN'T MUCH TIME FOR ANY OF US!
CLIMB ON!
IT IS GOOD TO SEE YOU AGAIN, GLASME.
WE THOUGHT WE LOST YOU TO THE RUBBLE!
FIRELINGS ARE NEVER LOST, YOUR EMBERS.
AS LONG AS THERE ARE QUEENS TO SERVE, WE ARE A KINGDOM, AND WE STAND TOGETHER.
YOUR EMBERS, YOU'RE SAFE! HAVE YOU STOPPED THE FIRE THAT STAYS?
WE UNDER-ESTIMATED HOW STRONG HE IS.
BUT HE'S UNDERESTIMATED WHAT WE ARE...

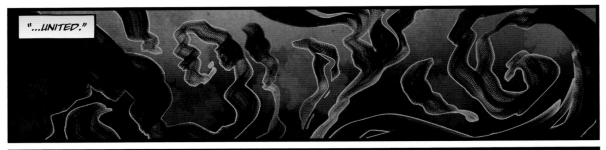

"...UNITED."

NO,
NO, NO,
NO...

I NEED TO GET BACK.
HOW DO I GET OUT
OF THIS CRYSTAL...
THERE ARE SO
MANY...

I CAN'T
LET THEM
SLIP AWAY.
I HAVE
TO--

WAKE UP,
KENSHO!

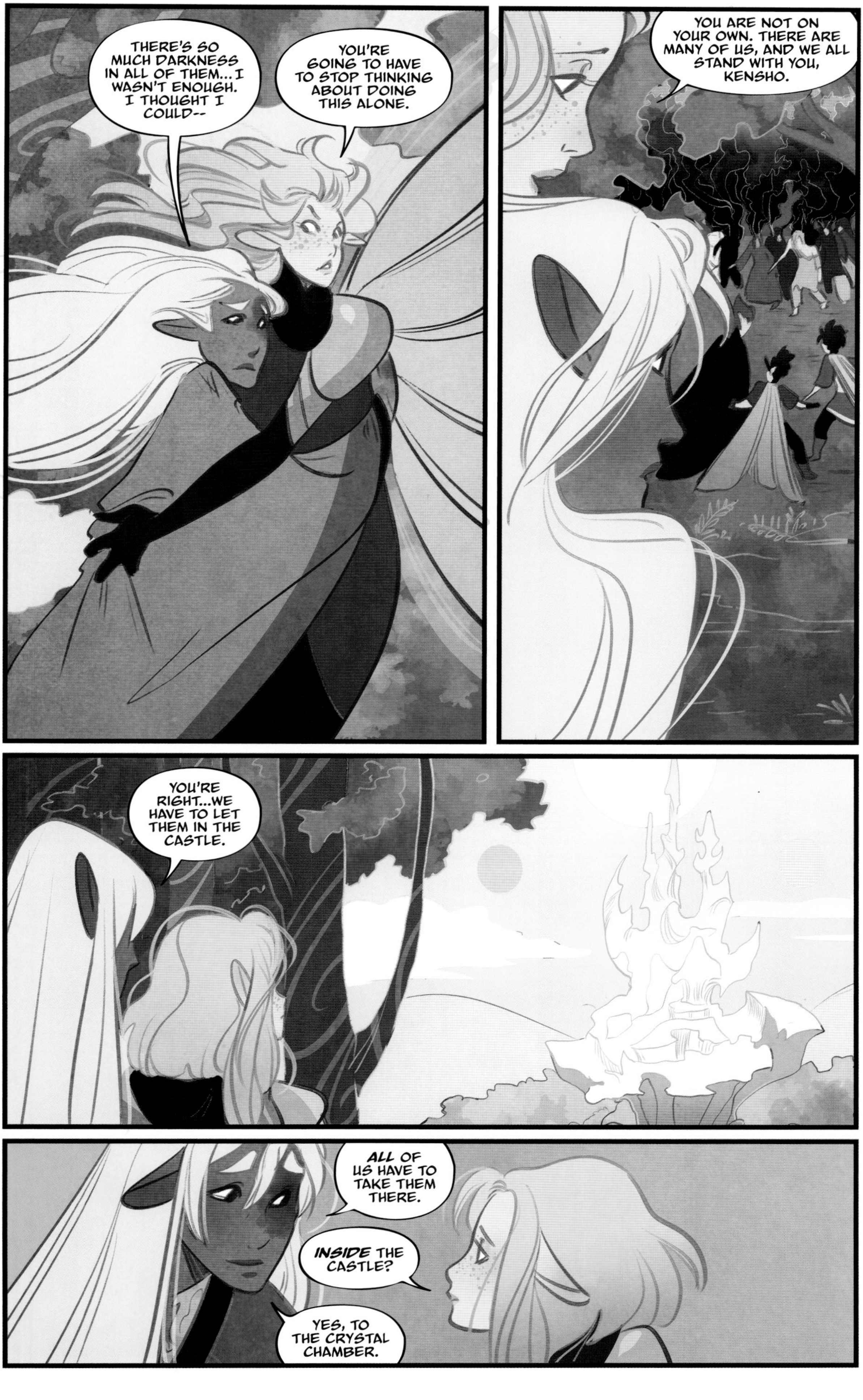
THERE'S SO MUCH DARKNESS IN ALL OF THEM... I WASN'T ENOUGH. I THOUGHT I COULD--
YOU'RE GOING TO HAVE TO STOP THINKING ABOUT DOING THIS ALONE.
YOU ARE NOT ON YOUR OWN. THERE ARE MANY OF US, AND WE ALL STAND WITH YOU, KENSHO.
YOU'RE RIGHT...WE HAVE TO LET THEM IN THE CASTLE.
ALL OF US HAVE TO TAKE THEM THERE.
INSIDE THE CASTLE?
YES, TO THE CRYSTAL CHAMBER.

AND WHAT DO WE DO WHEN THEY'RE WITHIN THE CHAMBER?

WE MAKE SURE I'M BETWEEN THEM AND THE CRYSTAL.

Oh, GOOD. I WAS CONCERNED FOR A MOMENT.

WE JUST NEED TO FIGURE OUT HOW TO BEAT THEM TO THE CRYSTAL...

I CAN HELP.

AIYANA, ARE YOU SURE ABOUT THIS?

OF COURSE. THE COUNCIL WANTS A WINGED LEADER ANYWAY.

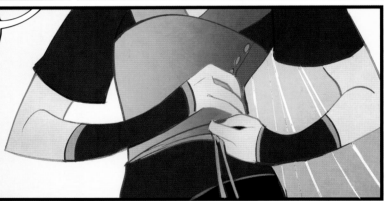

WE ALL WORK OUR WHOLE LIVES TO BECOME WHO WE ARE IN OUR HEARTS.

SOME GELFLING HAVE TO FIGURE IT OUT ON THEIR OWN. I HAVE BEEN LUCKY TO HAVE MY SISTER BY MY SIDE.

AND NOW, I AM HAPPY TO BE BY *YOUR* SIDE.

WE'RE NOT ALL BORN WITH WINGS, BUT WE CAN BE MORE. ISN'T THAT WHAT YOU ALWAYS SAY?

YOU ARE BEAUTIFUL, SISTER.

THANK YOU, AIYANA.

WITH THESE, AND ALL OF YOU...

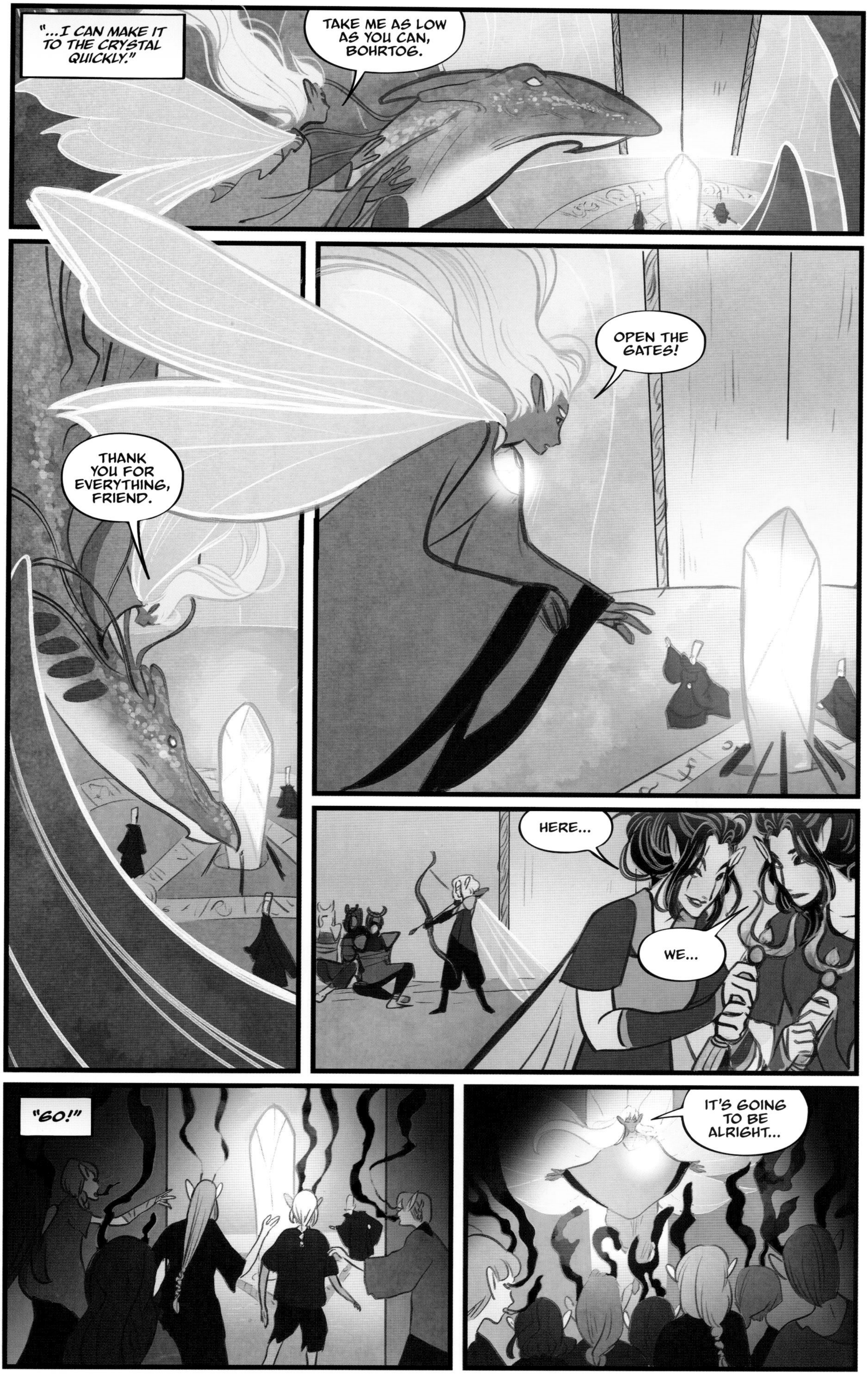
"...I CAN MAKE IT TO THE CRYSTAL QUICKLY."
TAKE ME AS LOW AS YOU CAN, BOHRTOG.
THANK YOU FOR EVERYTHING, FRIEND.
OPEN THE GATES!
HERE...
WE...
"GO!"
IT'S GOING TO BE ALRIGHT...

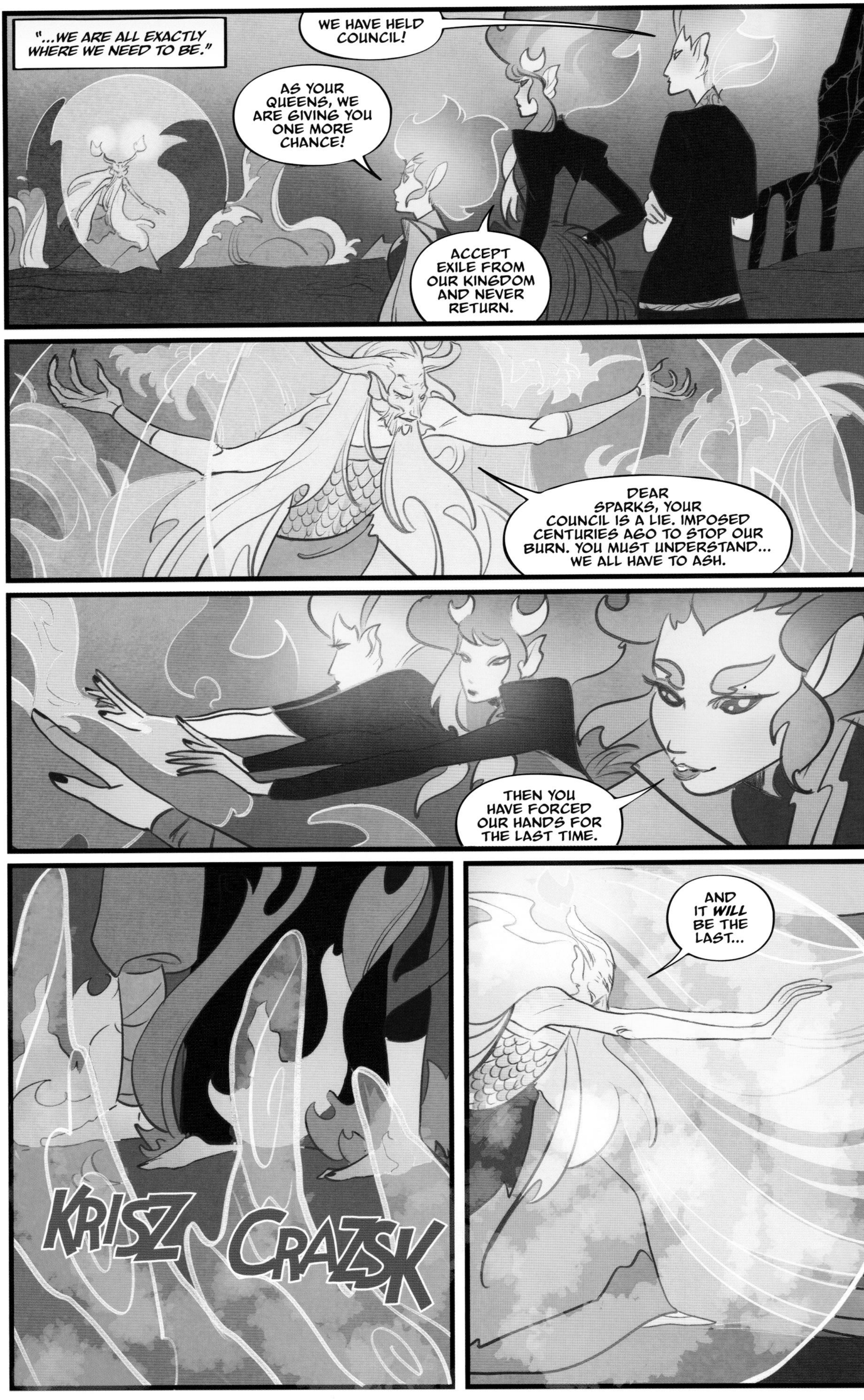
"...WE ARE ALL EXACTLY WHERE WE NEED TO BE."
WE HAVE HELD COUNCIL!
AS YOUR QUEENS, WE ARE GIVING YOU ONE MORE CHANCE!
ACCEPT EXILE FROM OUR KINGDOM AND NEVER RETURN.
DEAR SPARKS, YOUR COUNCIL IS A LIE. IMPOSED CENTURIES AGO TO STOP OUR BURN. YOU MUST UNDERSTAND... WE ALL HAVE TO ASH.
THEN YOU HAVE FORCED OUR HANDS FOR THE LAST TIME.
KRISZ
CRAZSK
AND IT *WILL* BE THE LAST...

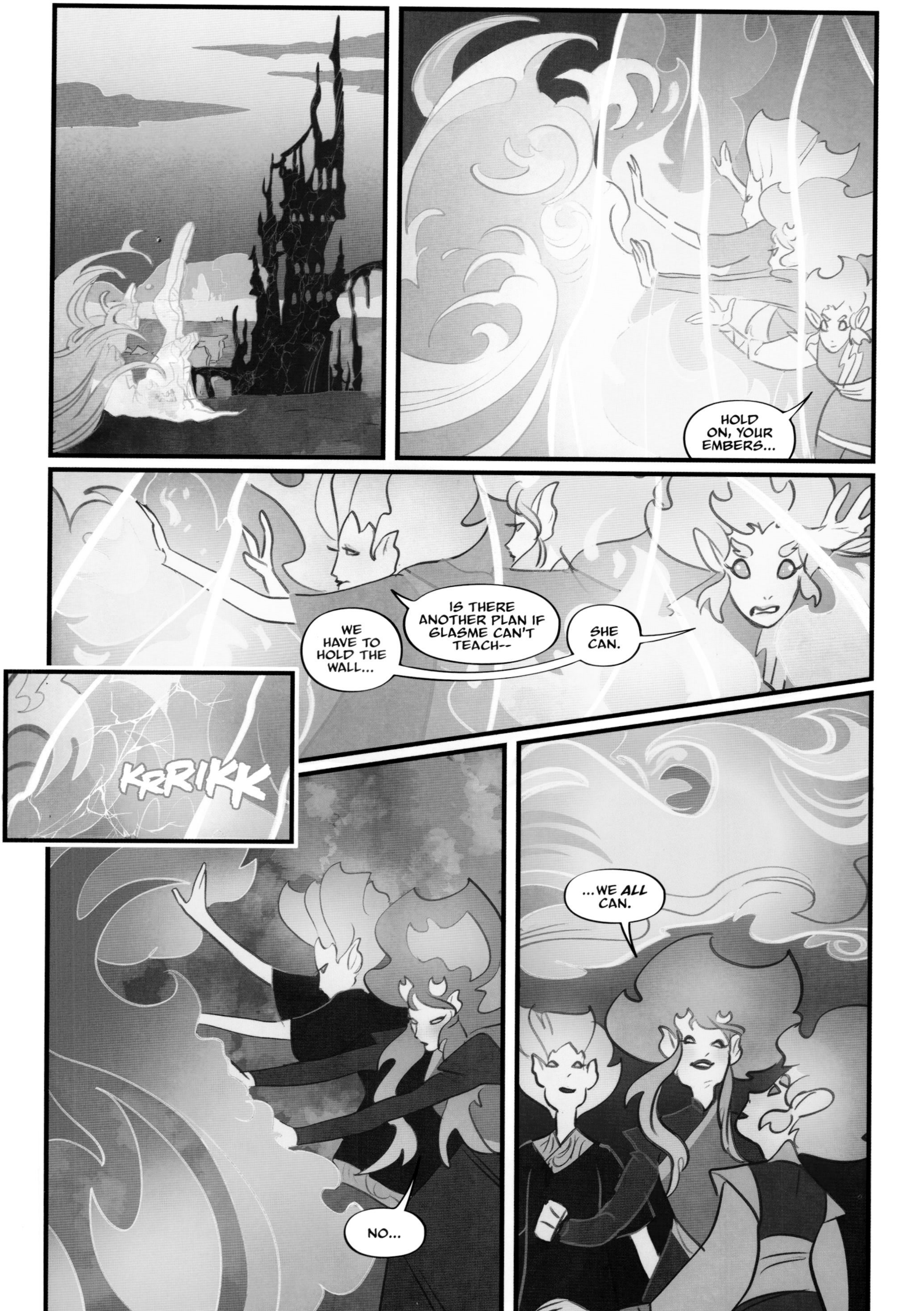
HOLD ON, YOUR EMBERS...
WE HAVE TO HOLD THE WALL...
IS THERE ANOTHER PLAN IF GLASME CAN'T TEACH--
SHE CAN.
KRRIKK
NO...
...WE ALL CAN.

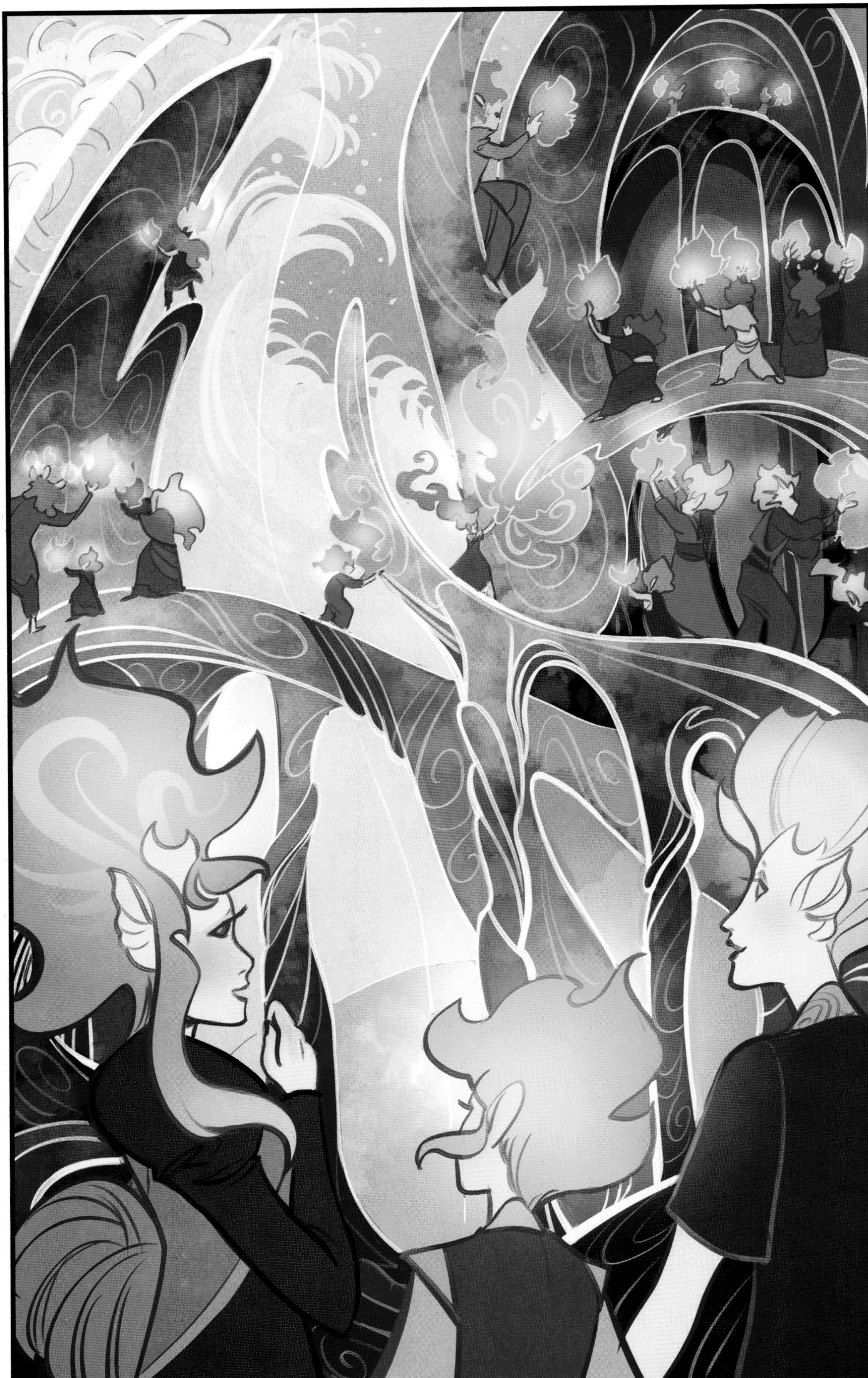

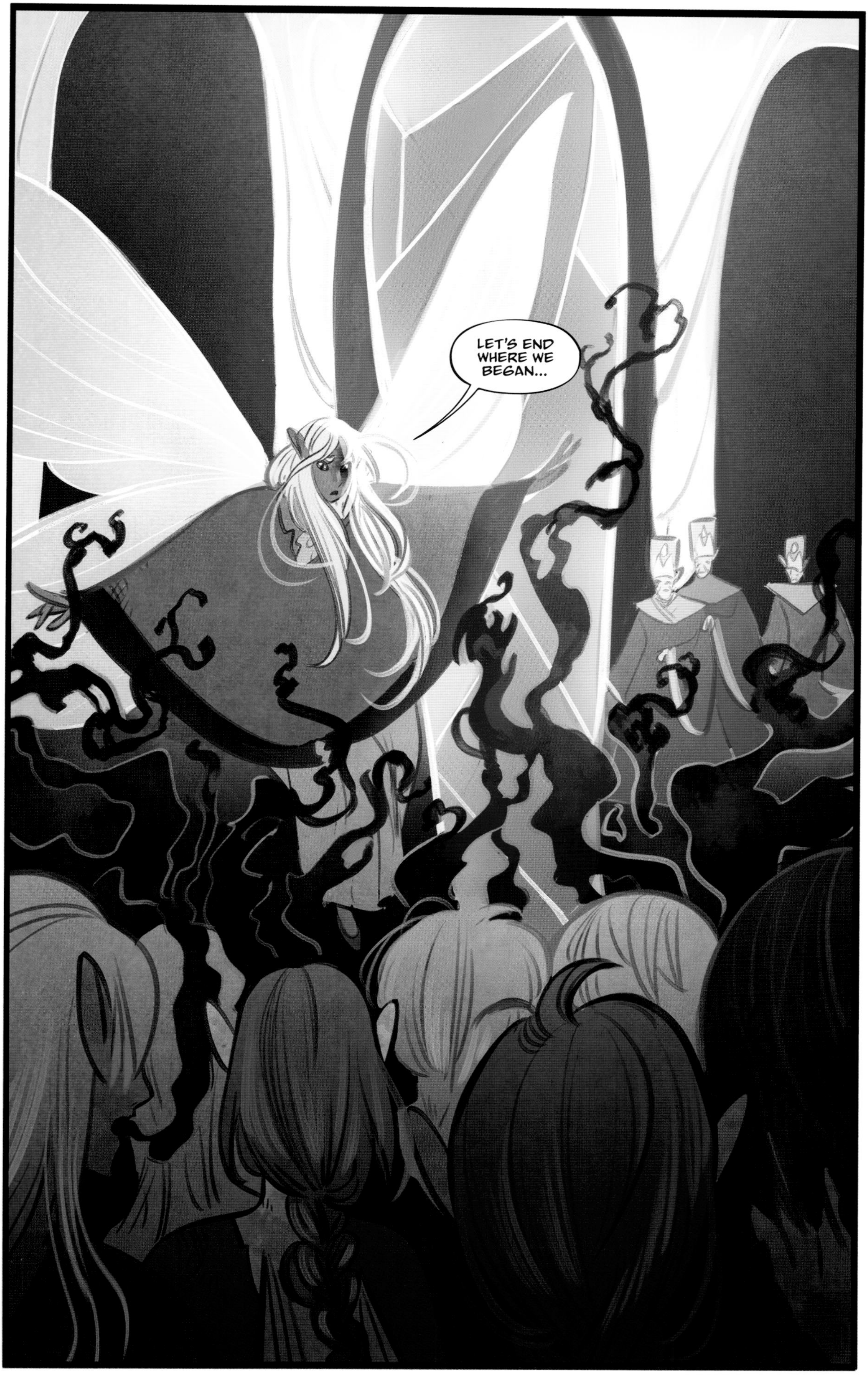
LET'S END WHERE WE BEGAN...

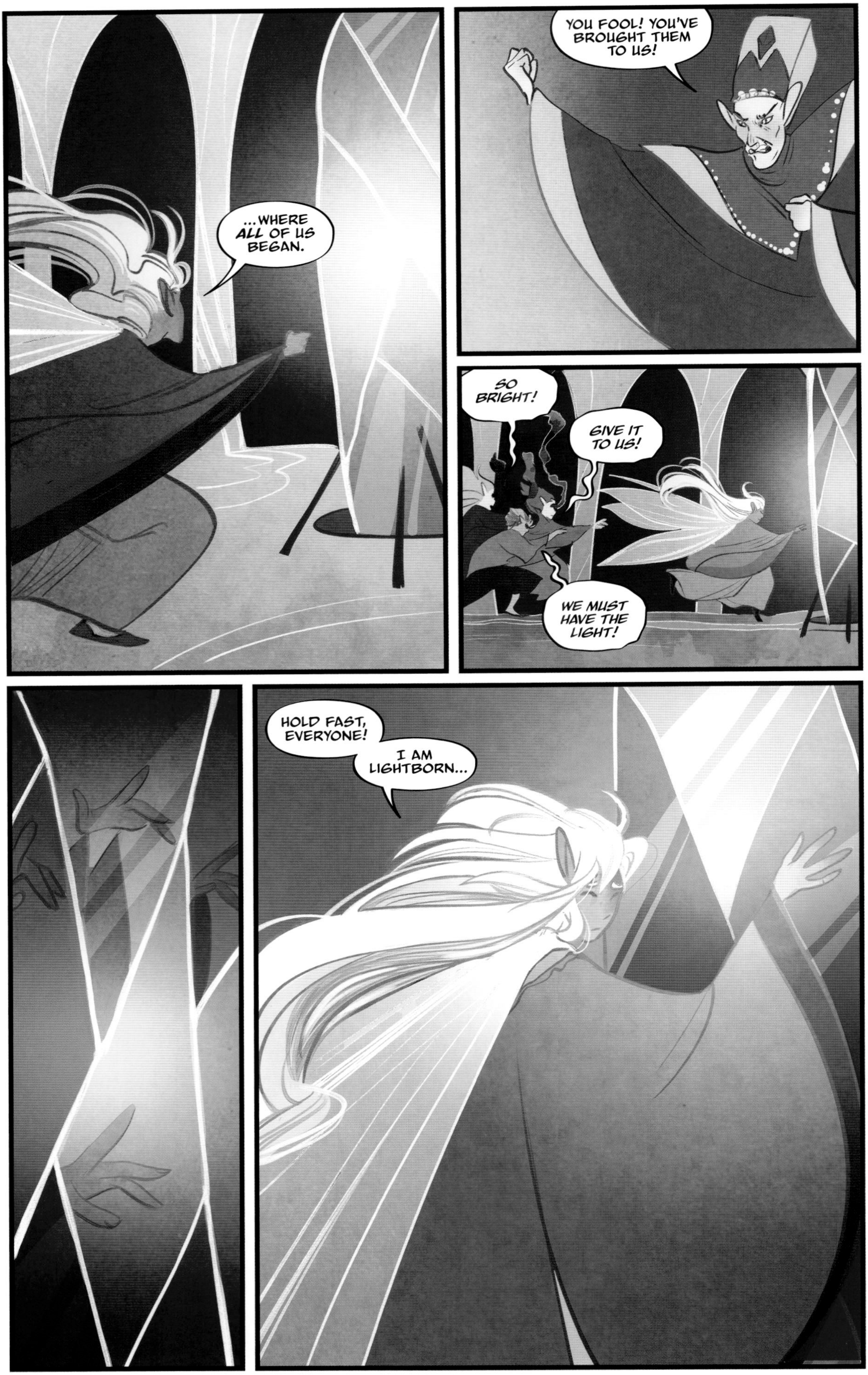
...WHERE ALL OF US BEGAN.
YOU FOOL! YOU'VE BROUGHT THEM TO US!
SO BRIGHT!
GIVE IT TO US!
WE MUST HAVE THE LIGHT!
HOLD FAST, EVERYONE!
I AM LIGHTBORN...

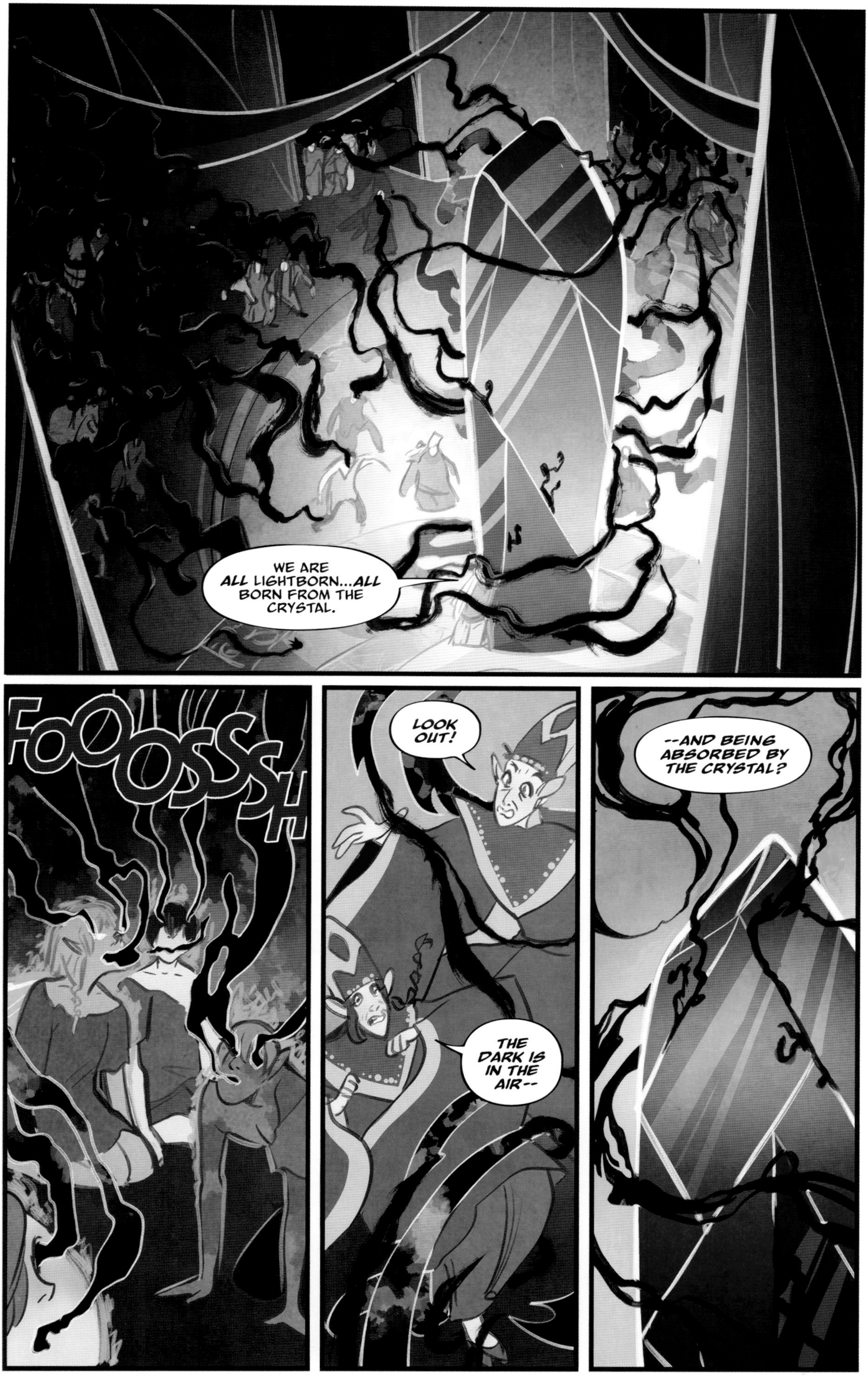
WE ARE ALL LIGHTBORN...ALL BORN FROM THE CRYSTAL.
FOOOSSSH
LOOK OUT!
THE DARK IS IN THE AIR--
--AND BEING ABSORBED BY THE CRYSTAL?

ARE YOU ALL ALRIGHT?

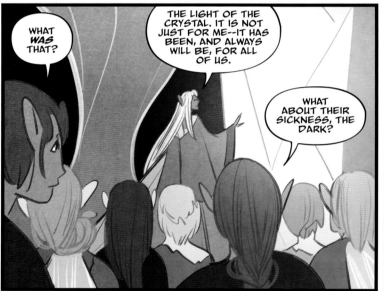

WHAT *WAS* THAT?

THE LIGHT OF THE CRYSTAL. IT IS NOT JUST FOR ME--IT HAS BEEN, AND ALWAYS WILL BE, FOR ALL OF US.

WHAT ABOUT THEIR SICKNESS, THE DARK?

IT'S A PART OF US AS WELL. WE HAVE TO ALWAYS WORK FOR BALANCE.

WISE WORDS...

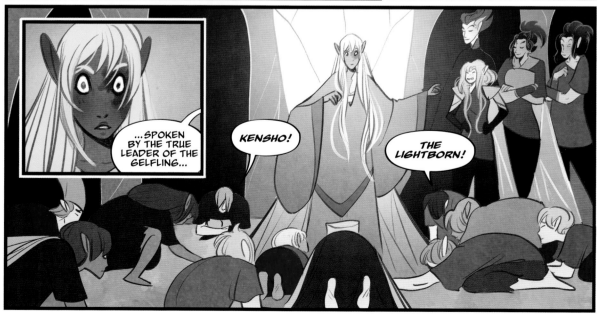

...SPOKEN BY THE TRUE LEADER OF THE GELFLING...

KENSHO!

THE LIGHTBORN!

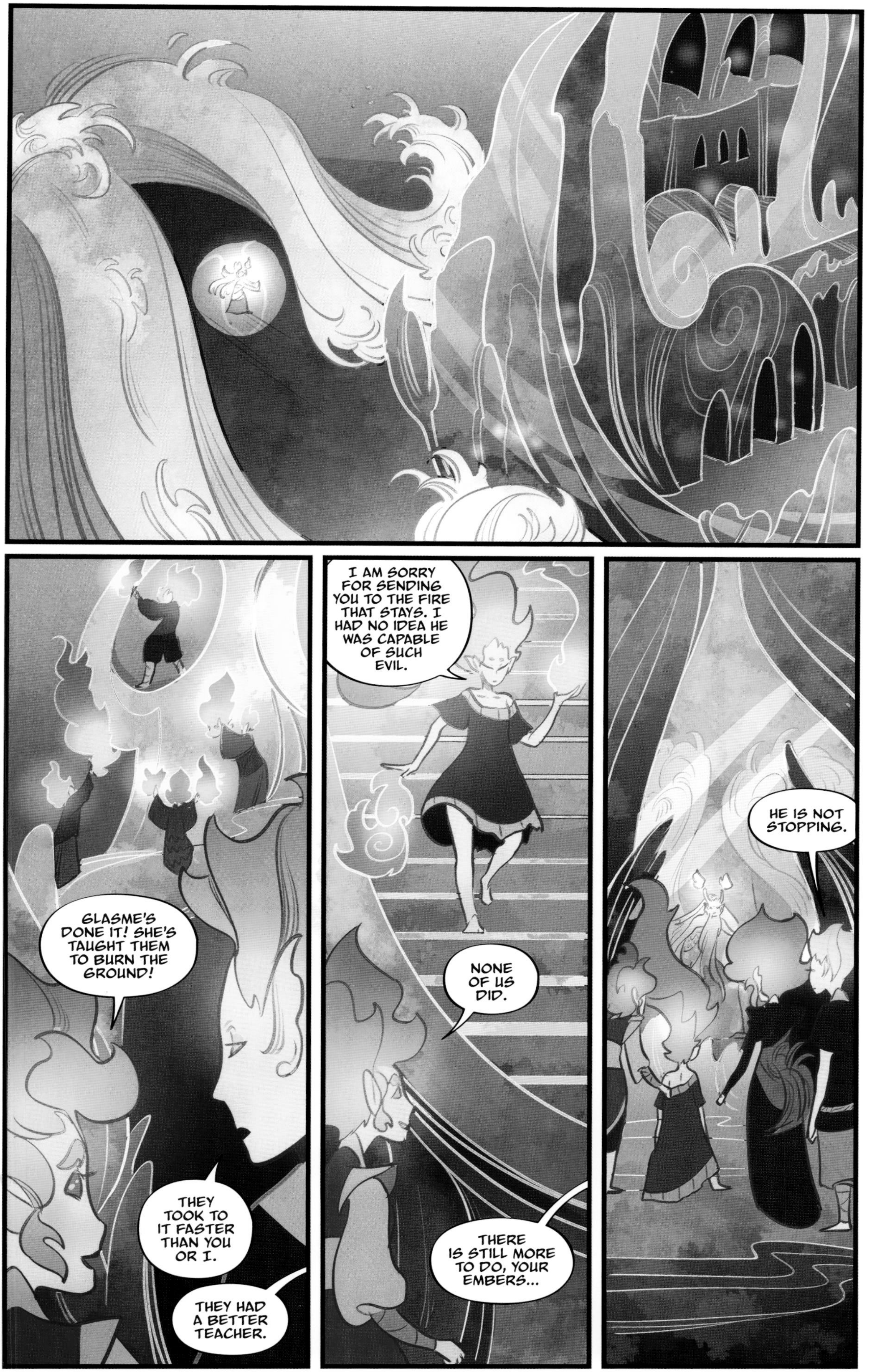
GLASME'S DONE IT! SHE'S TAUGHT THEM TO BURN THE GROUND!
THEY TOOK TO IT FASTER THAN YOU OR I.
THEY HAD A BETTER TEACHER.
I AM SORRY FOR SENDING YOU TO THE FIRE THAT STAYS. I HAD NO IDEA HE WAS CAPABLE OF SUCH EVIL.
NONE OF US DID.
THERE IS STILL MORE TO DO, YOUR EMBERS...
HE IS NOT STOPPING.

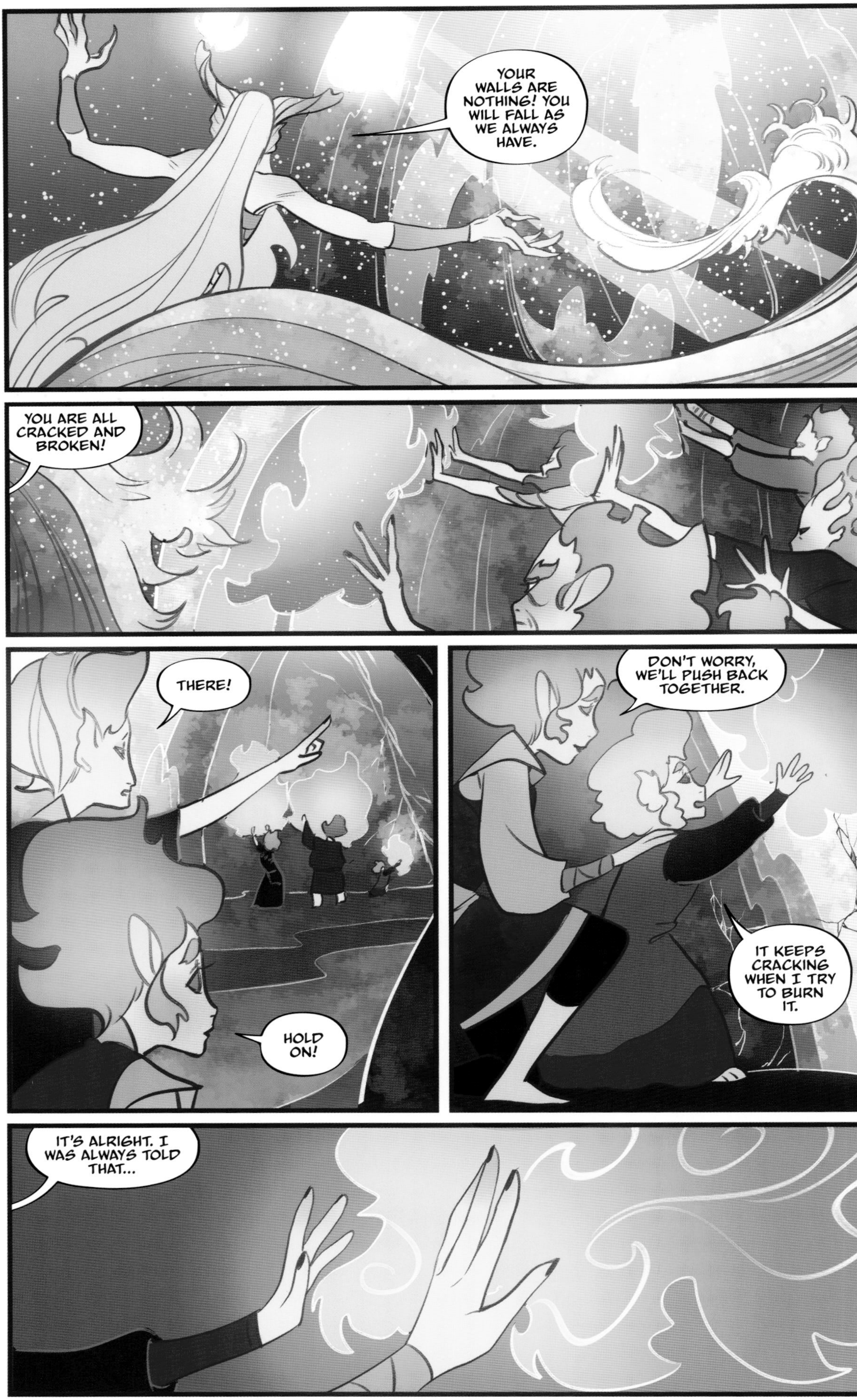
YOUR WALLS ARE NOTHING! YOU WILL FALL AS WE ALWAYS HAVE.
YOU ARE ALL CRACKED AND BROKEN!
THERE!
HOLD ON!
DON'T WORRY, WE'LL PUSH BACK TOGETHER.
IT KEEPS CRACKING WHEN I TRY TO BURN IT.
IT'S ALRIGHT. I WAS ALWAYS TOLD THAT...

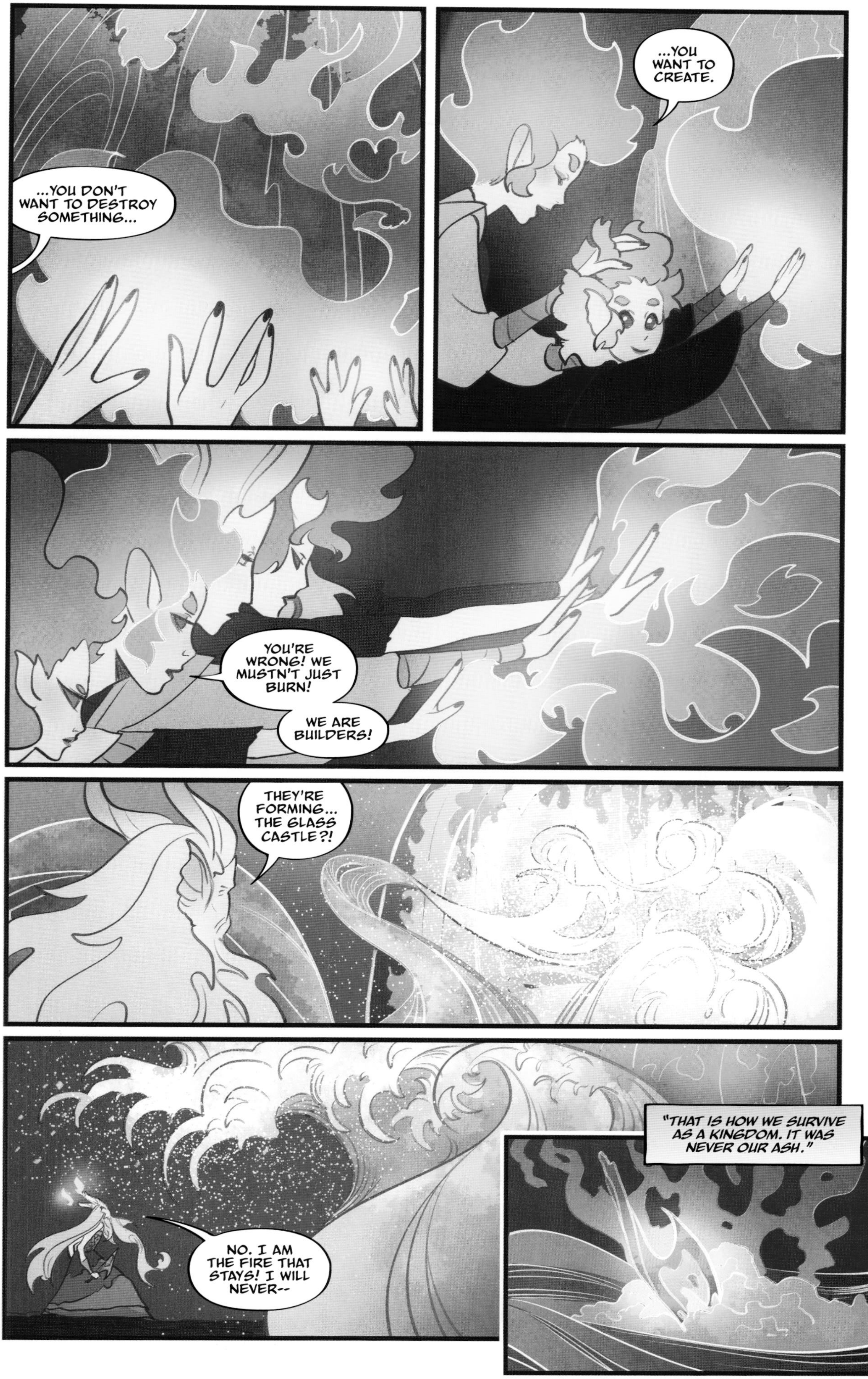
...YOU DON'T WANT TO DESTROY SOMETHING...
...YOU WANT TO CREATE.
YOU'RE WRONG! WE MUSTN'T JUST BURN!
WE ARE BUILDERS!
THEY'RE FORMING... THE GLASS CASTLE?!
NO. I AM THE FIRE THAT STAYS! I WILL NEVER--
"THAT IS HOW WE SURVIVE AS A KINGDOM. IT WAS NEVER OUR ASH."

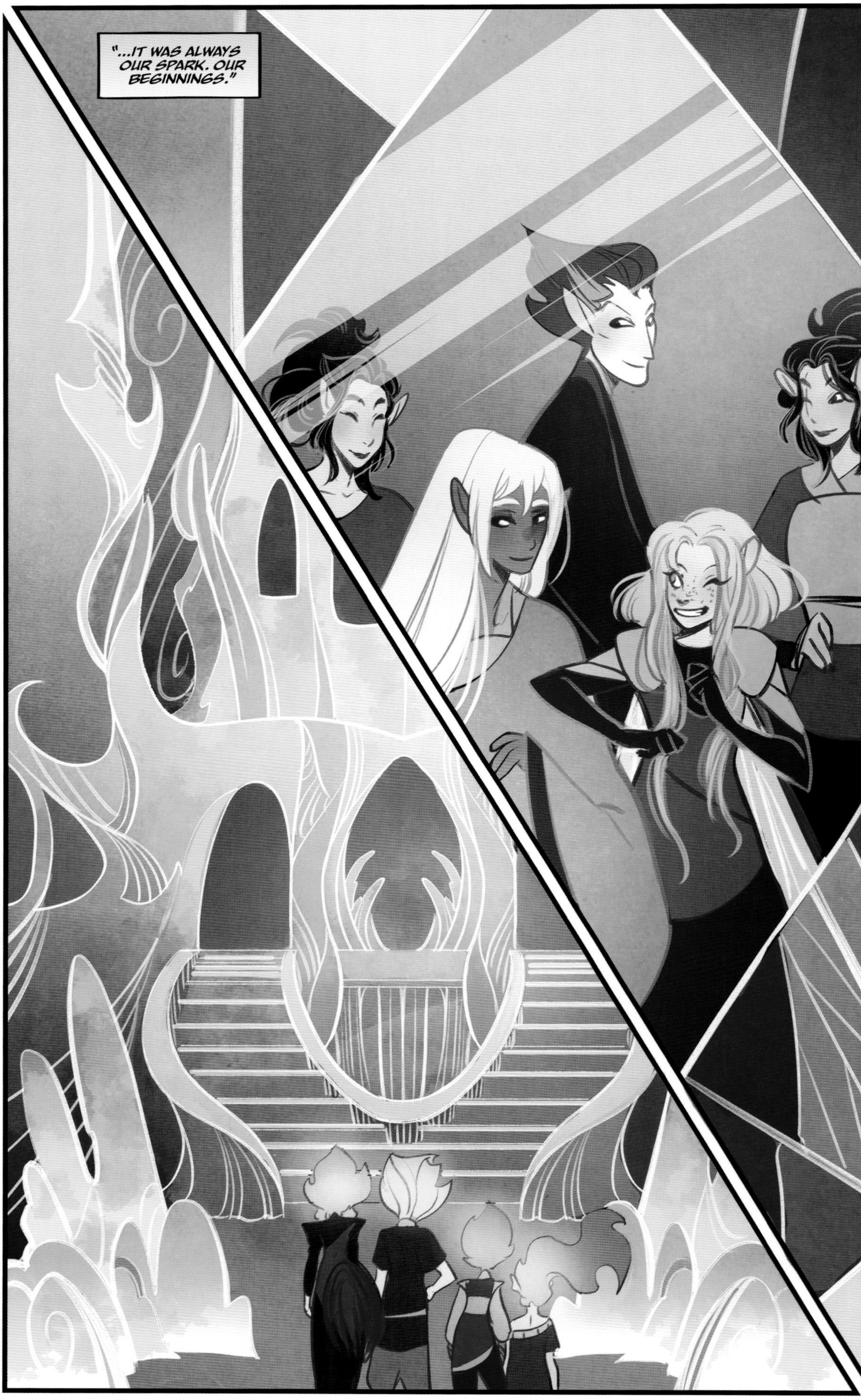
"...IT WAS ALWAYS OUR SPARK. OUR BEGINNINGS."

"WE CAN BE MORE."

WELL THEN, THE LIGHTBORN SEEM TO SHINE BRIGHTLY.

I AM TRYING. THERE'S MUCH TO DO...

...BUT WE HAVE A PATH.

WE'VE CLEARED THE SKEKSIS METAL AND ARE STARTING TO REBUILD.

IT'S A BEGINNING.

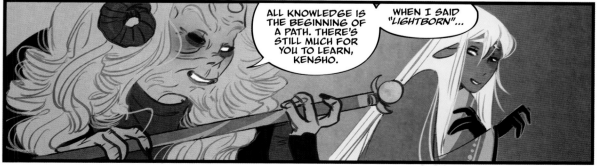

ALL KNOWLEDGE IS THE BEGINNING OF A PATH. THERE'S STILL MUCH FOR YOU TO LEARN, KENSHO.

WHEN I SAID "LIGHTBORN"...

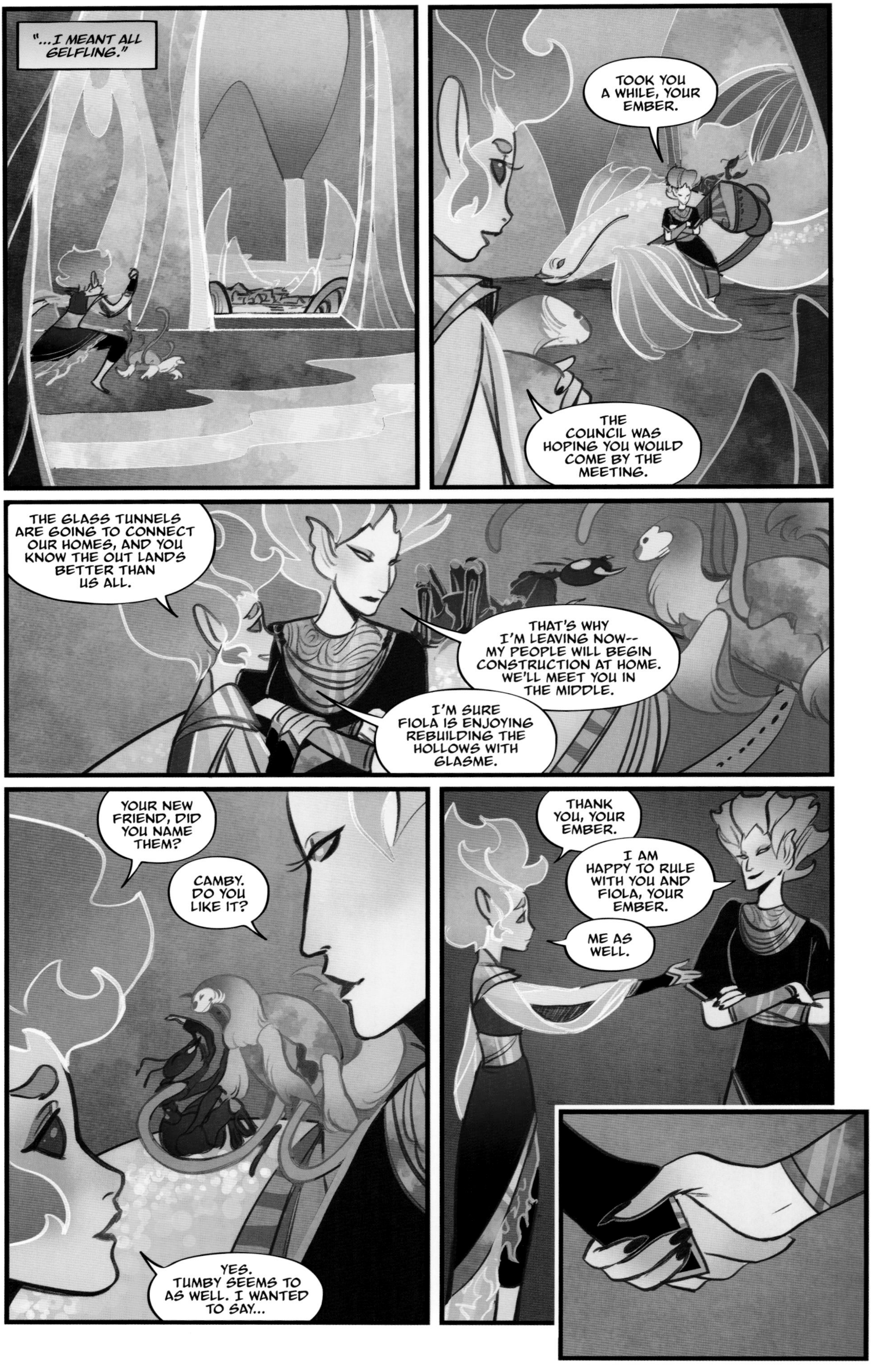
"...I MEANT ALL GELFLING."
TOOK YOU A WHILE, YOUR EMBER.
THE COUNCIL WAS HOPING YOU WOULD COME BY THE MEETING.
THE GLASS TUNNELS ARE GOING TO CONNECT OUR HOMES, AND YOU KNOW THE OUT LANDS BETTER THAN US ALL.
THAT'S WHY I'M LEAVING NOW-- MY PEOPLE WILL BEGIN CONSTRUCTION AT HOME. WE'LL MEET YOU IN THE MIDDLE.
I'M SURE FIOLA IS ENJOYING REBUILDING THE HOLLOWS WITH GLASME.
YOUR NEW FRIEND, DID YOU NAME THEM?
CAMBY. DO YOU LIKE IT?
YES. TUMBY SEEMS TO AS WELL. I WANTED TO SAY...
THANK YOU, YOUR EMBER.
I AM HAPPY TO RULE WITH YOU AND FIOLA, YOUR EMBER.
ME AS WELL.

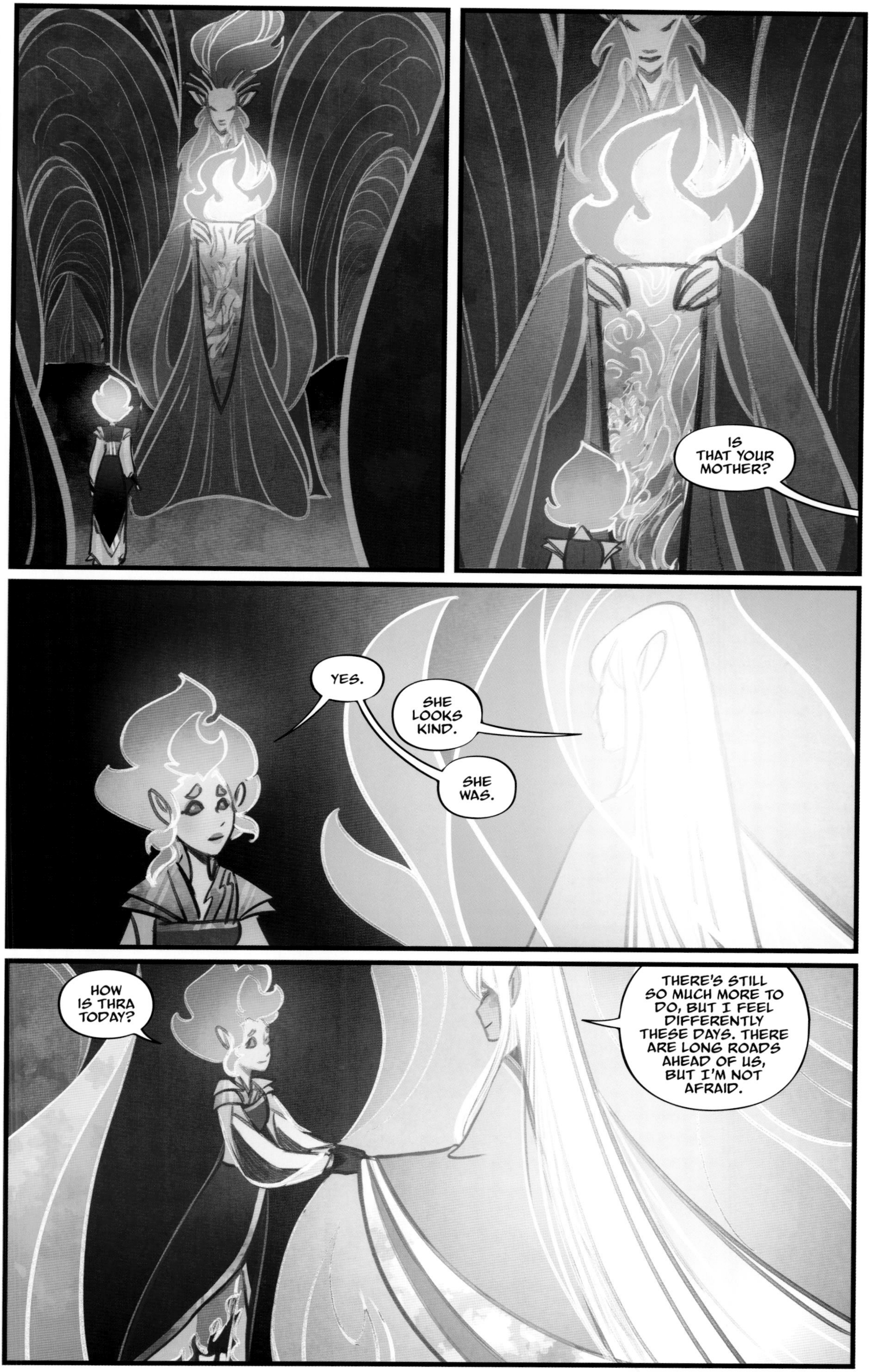
IS THAT YOUR MOTHER?
YES.
SHE LOOKS KIND.
SHE WAS.
HOW IS THRA TODAY?
THERE'S STILL SO MUCH MORE TO DO, BUT I FEEL DIFFERENTLY THESE DAYS. THERE ARE LONG ROADS AHEAD OF US, BUT I'M NOT AFRAID.

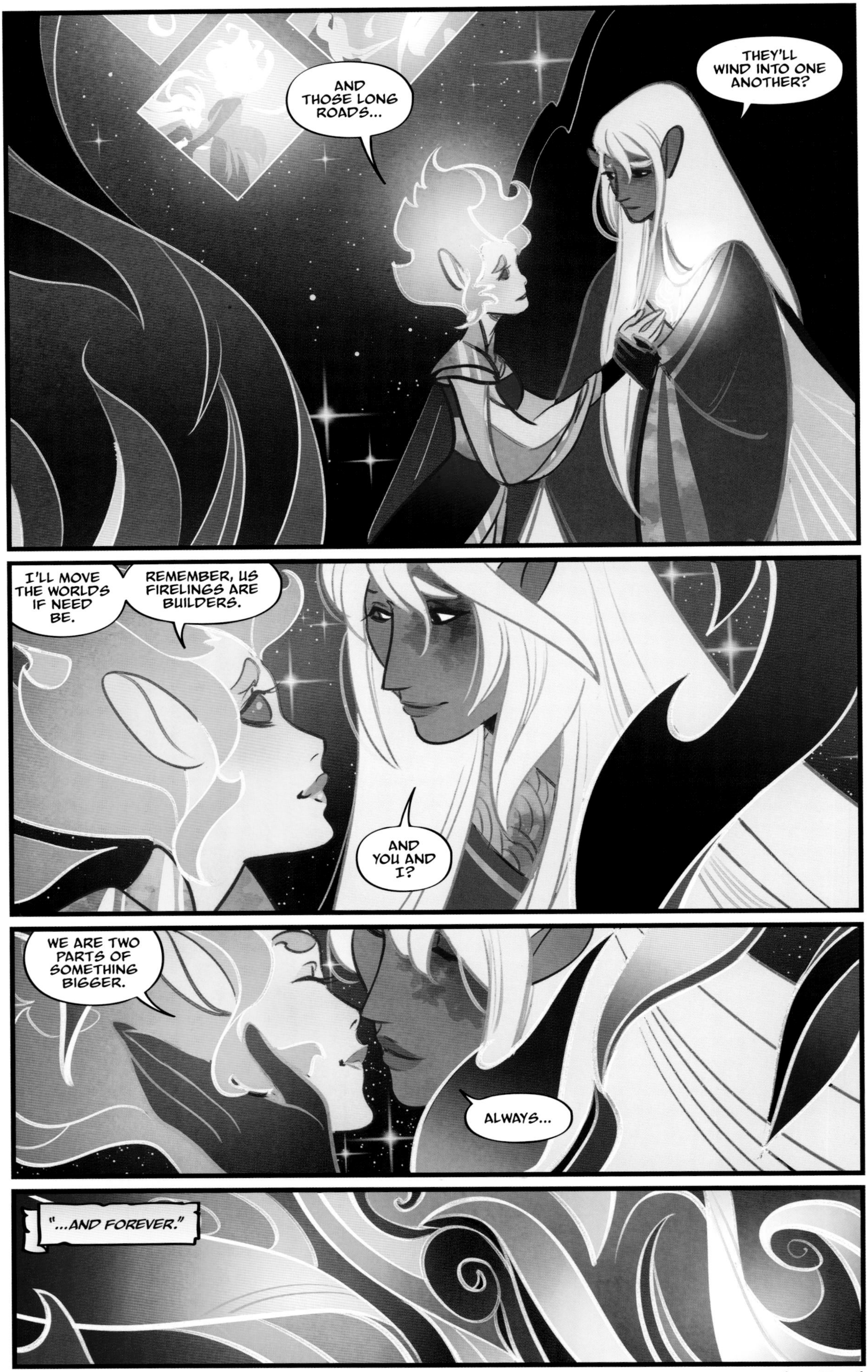
AND THOSE LONG ROADS...
THEY'LL WIND INTO ONE ANOTHER?
I'LL MOVE THE WORLDS IF NEED BE.
REMEMBER, US FIRELINGS ARE BUILDERS.
AND YOU AND I?
WE ARE TWO PARTS OF SOMETHING BIGGER.
ALWAYS...
"...AND FOREVER."

The End

COVER GALLERY

Following Pages: Issue #9-12 Subscription Covers by David Petersen

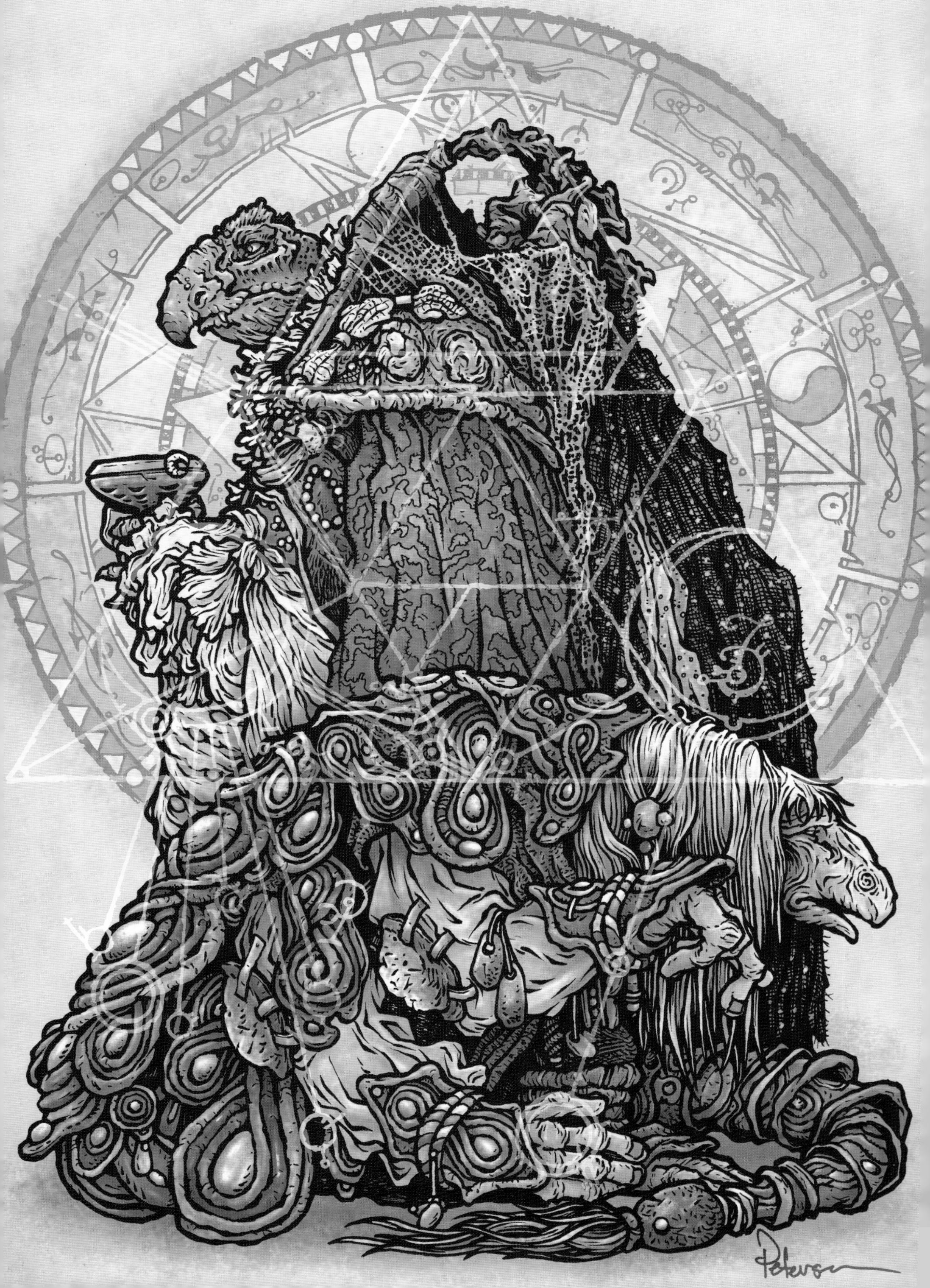

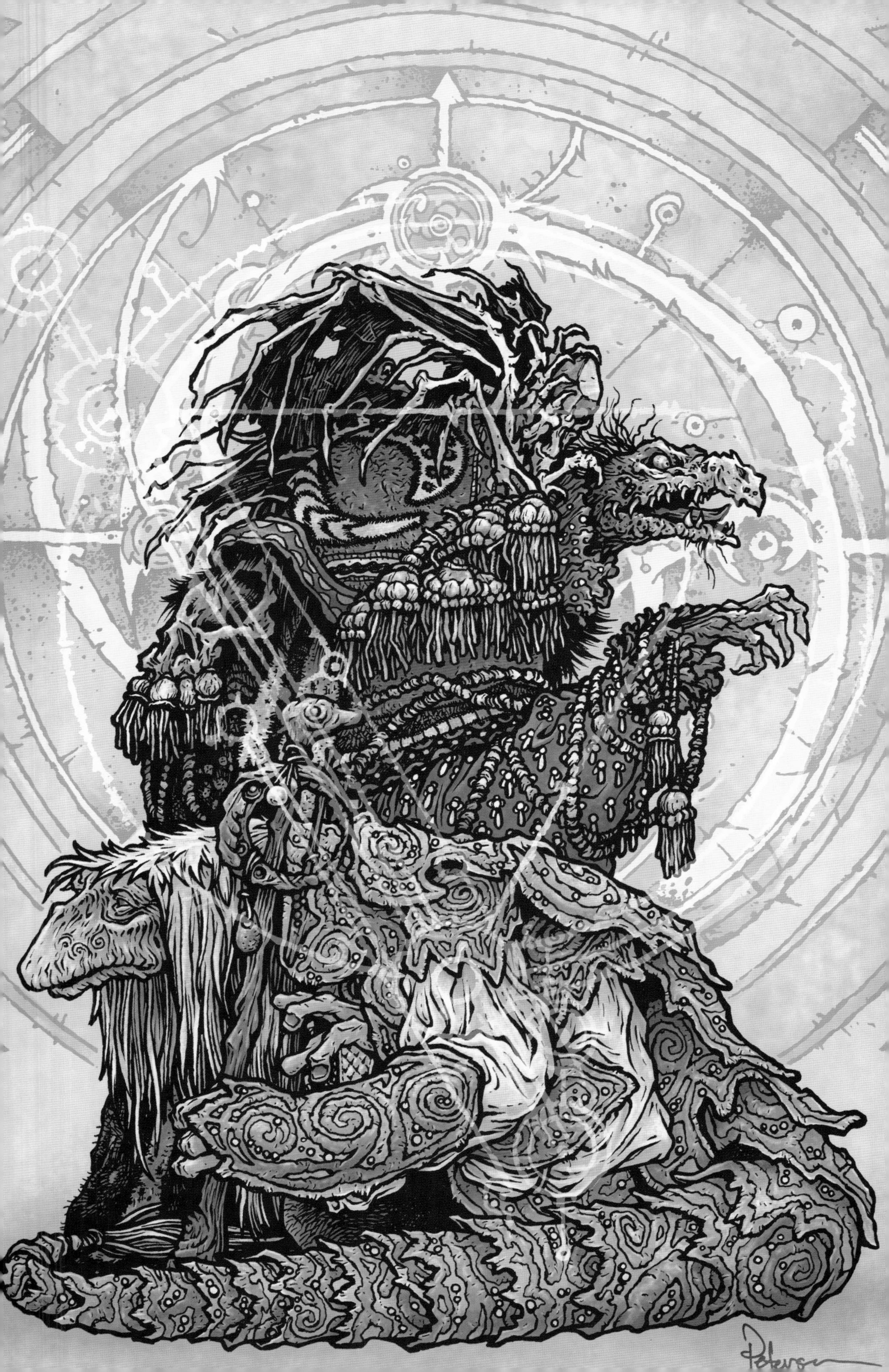

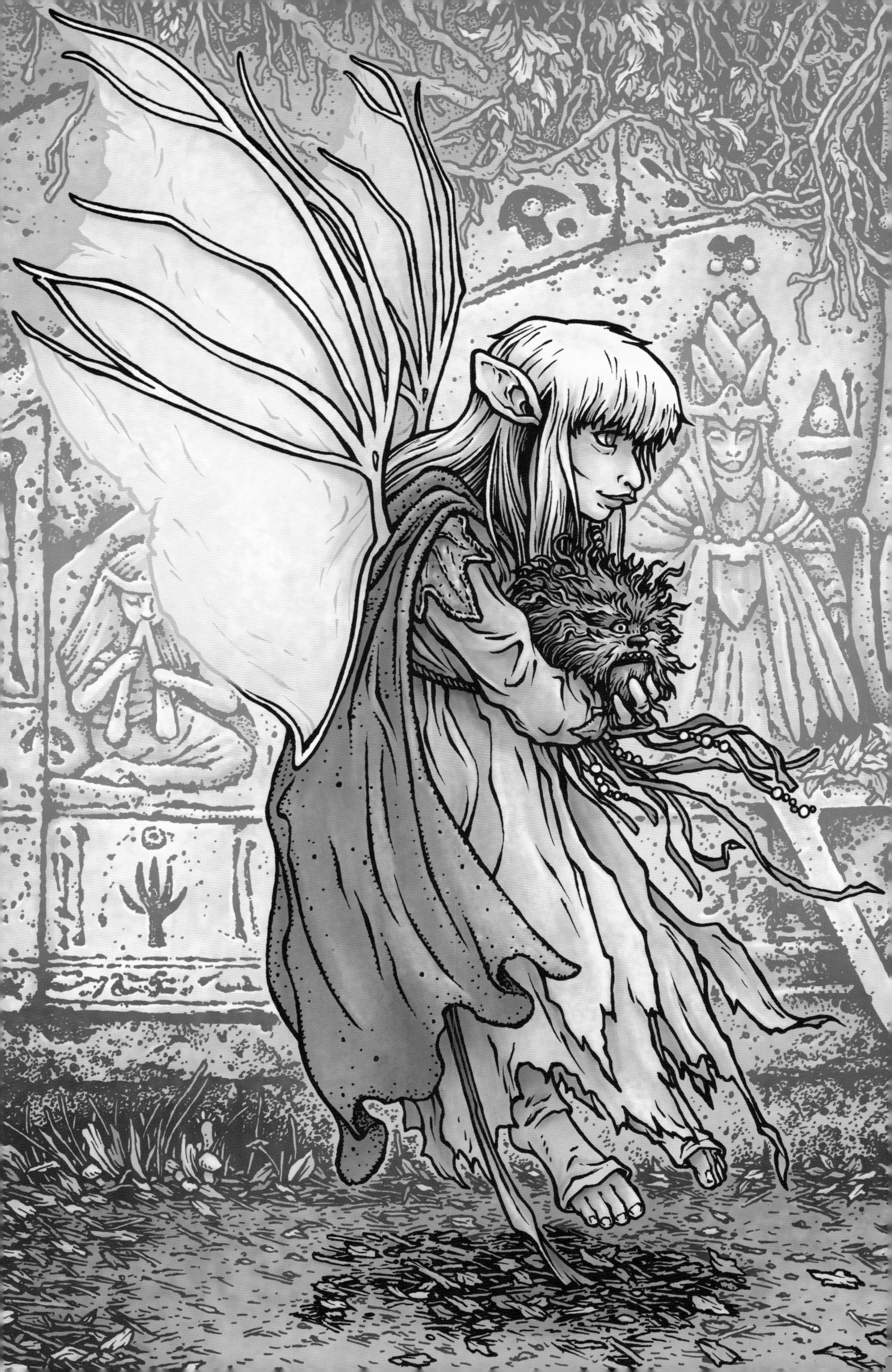

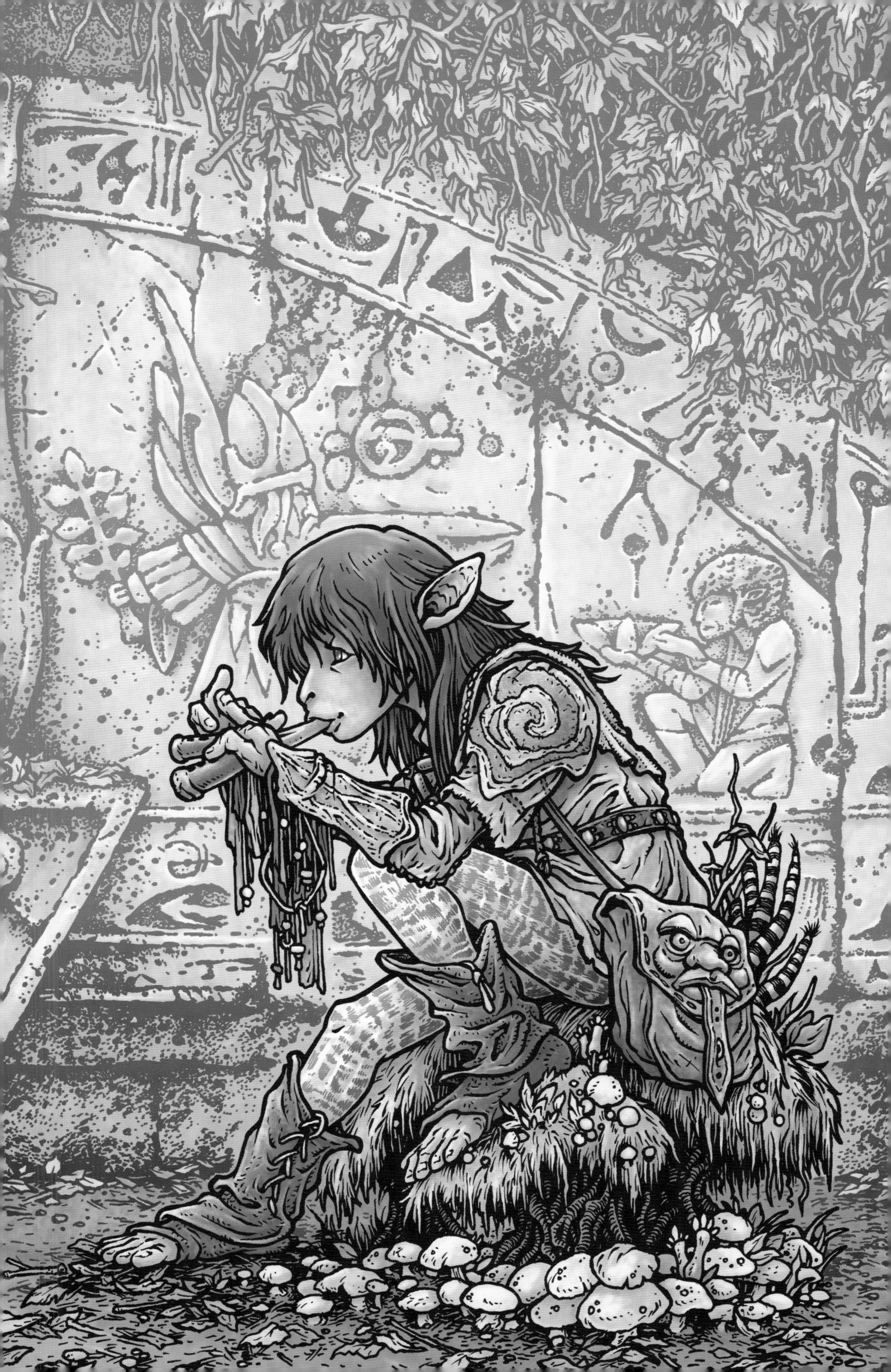

FROM SCRIPT
TO PAGE

ISSUE TWELVE: PAGE NINETEEN

PANEL ONE & PANEL TWO: Flashing forward a bit in time but still keeping the split/ splash format for the first two panels, taking the upper half of the page, where we see the KINGDOMS as they are now. On the Mithra side, what was left of the water as been covered in a glass, FIRELINGS bustle in through the large gates that they had used to defend themselves from TFTS. Houses have been built and erected around the CASTLE to show the FIRELINGS have made this their home after the destruction of their previous village. In THRA, we stay in the CRYSTAL CHAMBER as KENSHO and CO. carry the offerings out of the CHAMBER. In their place, they all building shops and workshops to make this a marketplace of sorts.

    THURMA(CAPTION): We can be more.

PANEL THREE: KENSHO stands with AUGHRA in front of the CRYSTAL as various GELFLING scamper around behind them in the MARKETPLACE.

    AUGHRA: Well then, the Lightborn seem to shine brightly.

    KENSHO: I am trying. There's much to do...

PANEL FOUR: TOOLAH and DIHNMOR hold a board up to a wooden frame as the TWINS hammer and nail the board together.

> *KENSHO (OFF-PANEL):* But we have a path. We've cleared the Skeksis metal and are starting to rebuild. It's a beginning.

PANEL FIVE: AUGHRA smiles as she nudges KENSHO with her walking stick.

> *AUGHRA:* All knowledge is the beginning of a path. There's still much for you to learn, Kensho. When I said "Lightborn"...

ISSUE TWELVE: PAGE TWENTY

PANEL ONE: In MITHRA, we see THURMA and TUMBY running towards the door of the bustling parlor towards the large doors leading outside.

    AUGHRA(CAPTION): "...I meant all Gelfling."

PANEL TWO: Outside, NITA and CAMBY lean on her STEED waiting for THURMA. The STEED is weighed down with sacks to show she's leaving for a while.

    NITA: Took you a while, Your Ember.

    THURMA: The Council was hoping you would come by the meeting.

PANEL THREE: THURMA looks to NITA as CAMBY and TUMBY sniff one another on the STEED'S back.

    THURMA: The Glass Tunnels are going to connect our homes and you know the Out Lands better than us all.

    NITA: That's why I'm leaving now--my people will begin construction at home. We'll meet you in the middle.

    THURMA: I'm sure Fiola is enjoying rebuilding the Hollows with Glasme.

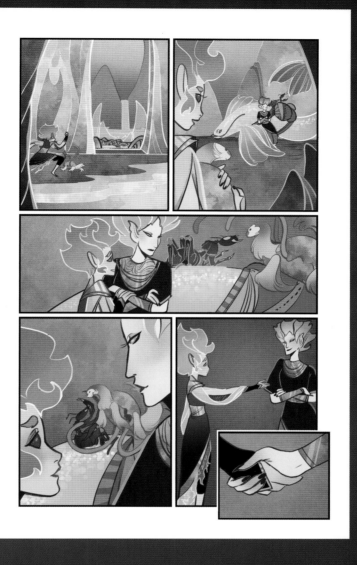

PANEL FOUR: THURMA and NITA look down to TUMBY and CAMBY as they begin to play on the ground.

    THURMA: Did you name it?

    NITA: Camby. Do you like it?

    THURMA: Yes. Tumby seems to also. I wanted to say...

PANEL FIVE: THURMA holds her hand out to shake NITA'S.

    THURMA: Thank you, Your Ember.

    NITA: I am happy to rule with you and Fiola, Your Ember.

    THURMA: Me as well.

PANEL SIX: The two QUEENS shake hands.

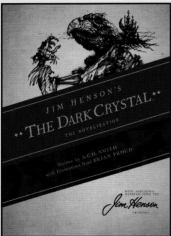